Broadcasters' Rights in the Digital Era

Broadcasters' Rights in the Digital Era

Copyright Concerns on Live Streaming

By

M. Sakthivel

BRILL
NIJHOFF

LEIDEN | BOSTON

The Library of Congress Cataloging-in-Publication Data is available online at http://catalog.loc.gov
LC record available at http://lccn.loc.gov/2019055549

Typeface for the Latin, Greek, and Cyrillic scripts: "Brill". See and download: brill.com/brill-typeface.

ISBN 978-90-04-41910-0 (hardback)
ISBN 978-90-04-41915-5 (e-book)

This book is printed on acid-free paper and produced in a sustainable manner.

Dedicated to my Guru

என் ஆசானுக்கு சமர்ப்பணம்

∵

Contents

Annexures

Preface

Copyright has always been accommodating technological advancements by express inclusion of the authors' right of 'dissemination of their works' for the enjoyment of public over the new medium both at the international and national level. These technological advancements led to the emergence of the concept of authors' right of Radio broadcasting, TV broadcasting, etc., which have been now grouped together under the umbrella of the authors' right of 'communication to the public'.

It was the broadcasting industry which at first flourished and consequently paved the way for the expansion of authors' right of 'communication to the public'. A socio-economic analysis of the development of broadcasting industry sheds light on the considerable investment required for the dissemination of works through broadcasting and the perils of unauthorized rebroadcasting. Such unauthorized rebroadcasting of content carrying signal of the broadcasting organizations by their competitors in the past created considerable revenue loss not only to broadcasting organizations but also to the authors of the copyright works. The major reason for the unauthorized rebroadcasting of content was the legal lacunae that existed in the authors' right of broadcasting, as the same was restricted only to the expression of content and not to the signals generated by the broadcasting organizations. This led to the emergence of the concept of 'neighbouring rights protection' including that of broadcasting organizations. In order to address the economic interest of broadcasters while generating the signal for disseminating authors' works to the public, the concept of 'broadcast reproduction right' was conceived and accepted by the Rome Convention in 1961. The same has been recognized with a limited scope in the TRIPS Agreement as well.

Even though the degree of legal protection accorded to the broadcasters' signal has remained constant, the technical advancements in signal protection i.e., signal encryption techniques have vastly improved in recent years. As a result of these enhanced techniques in encryption for signal protection, there is a need to examine whether the program carrying signal in digital broadcasting still requires any additional legal protection. Moreover in the digital context, it is pertinent to understand the scope and extent of authors' right in live streaming and to further examine whether there is any legal lacunae similar to that of unauthorized access of traditional broadcasters' signal while transmitting the work of authors through 'live streaming'. This book is an attempt to clear the fog around these questions and to provide a contoured answer to the same in detail among others.

Acknowledgements

The author is first and foremost grateful to the almighty for endowing him with the ability to complete the work and bestowing him with the good fortune of being mentored by the eminent teacher, academician, jurist and expert in IPR, Prof. (Dr.) N. S. Gopalakrishnan, Honorary Professor, Inter University Center for IPR Studies, Cochin University of Science and Technology who is an inexhaustible source of information and a beacon of inspiration. Being an Indian delegate to the SCCR, WIPO, his vast experience and critical thinking nurtured and nourished this work. The author knows that mere words of obeisance to his guru are insufficient to express the author's gratitude to him for his earnest encouragement in moulding this work. He has been a pillar of incessant support and guidance in shaping both the research and the researcher.

The author takes this opportunity to thank Prof. (Dr.) K.N. Chandrasekharan Pillai for his perpetual moral support & blessings, and is thankful to Prof. (Dr.) T. G. Agitha, Prof. (Dr.) N. S. Soman and Dr. P.S. Seema for their valuable insights to strengthen the arguments and stands taken in this book.

The author is also grateful to Prof. Basi, Director, members of faculty of IUCIPRS and the School of Legal Studies and the administration of Cochin University of Science and Technology for the inspiration they rendered all along this work. The author wishes to further place sincere gratitude to Prof. (Dr.) A.P. Singh, Dean, members of the faculty at USLLS and the administration of Guru Gobind Singh Indraprastha University, New Delhi for the smooth facilitation to complete the book.

The author expresses his special gratitude to Mr. Joel Joseph, for his assistance in editing and preparing the final manuscript and also to Mr. T.J. Raj Kumar, Ram Vinayak, Anjali & Shiv for their valuable assistance while finalizing this book. In addition, the author wishes to convey his special thanks to the editorial team of Brill Publishing for their excellent coordination to bring out this book on time.

The author also expresses his deep gratitude to his extended family and friends for their constant support and encouragement in completing the work. A special gratitude is reserved to the apple of his eye, his dear daughter Vaishnavi Sakthivel for being a constant refreshing breeze amidst the nerve wracking process of research.

Last but not the least, the author would like to extend his heartfelt gratitude from the deepest of reservoirs to his wife, Rajarajeswari for her unflinching support and unmeasurable love which became his palm fronds in times of unrelenting heat and to continue his intellectual pursuits. She has been a partner in the true essence of the word both in his personal and professional life.

Illustrations

Figures

Tables

Abbreviations

AM	Amplitude Modulation
BSNL	Bharat Sanchar Nigam Limited
CATV	Community Antenna Television
CDPA	Copyright Designs and Patent Act, 1988
CJEU	Court of Justice of the European
DSL	Digital Subscriber Line
e-UTRAN	Evolved Universal Terrestrial Access Network
ECJ	European Court of Justice
eMBMS	evolved Multimedia Broadcast Multicast Service
EPS	Evolved Packet System
FM	Frequency Modulation
ILO	International Labour Organization
IP	Internet Protocol
IPTV	Internet Protocol Television
ISRO	Indian Space Research Organisation
ITU	International Telecommunication Union
kHz	kilohertz
LTE	Long-Term Evolution
MBMS	Multimedia Broadcast Multicast Service
MPEG	Moving Picture Experts Group
NTP	National Telecom Policy
OECD	Organisation for Economic Co-operation and Development
OFC	Optical Fiber Cable
OFDMA	Orthogonal Frequency Division Multiple Access
P2P	Peer 2 Peer
SCCR	Standing Committee on Copyright and Related Rights
TCP	Transmission Control Protocol
TRAI	Telecom Regulatory Authority of India
TRIPS	Trade Related Intellectual Property Rights
TV	Television
UDP	User Datagram Protocol
UHF	Ultra High Frequency
UNESCO	United Nations Educational, Scientific and Cultural Organization
VHF	Very High Frequency
VOD	Video on Demand
WCT	WIPO Copyright Treaty
WPPT	WIPO Performances and Phonograms Treaty
WIPO	World Intellectual Property Organization

CHAPTER 1

Introduction

The origin and development of copyright law is closely associated with the technological advancements that took place in the printing and entertainment industries. The technological developments in the field of communication of sound and images have had its impact on the enjoyment of copyright works by the public. From gramophone to smart phone, invention of electronic equipments that facilitated 'access to works' had in fact accelerated the enjoyment of copyright works by the public. Similarly, the developments in communication of works through radio, television, satellite, DTH, IPTV, Internet TV etc., also created new demand for access to copyright works.[1] These developments also posed new challenges to copyright law which led to the evolution of new norms for communicating the works to the public. Of all the technological developments, it is the transmission of works through computer networks using 4th generation peer to peer (4G P2P) technology that is currently pushing the copyright law for new solutions to the problem of protecting the interest of authors while satisfying the new demands of public for faster and easy access to works. Copyright laws of the developed countries particularly US and EU, are already in need of review of their norms on 'communication to the public' of the works through new means/medium and India is no exception, given the speed at which technology is penetrating the Indian market.

Copyright law has always been accommodative to these technological changes by express inclusion of the authors' right of dissemination of their works for the enjoyment of public over the new medium both at the international and national level. These technological advancements have not only led to the emergence of the concept of authors' right of 'communication to the public' but also have paved the way for the creation of 'neighbouring rights' at the international level. Historically, the invention of the phonogram records or musical sheets gave birth to the concept of the right of communication to the public and has clearly distinguished itself from the public performance right. With the advent of wireless Herzian waves based communication technologies i.e., broadcasting, the scope for the exploitation of the authors' right has widened. However, due to legal uncertainty over the then emerged new mode of communication of the authors' work, the technology was used by

1 For detailed discussion, see Chapter 2.

 | DOI:10.1163/9789004419155_002

the broadcasting organizations to disseminate the copyright works without any authorization from the copyright owner.[2] After a prolonged legal battle, eventually, the authors' supremacy over the newly emerged technology for the exploitation of their works was upheld through judicial interventions which were followed by legislative changes around the world.[3] At the international level, it was recognized as authors' right of radio-diffusion in the Berne Convention in 1940's. Later on, this had transformed into the right of 'communication to the public' in the WIPO Copyright Treaty in 1996 (WCT) so as to accommodate the newly emerged and commercially exploited technologies such as television broadcasting, cable broadcasting, satellite broadcasting and internet transmissions. From the analysis of the evolution of the concept of the 'communication to the public' internationally, it is evident that as and when a new technology is commercially exploited, the right over the same has been extended to the authors. The language used in the Berne Convention even today stands as a techno-specific model which limits its coverage of emerging technologies.[4]

The socio-economic analysis of the development of the broadcasting industry clearly indicates that huge investment is required for the dissemination of works through broadcasting. It was also evident that unauthorized rebroadcasting of content carrying signal of the broadcasting organizations by their competitors created considerable revenue loss not only to broadcasting organizations but also to the authors of the copyright works.[5] The major reason for the unauthorized rebroadcasting was the legal gap that existed in the authors' right of broadcasting, since the same was restricted only to the expression of content and not to the signals generated by the broadcasting organizations. This led to the emergence of the concept of neighbouring rights protection including that of broadcasting organizations. In order to address the economic interest behind the broadcasters' role in generating the signal for disseminating the authors' works to the public, the concept of 'broadcast reproduction right' was conceived and accepted by the Rome Convention in 1961.[6] The same has been recognized in a limited way in the TRIPS Agreement as well.[7]

2 For detailed discussion, see Chapter 4.

3 *Ibid.*

4 *Ibid.*

5 For the detailed discussion, see Chapters 3 & 4.

6 International Convention for the Protection of Performers, Producers of Phonograms and Broadcasting Organizations, Rome, 1961.

7 For the detailed discussion, see Chapter 4.

The international copyright regime was further modified in 1996 through WCT to meet the new demands of the digital world especially file transfer and other means through which works are made available through Internet.[8] But, the adequacy of the new norms for communication to public in the WCT have been questioned, especially when live streaming or 4G P2P technology has become a commercial success since last decade. As the WCT has aimed at protecting the authors' interest in the digital environment, it may be possible to argue that the WCT provision is technology neutral and hence could be used to cover the future technologies including live streaming. On an analysis of the scope of Article 8 of the WCT on communication to the public, it is possible for one to reach a contrary view. It is true that Article 8 of WCT used terms such as 'communication to the public', 'wire or wireless means', and *making available to the public of their works in such a way that members of the public may access these works from a place and at a time individually chosen by them.* Though these terms have the potential to cover live streaming, the negotiating history of WCT gives the impression that these were intended to cover only the then existing technology of file transfer and on-demand services and not the live streaming technology that did not exist at that time.[9] Therefore, the usage of 'any communication to the public' and 'wire or wireless means' could be construed as if it covers only the then existing technologies and not beyond. In this context, it is felt that further clarification of the WCT norms may be required to cover the authors' right of communication to public in the context of 4G P2P technology.

It is important to note that in 4G P2P, the file is not actually transferred rather the files are merely transmitted for the enjoyment of the public without storing the works in the users' devices. Thus, live streaming is now equated to traditional signal based broadcasting even though the technologies are entirely different i.e., streaming is based on the packet technology whereas broadcasting is based on signal. Even the mode of communication and the medium through which the works are communicated are entirely different.[10] Nevertheless, from the end users' point of view, the live streaming mode of communication resembles with that of the traditional broadcasting. The streaming technology also enables the content received from the signal of the broadcasting organization to be simultaneously retransmitted through computer network generally known as 'simulcasting'. This resulted in the broadcasting organizations demanding for the extension of their traditional rebroadcasting right to

8 *Ibid.*

9 *Ibid.*

10 For the detailed discussion, see Chapter 2.

simultaneous live streaming of the content received from their signal. In the context of the evolution of technologies like encryption to prevent the unauthorized use of digital signals, it is worth examining whether there is any justification for the expansion of the rights of broadcasting organizations.

The experience of developed countries, particularly the United States and the European Union, reveal that the authors' right over the new medium has been extended through judicial interpretations. As far as US is concerned, the technology neutral language of public performance right in the US copyright law[11] has been interpreted by the judiciary to cover the new technologies including streaming.[12] With respect to EU, the scope of the Copyright Directive, 2001/29/EC[13] is capable enough to address live streaming, though it was not intended by the legislature at the time of enacting the Directive. However, the ECJ has extended the same by its interpretations.[14] An examination of the implementation of the EU Directives by the UK indicates that specific provisions are included in the Copyright, Designs and Patent Act, 1988 of UK to address the issue of protection of the right in live streaming of not only the authors but also the broadcasting organizations.[15] Therefore, from the individual countries perspective, it is clear that in the absence of express provisions, the judicial interpretations of the existing provisions enabled the authors to establish their right of communication to the public of works through the newly emerged communication medium to accommodate their economic interest. But, in all these jurisdictions, the judicial interpretations are not free from the wrath of dissent and criticism in the absence of express provisions in the law covering the new technologies. This also compels one to examine the need for legislative reforms in the changing technological environment.

Regarding the demand of broadcasting organizations to extend their rights of rebroadcasting to computer networks, the analysis of the technology behind broadcasting and streaming revealed that both are entirely different. While broadcasting is based on signal, streaming is built on packets which are transmitted using internet protocol. It is technically not possible to directly

---

11 U.S. Copyright Act, 1976.

12 *American Broadcasting Cos., Inc., et al.* v. *Aereo, Inc., FkaBamboom Labs, Inc.* 573 U.S. 2014 and for the detailed discussion, see Chapter 5.

13 Directive 2001/29/EC of the European Parliament and of the Council on the Harmonization of Certain Aspects of Copyright and Related Rights in the Information Society, 22 May 2001.

14 See *ITV Broadcasting Ltd.*, v. *TV Catchup Ltd.*, [2013] F.S.R. 36 and for the detailed discussion, see Chapter 5.

15 See U.K. Copyright, Designs and Patent Act, 1988, Sec. 6 (1A) and for the detailed discussion, see Chapter 5.

stream the signal. The content carrying signal needs to be fixed before it is simultaneously streamed through computer network.[16] Since streaming is an independent and different technology and targets a different market, authors' authorization is very much required to stream the content, even though it is received from the signal generated by the broadcasting organization. The experience of the developed countries makes it clear that the remedy is based on the right of the author through a contractual relationship between the author and broadcasting organizations. The major issue that emerged in these jurisdictions is regarding the streaming of sports content and that has been addressed through contractual agreements.[17] Irrespective of this, the WIPO is still engaged in the negotiation of a separate treaty for extending the rights of broadcasting organizations to computer networks. While developing countries are insisting for a signal based approach for the protection of broadcasting organizations in the traditional platform, developed countries argue for its extension to computer network. Due to a difference of opinion among member states, no final agreement has been reached till date on this issue.[18] In the face of the emergence of technological solutions to prevent unauthorized use of signal in digital context, it is worth examining whether there is any need for such a treaty when globally traditional broadcasting is going to be replaced by live streaming in the foreseeable future.

It is in the context of the above deliberations, one needs to examine whether the Indian law is adequate to protect the interest of authors and broadcasting organizations in the context of the emergence of 4G P2P technologies. The analysis of the right of 'communication to the public' under the Indian Copyright law from its very inception to the 2012 Amendment makes it clear that the Indian law is still based on signal based technology of diffusion and has a limitation of extending it to live streaming. This is evident from the definition of 'radio-diffusion' introduced in the Indian Copyright Act, 1957 which was replaced by 'broadcast' through the 1983 Amendment.[19] A plain reading of the new definition of 'communication to the public' introduced in 1993 and further amended in 2012 gives the impression that the law is still confined to the traditional technology. This demands one to make a critical examination of the technological developments that are taking place in India and to find out whether the law requires further amendment to take care of the interest of the authors in the context of emerging technologies particularly 4G P2P.

16 For the detailed discussion, see Chapter 2.
17 For the detailed discussion, see Chapter 5.
18 For the detailed discussion, see Chapter 4.
19 For the detailed discussion, see Chapter 6.

Broadcasting organizations were also given protection under the Indian copyright law since 1957. Serious amendments were introduced in 1993 to enhance the protection including post-fixation rights. But still, there exists a confusion regarding the nature and scope of protection and its relationship with the 'rights of authors'.[20] Unlike other jurisdictions, Indian Judiciary seems to have thoroughly failed to bring clarity to the nature and scope of protection. Since India is on the verge of switching over to digital broadcasting and moving towards absorbing the 4G P2P technologies, it is also important to have a reexamination of the protection currently afforded to the broadcasting organizations.

20 Ibid.

CHAPTER 2

Technological Advancements in Communication to Public of Works: From Radio-Diffusion to Streaming

2.1 Introduction

Technological advancements especially in the field of information and communication during the 19th Century in many ways influenced the expansion of the scope and content of copyright law. In this context, creation of new rights for the authors of works and the introduction of the concept of neighbouring rights assumed much significance. At the beginning of the 19th century, communication of the work to the public was broadened with the introduction of phonogram records or musical sheets.[1] Before this, works needed to be performed live before the public for them to enjoy it. Phonogram and music sheets enabled people to enjoy the works at home or in public if they had access to record players. Simultaneously, the wireless communication technology through radio which had just penetrated the US market for commercial gains was also used to communicate both copyright and public domain contents. When the radio wireless technology penetrated substantially in the US market, due to competition, the radio diffusion (broadcasting) companies facilitated unauthorized access of copyright contents to the public who had the radio sets in their homes. Due to this the copyright owners sued the radio broadcasters for the unauthorized access.[2] This resulted in the expansion or bringing of a new mode of exploitation of copyright i.e., right of 'wireless diffusion' which was later termed as 'communication to the public' to include new modes of communication due to the advent of technology such as TV, satellite, cable, internet, etc.

Though, technology has been advancing since 19th century, radio wireless diffusion brought important changes in the communication of the work to

1 For the detailed discussion about the expansion of copyright to the records and sheets, see Sidney A. Diamond, "Sound Recordings and Phonorecords: History and Current Law", *University of Illinois Law Forum*, (1981), pp. 337–372, at p. 337.

2 Makeen Fouad Makeen, *Copyright in a Global Information Society: The Scope of Copyright Protection under International, US, UK and French Law*, Kluwer Law International, London, (2000), at p. 35.

 | DOI:10.1163/9789004419155_003

the public. Prior to radio diffusion, if a copyrighted work had to be enjoyed by the people, either they must have possessed work embodied in material form (phonogram records or music sheets) or people had to go to a place where it was played in public. However, radio diffusion enabled public who had access to radio instruments to enjoy the content without possessing phonogram records or music sheets. In short, it may be initially observed that this radio diffusion substituted the traditional public performance of recorded works. In this chapter, an attempt is made to briefly explain the growth of technology in the field of communication to public from radio diffusion to internet streaming and the demand it created in evolving new norms in the copyright law for protection of the works and the carrier of the content.

2.2 Radio Diffusion

The underlying process in radio-diffusion involves the conversion of sound waves into electric current.

> The sound waves vibrate the microphone diaphragm and are converted into a varying electric current. The electric current is then converted to a varying magnetic field by an electromagnet, which makes a representation of the sound as magnetized areas on a plastic tape with a magnetic coating on it.[3]

The 'transducer' is used to convert the non electrical signals to electrical signals.[4] Hence, it is termed as 'signal' based technology. Converted waves are low frequency waves which are low power in nature; create huge noise at the receiver when they are diffused without carriers.[5] So as to deliver the content to the desired public, the low frequency waves are sent with the help of carrier

3 Steve Esomba, *Moving Cameras And Living Movies*, available at (Google Books) https://books.google.co.in/books?id=k5rFBgAAQBAJ&pg=PA1&source=gbs_selected_pages&cad=2#v=onepage&q&f=false (last accessed on 27/06/2019) and also K. Bijusha, "Sound Recording and Reproduction", available at http://dmmcfc.com/sound-recording-and-reproduction-2/ (last accessed on 25/10/2017).

4 S.K. Bhattacharya and S. Bhattacharya, *Electrical Measurement and Control*, Vikas Publishing House, (2015), at p. 3.

5 "Electromagnetic Spectrum", available at http://www.encyclopedia.com/science-and-technology/astronomy-and-space-exploration/astronomy-general/electromagnetic-spectrum (last accessed on 26/06/2019).

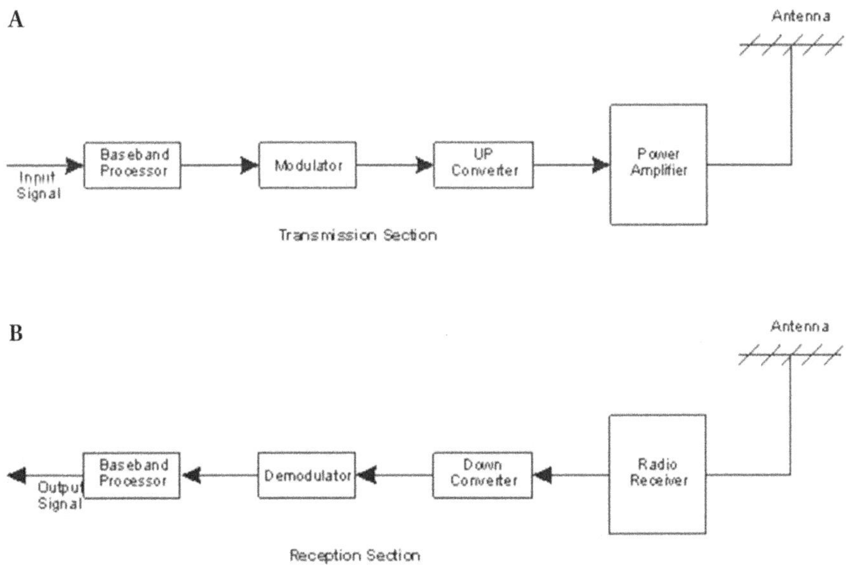

FIGURE 1 Radio communication system[6]

signals after encoding the content with signal for eliminating external and internal distortions. While receiving the content carrying signals by the receiver, the content carrying signals are decoded for the enjoyment. Figure 1 explains the nature of the technology employed in detail.

Due to this, content is dependent on carrier signals for moving from one place to another. This is being done either with the help of high frequency magnetic waves such as very high frequency (VHF) or ultra high frequency (UHF). These two types of the analogue diffusion are specially used for short range broadcasting just like radio magnetic waves broadcasting.[7] Once the content is diffused with the help of carrier signals, then the public by using an antenna, can receive the modulated signals around the same time. Once the signal is received, content would be dissected from the carrier signals and

6 See for the same, K.V. Prasad, "Radio Communication System", available at http://flylib.com/books/en/4.329.1.72/1/ (last accessed on 26/06/2019).

7 For detailed discussion about UHF and VHF, see Standing committee on copyright and related rights, WIPO 19th SCCR study paper on "Socio-Economic Dimension of the Unauthorized Use of Signals: Current Market and Technology Trends in the Broadcasting Sector", (2009–2010), at p. 9, available at https://www.wipo.int/edocs/mdocs/copyright/en/sccr_19/sccr_19_12.pdf (last accessed on 26/06/2019).

then the same can be enjoyed by the public. In this radio broadcasting, there are two different modes: the first is amplitude modulation (AM) and second is frequency modulation (FM).[8] In the AM method, electromagnetic waves could be affected easily by the natural barriers such as weather and other physical interferences. However, in the FM method, the possibility of external influence is far less than AM which is the reason why FM is preferred over AM for audio broadcasting in most of the cities at present.[9] The limitations of radio-diffusion are as follows:

1. As comparatively very low frequency waves are used for this radio broadcasting, the waves cannot travel beyond a particular point. So as to enable further transmission, boosting of content carrying waves has to done. By this way, it becomes an expensive process since many transmitting towers have to be employed for the purpose of further transmission. As a result, it is limited to a geographical region.
2. Content size has to be optimal in any mode of transmission. However, in this analogue model, it is huge in size, and storing of the same has to be done in volumes and volumes. This is considered as one of the negative aspects of this transmission.
3. The low frequency waves can be influenced by internal and external environment.
4. Quality of the content would be relatively low due to the frequency ranges.
5. Only audio contents can be diffused not video contents.

The above self-explained UHF and VHF waves are employed in television broadcasting too. Let us look into television broadcasting technology in brief.

2.3 Terrestrial TV Broadcasting

Initially, the terrestrial TV services were based on transmitter towers. The towers located within that region were used to relay the program from the station

8 For detailed discussion on radio broadcasting technology, "AM, FM Waves and Sound", available at http://www.cybercollege.com/frtv/frtv017.htm (last accessed on 26/06/2019).

9 See WIPO 19th SCCR study paper on "Socio-Economic Dimension of the Unauthorized Use of Signals: Current Market and Technology Trends in the Broadcasting Sector", (2009–2010), at p. 29, available at: https://www.wipo.int/edocs/mdocs/copyright/en/sccr_19/sccr_19_12.pdf (last accessed on 26/06/2019).

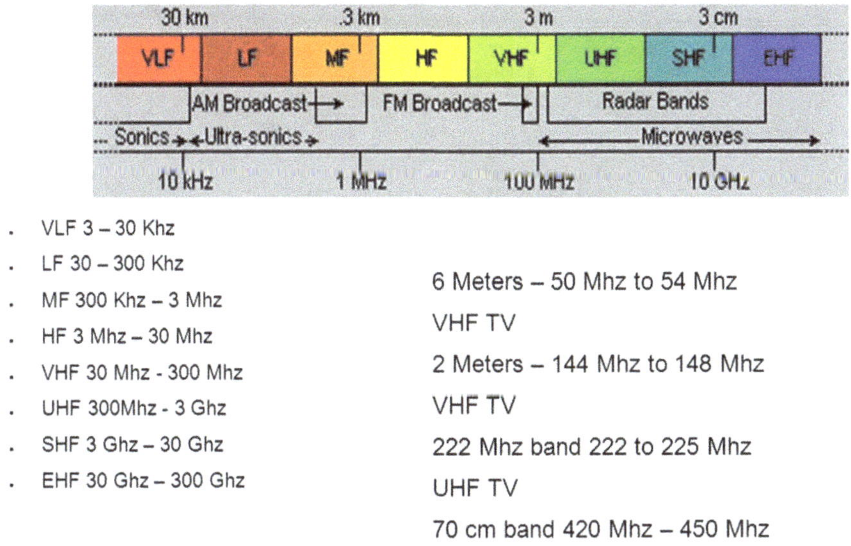

FIGURE 2 High frequency spectrum[10]

to the distant location. This terrestrial TV technology is known as 'analogue technology' due to the use of radio magnetic signals. In a terrestrial TV broadcasting, the signal comprises of two important parts: the first one is sound and the second one is picture.[11] In the terrestrial TV broadcasting, UHF waves are considered as more perfect one than VHF waves because of the quality of content delivery. Another reason is that the useable range in the spectrum has widened which has resulted in preference of UHF over VHF for television communication. Due to technological advancements, UK had completely switched to UHF in the 1980s.[12]

In this technology, sound carrier is put at the upper end of the spectrum due to the spectrum and the bandwidth. In general, the audio bandwidth ranges from 50 Hz to 15 kHz. In some extreme cases, 25 kHz is possible but not beyond

10 See for the same, available at http://images.slideplayer.com/15/4806805/slides/slide_30.jpg (last accessed on 26/06/2019).

11 See generally for the same from the technical point of view, K G Jackson and G B Townsend, *TV & Video Engineer's Reference Book*, Butterworth-Heinemann Ltd., (1991), at pp. 47–48.

12 See for the same WIPO 30th SCCR on "Current Market and Technology Trends in the Broadcasting Sector", (2015), at p. 18, available at https://www.wipo.int/edocs/mdocs/copyright/en/sccr_30/sccr_30_5.pdf (last accessed on 26/06/2019).

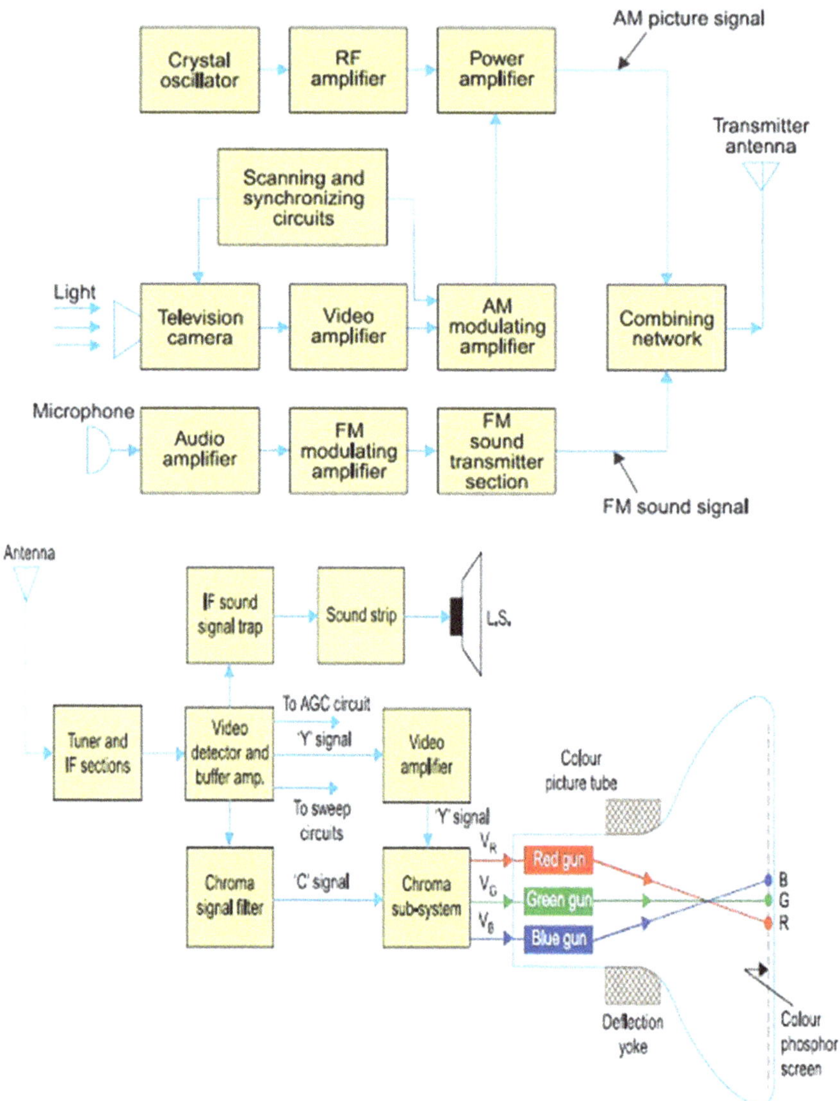

FIGURE 3 TV broadcasting[13]

that. In addition, the TV broadcasting sound content requires less bandwidth than FM sound content. Therefore, the method of diffusion employed in FM

13 R. R. Gulati, *Modern Television Practice: Transmission, Reception and Applications*, New Age International (5th edn., 2015), at pp. 5–7.

transmission is used in TV broadcasting of audio content. Whereas, the visual (video) part is concerned, it is transmitted with the help of carrier waves which is located lower than the sound carrier waves i.e., typically below 4.5 MHz. In TV broadcasting, frequency modulation is done for the audio content and amplitude modulation is done for the video content so as to avoid any interference between sound and video. Figure 3 shows us how TV broadcasting happens from the sender point to receiver point.

Since the technology used for radio broadcasting and terrestrial broadcasting is more or less the same, it is worth to understand the limitations of this technology. Both are based on radio magnetic waves. As stated above, radio magnetic waves are subjected to human interferences[14] and natural interferences.[15] The second limitation is that the receiving transmitter towers have the capacity of receiving signals ideally up to 30 miles not beyond that. For further communication to the left out geographical areas, transmitter towers in large numbers have to be placed, and the country like India requires plenty of it. These problems have been overcome by cable broadcasting.

2.4 Cable Broadcasting

Historically, Cable Television method was not considered as a mode of communication of works. It is not an independent technology because this technology has been used to fix the defects in the terrestrial TV broadcasting i.e., over the air model. As stated above,[16] when terrestrial broadcasting is done, signals may not be available to all places in a country or to all stations. For example, in the US, there were around 1544 authorized UHF TV stations out of which 102 TV stations were actually functioning in 1962. In 1965, Federal Communication Commission (FCC) strongly felt that when 82 channels were made available to all US Citizens, then the US would be considered to have TV service.[17] For achieving this target, over the air mode of broadcasting was

14 For the detailed discussion on the same, see "RF Design Guide", available at http://www.cdt21.com/resources/guide2.asp (last accessed on 26/06/2019).

15 *Ibid.*

16 *Ibid.*

17 Charles O. Verrill, "CATV's Emerging Role: Cablecaster or Common Carrier?", *Law and Contemporary Problems,* (1969), pp. 586–609.

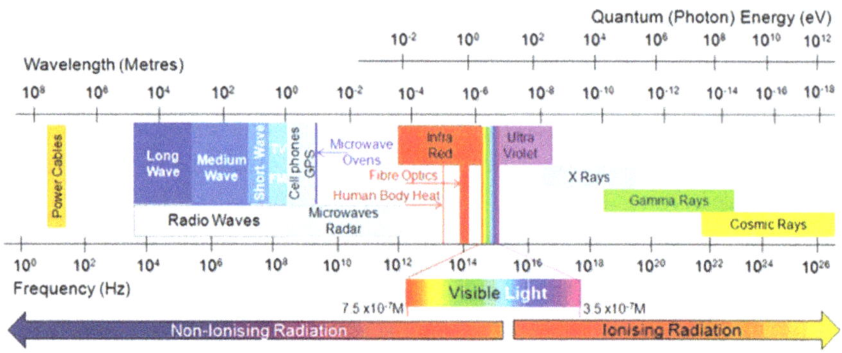

FIGURE 4 Complete view of the spectrum usage in communication[19]

inadequate. The solution was the introduction of community antenna system (CATV).[18]

The technology in the CATV is similar to that of over the air model. However, it is worth to be noted that it is not a terrestrial method. Though the fundamental technology behind these two is the same, the diffusion of content carrying signal was only through coaxial cable or copper cable rather than over the air. Over a period of time, due to digitalization, the optic fiber cable was used to deliver the carrier waves to the desired households.

Figure 4 and Table 1[20] explain the different uses of spectrum in communication. In cable broadcasting, UHF or VHF TV signals from the stations are received by using a common antenna which is ideally put at a suitable place. Then the same is further diffused at a very high spectrum in the UHF by using the wire. This frequency is much higher than the original signals transmitted by the VHF/UHF stations. TV sets that are connected with this cable, would receive the same signal at the same time at a relatively higher quality. When compared with over the air transmission, the time difference between the two

18 See for further details, John P. Cole, "Community Antenna Television, the Broadcaster Establishment, and the Federal Regulator", 14 *The American University Law Review*, (1964–1965), pp. 124–145 and also see Robert E R Huntley and Charles F Phillips, "CATV: A Regulatory Dilemma", 18 *Alabama Law Review*, (1965–1966), pp. 64–81.

19 See for the detailed discussion about spectrum usage in communication, "Electromagnetic Radiation and Radio Waves: Natural and Man-Made Miracles", available at http://www.mpoweruk.com/radio.htm (last accessed on 26/06/2019).

20 See for some updated uses Rajiv, "What are Radio Frequency bands and its uses?", available at https://www.rfpage.com/what-are-radio-frequency-bands-and-its-uses/ (last accessed on 26/06/2019).

TABLE 1 Common frequency ranges and uses

Name	Frequency range	Name Origin	Common uses
VHF	30 to 300 MHz	Very High Frequency	FM Radio, TV Broadcasts
UHF	300 to 3000 MHz	Ultra High Frequency	TV broadcasts, Microwave oven, Microwave devices and communications, radio astronomy, mobile phones, wireless LAN, Bluetooth.
L Band	1 to 2GHz	Long	Military telemetry, GPS, ATC radar
S Band	2 to 4 GHz	Short	Weather radar, surface ship radar, microwave ovens, microwave devices/ communications.
C Band	4 to 8 GHz	Compromise (between S and X)	Long-distance radio telecommunications
X Band	8 to 12 GHz	X for crosshair (used in WW2 for fire control radar)	Satellite communications, radar, terrestrial broadband, space communications
Ku Band	12 to 18 GHz	Kurtz Under	Satellite communications
K Band	18 to 26.5 GHz	Kurtz (German for short)	Radar, satellite communications, astronomical observations, automotive radar
Ka Band	26.5 to 40 GHz	Kurtz Above	Satellite communications

is again substantially less.[21] Therefore, this is considered as re-broadcasting, since, it could simultaneously diffuse the 'Over the Air' content.[22]

21 See *Carter Mountain Transmission Corporation* v. *Federal Communications Commission*, 321 F.2d 359 (D.C. Cir. 1963) also see *Clarksburg Publishing Co.* v. *Federal Communications Commission*, 225 F.2d 511, (1955), at p. 517.

22 WIPO 30th SCCR on "Current Market and Technology trends in the Broadcasting Sector", (2015), at p. 18, available at https://www.wipo.int/edocs/mdocs/copyright/en/sccr_30/sccr_30_5.pdf (last accessed on 26/06/2019).

The cable broadcasting started initially with the help of coaxial cable or copper which did not enable the consumers to interact with the content providers, since it was intended only for one way communication which meant that 'One to All'. In this type of communication, the information or content can only flow from the broadcasters. Therefore, the users do not have any option to interact with the broadcasters i.e., they have to remain passive viewers. Therefore, only one way communication was possible which was considered as a limitation of cable broadcasting. However, over a period of time due to the advent of digitalization, two way communications were enabled. With the optic fiber cable, TV, telephone and broadband i.e., 3 in 1 can be provided to all. This would be discussed in detail under the IPTV. In between the analogue and the digital phase, the satellite transmission had emerged as a mode of communication which is discussed below.

2.5 Satellite Broadcasting

Satellite transmission of the TV signal is considered as another milestone in the communication revolution. Through satellites, live simultaneous transmission of a TV broadcast by using analogue transmission methods around the world or at a particular region without the help of amplifiers was made real.[23] Satellite broadcasting started in the 1960s in a very limited way. However, it came into reality and has been widely used since the 1990s. The satellite broadcasting technology is a bit different from TV and cable broadcasting. Here, broadcasting is done again with the help of spectrum. However, this spectrum is not within the ambit of VHF and UHF. The frequencies utilized for satellite broadcasting cannot be used for TV broadcasting. In satellite broadcasting, the content carrying signal is transmitted with the help of a satellite to all. The signals are received by a specialized antenna which is known as the common antenna/community antenna/dish antenna and then the received signal is amplified and the noise & other interferences are filtered out. After this, the set-top boxes that decode the content carrying

23 *Ibid.* and also for the detailed discussion about the Satellite broadcasting Technology see Megumi Ogawa, *Protection of Broadcasters' Rights*, Martinus Nijhoff Publishers, Boston, (2006), p. 64. In addition to these references, see 19th SCCR study paper on "Socio-Economic Dimension of the Unauthorized Use of Signals: Current Market and Technology Trends in the Broadcasting Sector", (2009–2010), at p. 11, available at https://www.wipo.int/edocs/mdocs/copyright/en/sccr_19/sccr_19_12.pdf (last accessed on 26/06/2019).

signals enable the viewers to enjoy the content by using TV sets. In case of free to air TV broadcasting, due to the technological limitations, it is restricted to a geographical region. In those cases, if the contents have to be transmitted beyond a region, then the signal has to be aired through satellite and the same would be received by a common/community antenna. Further, the content transmitted will be decoded, then it transmitted via copper wires to desired houses that have paid/agreed to pay the subscription/entry fee. The privileged group will enjoy the content at their home by using the TV set. This may be considered as a paradigm shift from traditional broadcasting, because, for the first time, the free to air signal access is limited to a group of public not to all. Due to technological advancements in the cable based transmission, access has been enabled not directly by the consumers but only through a service provider.

Even in this technology, one to one communication is not possible even though the content could be in digital format. The reasons are the technology and the nature of signals. The objective of this mode of communication was to provide access to contents getting transmitted. In short, it was aimed to overcome the limitations of previous modes of transmissions such as cost factor; transmissions being limited to geographical areas, etc. It was not aimed at providing sophisticated mode of transmission wherein the users were allowed to choose the desired program in an interactive manner. This is considered as a limitation of satellite broadcasting when compared with internet protocol TV (IPTV). However, with the advancement of technology, the set-top boxes have been enabled to act as a modem of broadband connection, so that it would facilitate one to one communication. When this model is adopted, then it will fall under IPTV/Web TV and not under satellite broadcasting since the IPTV model is entirely based on P2P file transfer techniques. Therefore, the detailed aspect of the same is discussed below.

2.6 P2P File Transfer Technology: 1st Generation to 3rd Generation

Usually file transfer over internet takes place through Peer 2 Peer (P2P)[24] file transmission techniques. The P2P file transfer is entirely based on packet

24 For the detailed discussion about the Peer to Peer and its nature, available at https://www.lifewire.com/introduction-to-peer-to-peer-networks-817421 (last accessed on 26/10/2019).

technology. It means the content is compressed and protected with encryption technology[25] by using dedicated software and then it is converted into small packets which could be transported over IP. Delivery of the packets is also regulated by the technology. Over a period of time, P2P has occupied an important position in the digital transmission of context, since, it has been modified from time to time from its inception to adoption. At present, there are four generations of P2P file transfer models available; first, Napster[26] which is considered as the 1st generation file transmission model. It was developed with a search engine, a centralized server and a relay chart or list.[27] The whole idea behind the technology was to enable the users to share MP3 music files with others through this technology.[28] Users who had installed this software on their PCs, had to search through the dedicated search engine to find out whether the desired file was available and with whom. With the help of a relay chart and a centralized server, the user would be connected with other user(s) who were in possession of the desired MP3 file and then the file would be downloaded to the user's PC. Further, the user who downloaded the file, could also share the same with others through the same process. In the centralized server, the file was neither kept nor supplied by the server. All it did was to connect users who wished to share the files. In this model, it was possible to monitor who transferred the file to whom. Like Napster, edonkey2000 and Soulseek are a few other examples for the 1st Generation P2P systems.[29] Due to a copyright issue, Napster was ordered to close down which led to the development of the 'Second Generation' P2P system.[30]

---

25 See for the detailed discussion on the technology, Chapter 3 of this book.

26 Napster is a model/software which was developed to share MP3 files among the users who have the software in their PC.

27 See for the detailed discussion on the Napster and the technology behind i.e., 1st generation P2P file transfer, Jeff Tyson, "How the Old Napster Worked", available at http://computer.howstuffworks.com/napster1.htm (last accessed on 26/06/2019) and also see Michael Nwogugu, "Economics of Digital Content: New Digital Content Control and P2P Control Systems/Methods", *Computer and Telecommunications Law Review*, (2008), pp. 140–149, at p. 141.

28 See for the same, "Napster: The Day the Music was Set Free", available at https://www.theguardian.com/music/2013/feb/24/napster-music-free-file-sharing (last accessed on 26/ 06/ 2019).

29 See Michael Nwogugu, "Economics of Digital Content: New Digital Content Control and P2P Control Systems/Methods", *Computer and Telecommunications Law Review*, (2008), pp. 140–149, at p. 141.

30 See for the same, Okechukwu Benjamin Vincents, "When Rights Clash Online: The Tracking of P2P Copyright Infringements Vs. the EC Personal Data Directive", 16 (3) *International Journal of Law and Information Technology*, Autumn 2008, pp. 270–296.

In the second generation P2P system (2G P2P), centralised server concept was replaced with the 'hybrid centralised server'. Therefore, the centralized file server was decentralized. Even though, it had no centralised server, it was alleged of copyright infringement activities just like the 1st Generation P2P system.[31] In order to avoid the problems in the 2G P2P system, further technological advancement took place. As a result, the 'Third Generation' P2P system (3G P2P) emerged. 3G P2P system was fully decentralized. At present, most of the file transmissions take place with the help of '3G P2P system'. Currently there are two types of P2P System in the 3G P2P system. They are Friend-to-friend (e.g. Metanet, Waste and Mute) and Anonymous (e.g. GNUnet, Entropy and Freenet).[32]

All the above said 3G P2P systems transmit the entire file from one to another. It means that the entire data is transferred. As a result of this, users can have a copy of the transmitted file. When the P2P system comes to the fourth generation (4G P2P), there is a tremendous change in the file transmission. The very nature of the 4G P2P is entirely different from the previous modes of P2P transmissions. Therefore, it is worth observing that there is no nexus between streaming/4G P2P and other previous P2P. 4G P2P is an improved mode of file transfer so as to overcome the limitations of previous generations of P2P. In 4G P2P system, the data is transmitted in the form of streams instead of sending it as a file. It means that the information is shared instead of the entire file. Due to this reason, end users cannot save any transmitted file. When the streams reach the users monitor, within a few seconds they will disappear. They cannot be saved. Unlike other generations, 4G P2P employs no server (centralised or decentralised servers) and no list.[33] Let us discuss the 4G P2P in detail.

2.6.1 *4G P2P Technology (Streaming Technology) and Its Nature*

From the technology point of view, terms like webcasting and streaming are used to describe the mode of transmission taking place using 4G P2P.[34] In

31 See Michael Nwogugu, "Economics of Digital Content: New Digital Content Control and P2P Control Systems/Methods", *Computer and Telecommunications Law Review*, (2008), pp. 140–149, at p. 141.

32 See *Ibid.*

33 See Michael Nwogugu, "Economics of Digital Content: New Digital Content Control and P2P Control Systems/Methods", *Computer and Telecommunications Law Review*, (2008), pp. 140–149, at p. 141.

34 David Austerberry, *The Technology of Video & Audio Streaming*, Focal Press, London, (2nd edn., 2005), at p. 7.

general, video or audio streaming over internet is considered as webcasting. Though, the streaming process is similar to broadcasting, it differs in the mode of delivery. In the rest of the broadcasting modes, the content is transmitted via over the air, cable and satellite using signals. In the streaming context, content is delivered over the internet.[35] Due to this reason, the technologists generally consider the streaming process as 'internet broadcasting' or 'webcasting'.

Form the technological point of view, webcasting has been very loosely defined as broadcasting of contents over the World Wide Web. According to Victorian State Scrutiny of Acts and Regulations Committee Report, 2005:

> Webcasting means the distribution of audio and/or video content over a computer network. Webcasting can be episodic (sporadic) or continuous (such as a radio broadcast), temporal (ephemeral) or permanent (stored). Webcasting takes advantage of "streaming" to allow the user to watch or listen to the content as it is transmitted, rather than having to wait for a complete file to be downloaded.[36]

Though these definitions are aimed at defining the nature of technology, the same have not been accepted by any legal system in the world.[37] From the above, it may be noted that the term streaming or streaming media have been employed in the same sense. It means transferring of data in a manner that allows it to be processed as the data is transferred, rather than requiring all the data to be transferred before it can be used. Streaming is often useful in accelerating access to large audio or video files, or where the stream is ongoing.

The streaming technology is different from web page delivery which is also known as Download and Play. In the web page delivery, the entire audio/video files are transferred and the user needs to wait till the entire file is downloaded to be enjoyed. In the web page delivery, larger content files take considerable time to download. It depends on the availability of bandwidth. In case of a progressive download, while downloading the file, the user can open it. It means

35 For the further detailed discussion about the difference between the broadcasting and webcasting, see Chapter 3 of this work.

36 See for the same, is available at https://www.parliament.vic.gov.au/archive/sarc/E-Democracy/Final_Report/Glossary.htm (last accessed on 01/09/2017).

37 For the detailed discussion about the legal definitions, see the subsequent Chapters.

the progressive download enables the user to access as well as to save the file in the local disk simultaneously.[38] However, in case of streaming, the audio/video content is transmitted like small packets. This enables the end user to use the content while receiving them rather than downloading and storing in the local disk. After seeing these packets, no copy of the file is automatically left in the users' system.[39]

In the terrestrial TV broadcasting, users have no option to do anything with the transmitted content. When they want to enjoy the content, they can (may) switch on the TV and switch it off when they do not want to see the content. In case of live streaming also, the clients do not have the options to pause or forward or replay the streaming content. Even though, there is an option for having interaction with the content provider, but at the time of transmission, clients can not have any interaction with the content providers. Therefore, it cannot be considered as an interactive transmission and is just like traditional broadcasting even though the technology is substantially different.

Even in live streaming, stored contents can be used. While using the stored contents, the content shall be streamed to all clients at the same time. They will not have any option to interact with the content providers unlike on demand service. It means when a film is streamed, all the clients will be watching the same content at the same time. At the time of stored content live streaming also, clients do not have the options for interaction because a single stream is transmitted to all at one time unlike on-demand streaming.[40]

As a result of the above discussion, live streaming may be considered as net based broadcasting in its nature and content, though the technology used is substantially different. However, as discussed above, both the technologies are entirely different. In addition, as the streaming technology is based on IP, there is no geographical limitation on content delivery and thus once transmitted

38 Streaming is also different from the progressive download. The progressive download can be considered as intermediate step between the streaming and the web page delivery. The main difference is that when the files are being received, the user can use the file also can save the file. In case of streaming the later one is absent.

39 See Michael Nwogugu, "Economics of Digital Content: New Digital Content Control and P2P Control Systems/Methods", *Computer and Telecommunications Law Review*, (2008), pp. 140–149, at p. 141 and also see David Austerberry, *The Technology of Video & Audio Streaming*, Focal Press, London (2nd edn., 2005), at p. 8.

40 See *Id.*, p. 209.

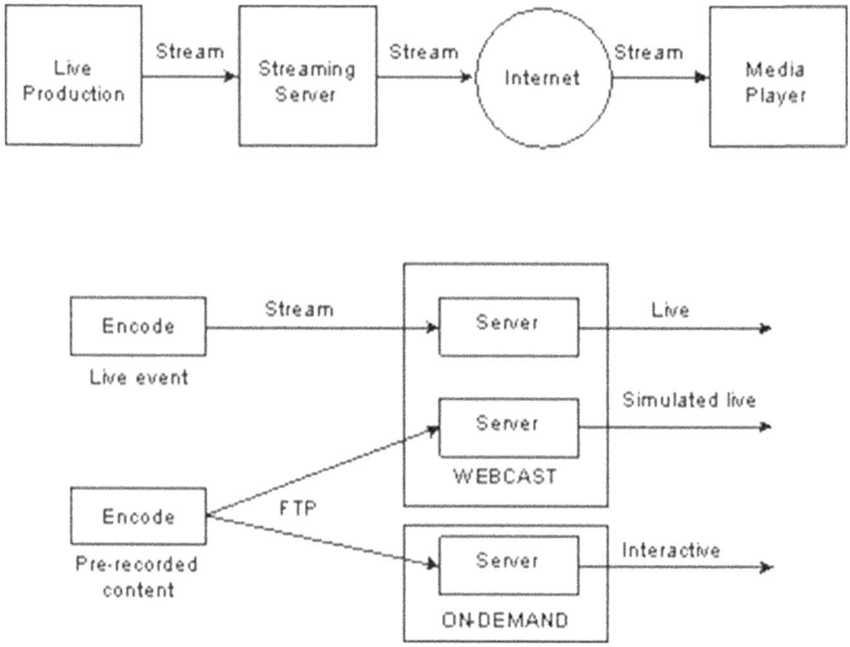

FIGURE 5 The technology of video and audio streaming[41]

it would be received by all those who are provided with access irrespective of geographical location. Whereas in broadcasting, it is very much restricted by the geographical limitations. Figure 5 shows the functioning of streaming technology.

2.6.2 *IPTV*

Internet protocol television(IPTV), is a medium by which TV content is transmitted via internet protocol to suite over a packet-switched network such as a local area network or internet, rather than transmission of signals over traditional terrestrial, cable and satellite.[42] Since, it was the first ever full fledged

41 See David Austerberry, *The Technology of Video & Audio Streaming*, Focal Press, London, (2nd edn., 2005), at p. 8.

42 See for the same, available at https://en.wikipedia.org/wiki/IPTV (last accessed on 26/06/2019).

interactive TV service, its features attracted many consumers to switch over from cable TV. The main features[43] are:

- Interactive services i.e., 2 way communication by which video on demand (VoD) can be provided
- Time Shifting
- Requirement of Low Bandwidth
- Enjoyment via multiple devices not limited to TV only.

IPTV employs a streaming transmission model. Generally streaming technology is understood as a technology through which file transmission would take place without transferring the file as such to the end-users. It means the file could be transmitted only for the enjoyment of the content and not to store the same for future use. It is entirely based on internet protocol. This streaming technology works based on streams which is nothing but packets of content encrypted and converted into binary codes which could be transmitted easily over internet protocol even when the bandwidth is at an average level. Whereas, in traditional broadcasting, it is entirely based on signals as discussed above. Thus, it would be possible to conclude at the preliminary inquiry itself that the streaming technology and broadcasting are two different technologies as the initial one is based on streams and packets which would be used over IP and the latter one is completely based on signals which would be used along with radio magnetic waves.

The streaming process can be divided into two types. One is live streaming and the other one is on-demand streaming. In case of live streaming, the streams (small packets which have been made by using compressing and encoding with the help of the specific software) are transmitted to the streaming server. Here, the streaming server regulates the delivery of packets into the network. Delivery of packets depends on the availability of the bandwidth. If the bandwidth rate is very high, delivery of the packets will take place at high speed. In order to receive the packets, buffering will take place for a few seconds. After decoding and decompressing, the user's system will play the stream with the help of the media player.[44] The entire process will be completed within a fraction of a second.

---

43 Jan Loskowski, "IPTV services and Technologies", available at https://www.tu-braunschweig.de/Medien-DB/ida-kn/seminar_komm_syst/laskowski_ws09.pdf (last accessed on 26/06/2019).

44 See David Austerberry, *The Technology of Video & Audio Streaming,* Focal Press, London, (2nd edn., 2005), Chapters 7 to 13.

Generally, a multicast model is used in live streaming. The content that is transmitted by using multicast is made available to all the clients at the same time.[45] Here, multicast means transmission of single stream for all the clients.[46] Therefore, there will not be any active interaction with the service provider in this context. For this reason, it may be possible to equate live streaming with terrestrial broadcasting even though the technology is entirely different.[47] In the terrestrial analogue transmissions, a single content is transmitted to all the households. This unicast model is widely employed in IPTV, however unicast is employed by some of the live streaming sites as well.[48] In this unicast model, the live streaming service provider sends single set of streams to signal subscriber thereby the authenticity of the subscriber is verified. Even though the transmission would be simultaneous, each individual subscriber is given with a predetermined access to the dedicated streams based on their subscription.

In IPTV, the video is encoded at the national head-end where the network feeds are accessed from satellite. While encoding the same, the MPEG 2/ MPEG 4[49] is used for the compression of video. Then the streams are pushed through the network which is an IP network. Then the local office will be enabled to mix the advertising content where the channel changes requests, VoD, etc., are handled.[50] At the receiver end, the specialised set-top box which is connected with DSL would reassemble the streamed packets into the right flow for the enjoyment.[51] Figure 6 shows how the IPTV technology works.

45 For the detailed discussion about the live streaming, see *Ibid.*

46 For the detailed discussion about the IP unicast and Multicast, see Steve Mack and Dan Rayburn, *Hands on Guide to webcasting: Internet event and Av production*, Focal Press, London, (2006), at p. 167.

47 For the same argument see *Ibid.*

48 See for the detailed discussion on the same, refer next Chapter.

49 See Nate Anderson, "An introduction to IPTV", available at https://arstechnica.com/information-technology/2006/03/iptv/ (last accessed on 26/06/2019).

50 William D. Hong, "IPTV Technology, Trends and Challenges", available at http://www-inst.eecs.berkeley.edu/~ee233/sp06/student_presentations/EE233_IPTV.pdf (last accessed on 26/06/2019).

51 See Amal Punchihew, "Internet protocol television (IPTV)", Multi Media Research Group, School of Engineering and Advanced Technology, Massey University, available at https://www.researchgate.net/publication/299410032_IPTV-Internet_Protocol_Televsion (last accessed on 26/06/2019).

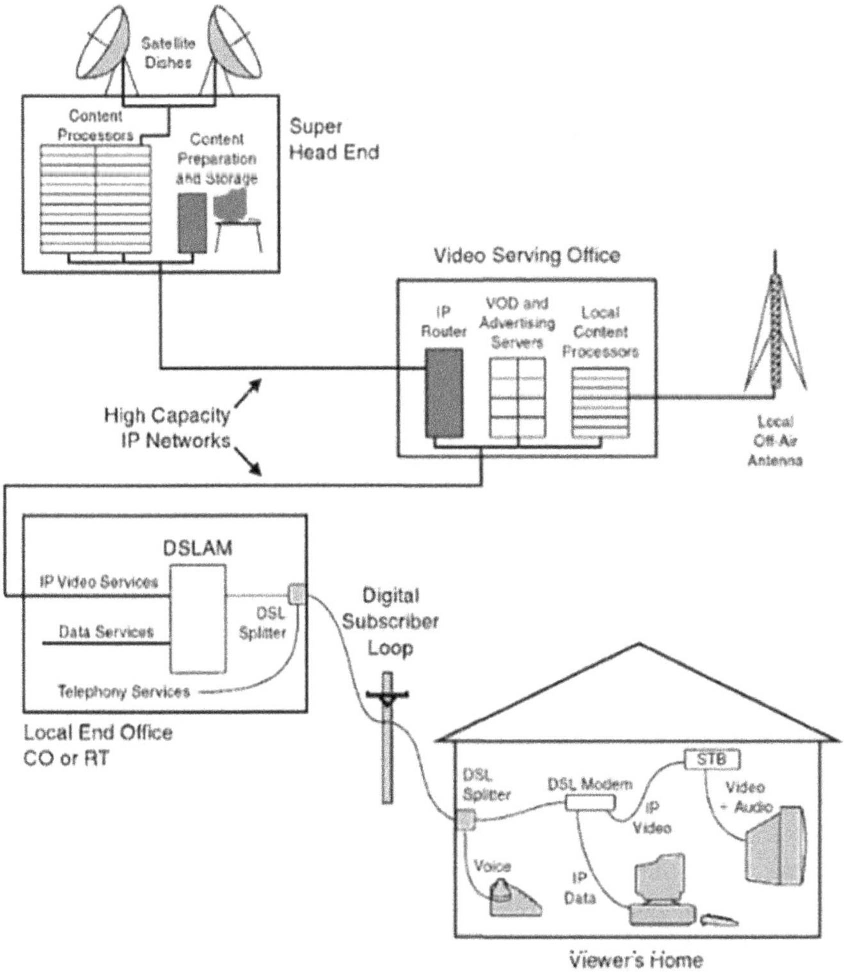

FIGURE 6 IPTV layout[52]

Though IPTV transmission is over IP, it is not similar to web-TV or watching live/real time content over internet.[53] In IPTV, the contents are delivered via dedicated limited bandwidth connection either by a telecom provider or a broadband provider.[54] In addition, though the dedicated line/connection is

52 *Ibid.*

53 *Ibid* and also see WIPO 30th SCCR on "Current Market and Technology trends in the Broadcasting Sector", (2015), at p. 18, available at https://www.wipo.int/edocs/mdocs/copyright/en/sccr_30/sccr_30_5.pdf (last accessed on 26/06/2019).

54 *Ibid.*

provided to each consumer, in total, it is considered as a closed group. Therefore, this is not open to all unlike web TV. Whereas, in web TV, content is open to all. All you need to have is a good bandwidth connection. As far as content delivery is concerned, in IPTV & web TV, it happens at the same time when compared with signal based transmissions since the contents are compressed with MPEG 2/MPEG 4.[55] Let us now discuss the technology of web TV in detail.

2.6.3 *Web TV/Internet TV*

Web TV or online streaming is again based on the same technology employed in IPTV with some modifications. As said above, since IPTV is a closed network, the access is limited to pre-determined consumers whereas web TV is open to all. It is not even restricted to a geographical location. What is required for accessing the content is a good bandwidth broadband connection and a personal computer (PC). Quality of the content being delivered over this would be similar to IPTV; however, it is subject to bandwidth. Good bandwidth connection determines the quality of service as well as uploading and downloading content size. Both the service provider as well as the users should have good bandwidth so that delivery can be effective e. This type of transmission method is known as 'streaming technology' or '4G P2P file transferring technology'. It has been developed over a period of time so as to effectively utilize the internet and bandwidth.

In this transmission, like previous generation file transfer methods, the content is digitized and then delivered in the form of packets which is nothing but binary codes i.e., (0 and 1). The content which has to be transmitted would get divided into multiple pieces in a particular size which can be transmitted over internet. The content is encrypted with identification markers and the packets which carry the content will be transported through network. The software which is employed for this streaming technology is TCP/UDP model. This is the main difference between 4G P2P and the rest. Though IPTV is also based on this streaming technology, it is highly imperative to understand the key differences[56] and commonalities between IPTV and the Web TV.

In the light of the above discussion, as the same live streaming techniques are used over mobile communications, the mobile based live streaming also needs to be discussed in detail.

---

55 See Nate Anderson, "An introduction to IPTV", available at https://arstechnica.com/information-technology/2006/03/iptv/ (last accessed on 26/06/2019).

56 For Detailed discussion about the IPTV and Web TV, see Anil Sharma, "What is the difference between IPTV and Internet TV?", available at https://www.quora.com/What-is-the-difference-between-IPTV-and-Internet-TV (last accessed on 26/06/2019) and also see "Internet TV", available at https://en.wikipedia.org/wiki/Internet_television (last accessed on 26/06/2019).

TABLE 2 Difference between IPTV and Web TV

Key Points	IPTV	Web TV
Technology	Streaming	Streaming
Protocol	Delivered content over UDP in combination with FEC (Octoshape)	Delivered content over UDP in combination with FEC (Octoshape)
Content Delivery Medium	Private, Dedicated, Well Managed Network	Public Open Internet
End Users' Medium	Set top Box which will enable to decode the encoded contents	PC which is connected with Internet
Quality of Contents Delivered	higher quality, more reliable, and more consistent viewing experience	subjected to delays due to lower bandwidth, high traffic or poor connection

2.6.4 *Mobile Streaming*

With the advent of smart phones in the east of the globe, we have been witnessing a new type of content delivery over a new platform i.e., mobile phones. Broadcasted content is being delivered to the users through their hand devices provided they are equipped with such hardware receiving equipments. As we all know that in the mobile communication technology, 3rd generation (3G) and above are used for speedier communication and fast data delivery when compared with GPRS in the 2nd generation (2G). Still there are many jurisdictions wherein 3G services are yet to be utilized effectively in its fullest extent and thus these mobile broadcast techniques based on 3G are not so popular among the people. However, countries like South Korea, Japan, US EU and India[57] have been using these techniques for transmitting TV contents over mobile. Based on the real time delivery of content and non-interactive services, there are many methods of content delivery through mobile streaming. The LTE mobile transmission is focused here as it is more relevant and suitable, as it is based on streaming.

57 Service providers like Jio, Airtel, Vodafone-Idea, etc. provide high speed 4G mobile communication services in India.

2.6.4.1 LTE Mobile Transmission

LTE (Long Term Evolution) or the E-UTRAN (Evolved Universal Terrestrial Access Network) has been introduced with the objectives of high spectral efficiency, high peak data rates, short round trip time as well as flexibility in frequency and bandwidth. With this new mode of mobile communication, data can be communicated real time to multiple people without compromising the quality of the content too.[58] Figure 7 shows the functioning of this technology.

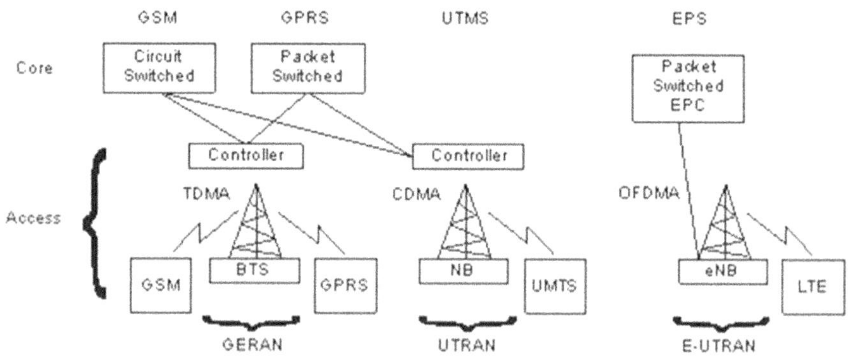

FIGURE 7 Mobile networks: GSM to LTE[59]

By using this new LTE, the existing MBMS or the eMBMS (evolved Multimedia Broadcast Multicast Service) can be used to stream the content to multiple users by multicast. Here, it is worth to be noted that it is an IP based service i.e., similar to internet transmission. This technology is explained:

> The Evolved Packet System (EPS) is purely IP based. Both real time services and datacom services will be carried by the IP protocol. The IP address is allocated when the mobile is switched on and released when switched off. The new access solution, LTE, is based on OFDMA (Orthogonal Frequency Division Multiple Access) and in combination with higher order modulation (up to 64QAM), large bandwidths (up to 20 MHz) and spatial multiplexing in the downlink (up to 4×4) high data rates can be

58 See WIPO 30th SCCR on "Current Market and Technology trends in the Broadcasting Sector", (2015), at pp. 22–27, available at https://www.wipo.int/edocs/mdocs/copyright/en/sccr_30/sccr_30_5.pdf (last accessed on 26/06/2019).

59 See for the same "LTE", available at http://www.3gpp.org/technologies/keywords-acronyms/98-lte (last accessed on 26/06/2019).

achieved. The highest theoretical peak data rate on the transport channel is 75 Mbps in the uplink, and in the downlink, using spatial multiplexing, the rate can be as high as 300 Mbps.[60]

The IP multicast model is deployed for mobile streaming over the internet by using IP protocol in the name of eMBMS. In this model, both stream to all and to group are possible and the same is well explained through Figure 8.

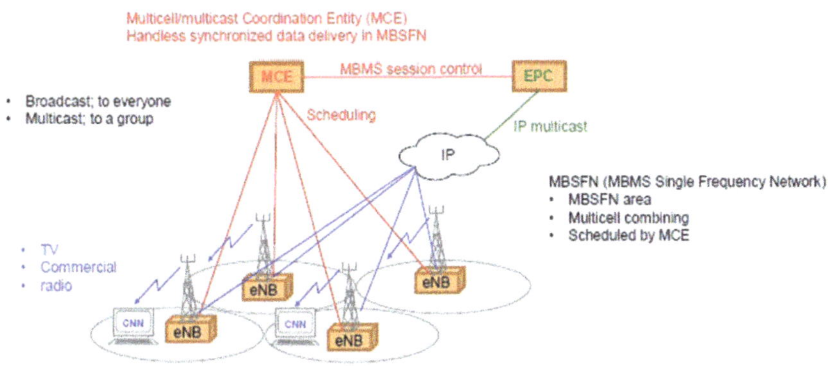

FIGURE 8 Mobile multicast[61]

From a technological perspective, when compared with previous generations of mobile communication technology, LTE stands ahead. Though 3G has been employing both MBMS which is a multicast in nature, and unicast model, it did not attract the consumers due to the above stated reasons. However, in countries like India and China, LTE has already gained popularity. With this cost effective model, the content can be distributed at a higher quality. However, affordability will be an issue because it will determine users' choice whether to access through mobile or through PC. From a technological point of view, it is important to clarify that the 4G or LTE transmission is nothing but internet protocol based transmission. Therefore, there is not much of difference between access of the content through PCs or mobiles because both are based on the software.

60 *Ibid.*
61 *Ibid.*

2.7 Conclusion

From the above discussion on various communication technologies that have been widely used for communicating both copyrighted and non-copyrightable content, we may safely arrive at the following conclusion. From the users' point of view, cable broadcasting, satellite broadcasting, radio diffusion and TV broadcasting can be considered as one and the same because of the fact that the users do not have any option in selecting the content. They cannot interact with service providers and can only remain as passive viewers. In IPTV, web TV and mobile streaming as discussed above, the real time transmission also does not provide any option in selecting the content to be enjoyed like radio diffusion and TV broadcasting. Thus, it can be summarized that from the end users' point of view, all the above highlighted technologies can be grouped into a single category of broadcasting due to their non-interactive character. However, the issue at hand is whether all these technologies can be termed as "broadcasting" technologies for the purpose of conferring neighbouring rights on broadcasters under the copyright regime?

The analysis of the above technologies makes it clear that the technology used in the terrestrial communication is the same in both radio diffusion and TV broadcasting. While comparing cable broadcasting with traditional broadcasting, it is different because the signal emitted in the terrestrial broadcasting is free to air i.e., it is open to all. Once, the content carrying signal is out of the broadcasters' control; it is not possible to restrict the access to selected or pre-identified audience. Whoever has the receiving equipment with the facility to decode the encoded contents from the emitted content carrying signal, can enjoy the same. Whereas, in cable broadcasting the access to the emitted signal is restricted only to the desired public who has paid/agreed to pay the subscription. Therefore, the communication is accessible to a section of public, and not to all. Though the end communication is through wire, the cable broadcasting retains the same conventional broadcasting technique in it.

In satellite broadcasting, the signal is emitted to all geographical areas unlike TV broadcasting and cable broadcasting, the content carrying signal is sent to satellite then the satellite transmits that signal to all. Whoever has the receiving equipment, will receive the signal with the help of a small dish and then will be decoded for further enjoyment which is the same in case of digital transmission too. A set-top box which is placed between TV and the dish, will decode the encoded contents for further enjoyment. In case of conventional and cable broadcasting, the set-top box is not required.

Even though there are many differences in the very nature of all these technologies, the so called commonality among them is the use/employment of 'signal'. The content is converted into signal and then communicated with the help of carrier signal i.e., radio magnetic wave at different frequencies. From the technology point, it is content carrying signal which is diffused in case of traditional TV & Radio broadcasting, cable broadcasting and satellite broadcasting and the content carrying signal remains as signal (encrypted/encoded for protection) till the receiving equipments receive the same for enjoyment. Even in the cable broadcasting, the signal is sent via cable to homes. Since, all these technologies are entirely based on 'signal' alone, it would be justified to use 'broadcasting' as an umbrella term for these technologies. However, in case of cable broadcasting, there may be a reservation since the signal cannot be directly received by the public unlike other modes of broadcasting. As the received signal using common antenna is further diffused through wire to the public by the intermediary for the enhancement of viewing quality and that too simultaneously, they would also definitely fall under the category of broadcasting. In a way, the intermediary do not generate new signal rather they further diffuse the same signal of the initial broadcasting organization. Therefore, there cannot be any difference of opinion with respect to using of the word 'broadcasting' for cable and satellite based communication that have been discussed above.

When, a copyright content is communicated using these technologies then it has to be converted into terrestrial signal first, then content carrying signal has to be communicated. To protect the rights of the authors over this technology, right to broadcast the works is recognized as authors' right.[62] But, for realizing the same, the author needs the technological infrastructure which requires huge investment for communication. Since, it is generally not possible for the authors to create infrastructure and fix these technological problem like unauthorized access of pre and post broadcast signal, the broadcasting organizations become relevant and imperative. The broadcasting organization can communicate the copyright work only with the permission of authors. However, the copyright permission given to the broadcasting organization by the author seems inadequate to protect the technical efforts taken by them to generate the content carrying signal and transmit the same to the public without being misappropriated by third parties. This has led to the evolution of neighboring rights and the details of the same will be dealt in subsequent chapters.

When we compare IPTV, Web TV and mobile TV with traditional broadcasting, it is found that the former uses streaming technology and the latter uses as referred above the diffusion technology. This streaming technology is based on file transmission methods of converting content into packets (which is known as stream) by compressing & encoding with the help of specific software and then transmitted to a streaming server which is further transferred to users using internet protocol. It is the streaming server which regulates the delivery of packets into the network depending on the availability of bandwidth. After decoding and

62 See for the detailed discussion on the rights, refer Chapters 4,5 and 6 of this book.

decompressing, the user's system will play the stream with the help of the media player.[63] From the beginning to end, the content is transmitted as stream and the same is received by the equipment, and then, decrypted for further enjoyment. As a result, it may be found that the concept of 'stream' is common among IPTV, Web TV and Mobile TV. In this regard, it is highly pertinent to raise the issue, i.e., whether all these mode of internet based transmissions can be termed as broadcasting?

If one has to answer the above question, it is highly imperative to answer the question i.e., whether signal and stream are one and same? The answer is in negative from the technology point of view. Even with respect to the infrastructure required they are different. While the traditional broadcasting requires huge investment for creating infrastructure as explained above, streaming does not require huge infrastructure requirements due to the fundamental differences in technology, which makes it possible for anyone with a computer equipped with a streaming software and internet access to stream the content over internet. The same will be discussed in detail in the next chapter.

As a result, from the technological point of view, signal and stream cannot be considered as same. If so, then the IPTV, Web TV and Mobile TV cannot be considered as broadcasting due to the technological differences. However, it may be treated as 'transmission'. Therefore, it can be safely concluded that the IPTV, Web TV, Mobile TV and other streaming based transmissions cannot be considered as part of the right of broadcasting of the author rather it would be covered by the authors' right of internet transmission under the umbrella of communication to the public.

In order to address this lacuna, the copyright law in major jurisdictions replaced the right of broadcasting of the author with the right of communication to public using technology neutral language to cover all forms of technology used for transmitting the work to the public.[64] The providers of IPTV, Web TV and other streaming based services can transmit the copyright works only with the permission of the authors. Since, this is not a broadcasting, (based on signal), it is interesting to examine whether these service providers also require conferring of rights similar to broadcasters' reproduction rights/neighbouring rights. As it is possible for the content carrying signal of the broadcasting organizations to be simultaneously retransmitted using streaming technology, it is also worth examining whether the broadcasting organizations' rights require further extension. In order to address the above copyright issues, the socio-economic impact of broadcasting and live streaming are deliberated in the next chapter.

---

63 See David Austerberry, *The Technology of Video & Audio Streaming*, Focal Press, London (2nd edn., 2005), Chapter 7 to 13.

64 See for the detailed discussion on the rights, refer Chapters 4,5 and 6 of this book.

CHAPTER 3

Socio-Economic Dimensions of Communication to Public of Works: New Challenges to Broadcasting Industry in the Context of 4G Peer to Peer Technology

3.1 General Introduction

Communication of works to public through broadcasting requires the work to be converted into signal first and then the content carrying signals have to be diffused to the public for reception and to enjoy it in the television or radio. So as to exploit the works through broadcasting, the authors' have been given the right of broadcasting.[1] In order to realize the authors' right of broadcasting, authors require the technological infrastructure which involve huge investment for communication. As discussed in the previous chapter, technology made it possible for unauthorized uses of signal by capturing the signal and then diffusing it further to the unintended audiences of the initial broadcasters. These subsequent unauthorized diffusions would result in potential economic loss not only to the initial broadcasters but also to the content creators. Due to the limitations on the content creators' right to address the technical problem i.e., unauthorized access and use of signal, it was felt pertinent to frame new norms for the protection of the investment of the broadcasters.[2] Due to technological changes in the broadcasting, including the emergence of digital technology, it was felt that the norms developed based on earlier technology was inadequate to address the problem of unauthorized use of signal. Similarly, in the context of the emergence of the streaming technology, there also emerged the possibility of the simultaneous transmission of the content received from the signal though computer networks. This resulted in the new demand from the broadcasting organization to extend the protection to prevent unauthorized streaming of the content received from their signal. WIPO has already taken up these demands and discussions are in progress to identify the gaps in the law and to find appropriate solutions. An analysis of the socio-economic conditions of broadcasting industry is necessary to find out whether such demands need to

1 See for the detailed discussion on the rights, refer Chapter 3 of this book.
2 *Ibid.*

 | DOI:10.1163/9789004419155_004

be accepted in the changing technological environment. Streaming technology also created a new market for the authors to exploit their work through new modes of transmission like IPTV, mobile TV, internet TV, etc. In the context of a relatively limited probability of unauthorized use of streams when compared to signals, we need to further explore the true nature of investment requirement and the possibilities of potential economic loss, if any, to the authors and the intermediaries facilitating streaming. This chapter first focuses on the socio-economic justifications for the special protection to the broadcasting industry followed by the emerging live streaming based transmission industries.

3.2 Socio-Economic Dimensions of the Broadcasting Industry and the Justification for Its Protection under the Copyright

3.2.1 *Introduction*

"*Television: A Scientific Success but a Commercial Headache*"[3] – It was the heading of an article covered by the *Life Magazine* of US in 1939.[4] Commercial failure even after spending more than $ 1,00,00,000 for the commercialization of television till 1939 was the reason for this report. Commercial success of the TV industry progressed parallel to the Second World War.[5] In 1936, New York City had only 50 TVs when UK had 3000. In 1939, it was produced at the rate of $200/ piece. In 1946, the number in UK went up to 26,000.[6] Commercial production of TVs in its fullest extent commenced then onwards. As on 2017, the world has around 1.63 Billion TV sets and it is expected to reach 1.74 Billion by 2023.[7] Let us have a brief look at the penetration and the reach of TV among the global population.

3.2.2 *Penetration of TV in the Households: a Global Outlook*

According to an OECD Study of 2009,[8] around 78% of the world population had television sets in their homes.[9] The TV penetration was much higher in

---

3 3 (26) *Life*, (27/12/1937). It is a magazine based in USA.

4 Emphasis added.

5 Peter Dunnett, *The World Television Industry: An Economic Analysis*, Routledge Publishing, (1990), at p. 8.

6 *Ibid.*

7 See for the same data, available at http://www.statista.com/statistics/268695/number-of-tv-households-worldwide/ (last accessed on 26/06/2019).

8 "The OECD Global Forum on Competition: Competition Issues in Television and Broadcasting", *Organisation for Economic Co-operation and Development* (OECD, 2013), at pp. 13–14, available at http://www.oecd.org/daf/competition/TV-and-broadcasting2013.pdf (last accessed on 26/06/2019).

9 *Id.*, at p. 13.

the developed economies when compared with developing and the least developed economies. When we closely look at the penetration of the TV sets at the global region wise, the Commonwealth of Independent States which is also known as the Russian Commonwealth, the Europe and USA, around 95%–97% of the total houses had TVs followed by the Arab states with 82%. The Asia-Pacific had only 75% and Africa, 28%.

However, according to WIPO SCCR Document of 2009,[10] TV penetration in North America is around 100% followed by Western Europe with 97% -98%. The least penetration is in the Middle East and African Region with around 70%. In the categorization, among the developed countries TV penetration is around 98%-99% and in the developing world, it is around 82%-83%.[11]

As per the 2011 study,[12] the world households have been divided into three categories based on the country's economic capabilities such as:

- 'Industrialized world' – i.e., the western countries such as Europe, USA, Canada and the advanced Asian Countries such as Japan, South Korea, Taiwan, Singapore, Hong Kong etc.
- 'Global Digital Divide' – i.e., the 'Emerging World' such as Latin American countries, Africa and less-affluent parts of Asia such as China, India, Indonesia etc. (Developing Countries).
- 'Underdeveloped' – i.e., least developed nations/3rd world countries.

As per the study,[13] industrial world's combined population of 1.2 billion (17% of world population) have been put into 480 million households (an average of 2.5 people/per house) which possess nearly 630 million TVs. Out of this, it has been projected that the viewership is around 1.05 billion. The Developing countries which comprises of 5.7 billion people (83% of world population) have been put into 1.32 billion households[14] (an average of 4.3 people/per house) which possess 970 million TV sets. Out of this, it has been projected that the viewership is around 3.15 billion.[15] However, there is no mention of the

10 WIPO 19th SCCR "Study on the Socio-Economic Dimension of the Unauthorized Use of Signals: Part I: Current Market and Technology Trends in the Broadcasting Sector", (2009–2010), available at http://www.wipo.int/meetings/en/doc_details.jsp?doc_id=142819 (last accessed on 26/06/2019).

11 *Id.*, at p. 58.

12 "Digital Divide: Global Household Penetration Rates for Technology", available at http://vrworld.com/2011/01/26/digital-divide-global-household-penetration-rates-for-technology/ (last accessed on 28/06/2019).

13 *Ibid.*

14 Out of which, around 370 million households have no access to electricity. See for detailed discussion on the same, *Ibid.*

15 *Ibid.*

least-developed nations' data on TVs. Another study[16] has estimated that as of 2015, the number of households with TV around the world is 1.57 billion and has projected that in 2016 it would be 1.59 billion & 1.68 billion in 2020.

As far as, India is concerned, in 1999, it was estimated that 130 million households out of total households i.e., 220 million had a TV set.[17] However, in 2015, there was a substantial increase in the figure, i.e., 277 million households out of 312 million households owned TV. Thus, only 11% of Indian population was projected as not owning TV Sets.[18] According to WIPO, as on 2015 out of 265 million households in India, 168 million households had TV.[19] Around 63% of homes had TV.[20] As of now, according to the BARC[21] India Universe Update-2018,[22] India has over 197 million households with television sets, with a 66% TV penetration.

3.2.3 *Penetration of TV Platforms: an Overview*

When TV was introduced, the only mode for receiving content that were broadcasted was 'free to air'. In this free to air model, the source of income for meeting the expenditure for broadcasting was revenue earned through advertisements. The free to air technology i.e., terrestrial broadcasting was somewhat similar to that of radio broadcasting. Due to its limitations, this model could not provide expected quality of service to the viewers. Thus, Cable TV model of broadcasting was introduced then followed by Satellite broadcasting which provides service to a larger section of the public at a lower cost when compared with cable. By the advent of the internet, IPTV model has also emerged.

---

16 See for the same, available at http://www.statista.com/statistics/268695/number-of-tv-households-worldwide/ (last accessed on 28/06/2019).

17 WIPO 19th SCCR "Study on the Socio-Economic Dimension of the Unauthorized Use of Signals: Part I: Current Market and Technology Trends in the Broadcasting Sector", (2009–2010), at p. 40, available at http://www.wipo.int/meetings/en/doc_details.jsp?doc_id=142819 (last accessed on 28/06/2019).

18 "TAM Annual Universe Update – 2015", available at https://www.tamindia.com/wp-content/uploads/2018/03/Overview_Universe_Update_2015.pdf (last accessed on 28/06/2019).

19 WIPO 30th SCCR on "Current Market and Technology trends in the Broadcasting Sector", (2015), at p. 48, available at http://www.wipo.int/edocs/mdocs/copyright/en/sccr_30/sccr_30_5.pdf (last accessed on 28/06/2019).

20 *Id.*, at p. 49.

21 Since 2016, BARC India is the sole TV viewership data provider in India, the committee consists of representatives from TRAI and industry experts.

22 See for the same details, available at https://www.barcindia.co.in/resources/pdf/BARC%20India%20Universe%20Update%20-%202018.pdf (last accessed on 28/06/2019).

Due to the technological advancements in the field of broadcasting, along with the free to air model, pay TV model has also come into existence. As of now the broadcasting industry is working based on the following two modes of broadcasting i.e.,

- Initial mode of broadcasting i.e., free to air model
- Pay TV model

The terrestrial/free to air model was completely based on analogue signal. Due to its limitations i.e., expenditures involved in broadcasting and the poor quality, this was transformed into digital free to air model. As stated above, the source of revenue for this type of broadcasting was from advertisements. Thus, the advertisement revenue data has become relevant to assess the growth of the broadcasting industry. In addition to that, the countries that have strong public service broadcasting are based on free to air model.[23] Therefore, it may be pointed out that due to a lack of strong public service broadcasting entities, pay TV model gained popularity as that was the only option available. In the pay TV model, the subscriber has to pay monthly/annual subscription fee to enjoy the content. Here, the pay TV means paying for the channels that are made available only on payments like sports, movies, songs, news, etc.[24] It is important to have a look at the current data of these platforms.

Before getting into the details of the platforms, it is necessary to have a basic understanding about each platform used for broadcasting. The following platforms are being used in broadcasting:

- Terrestrial broadcasting
- Cable broadcasting
- Satellite broadcasting
- IPTV

As IPTV is discussed in detail in the subsequent part, the other three platforms are discussed here in detail. In each broadcasting platforms, there are three models of broadcasting. i.e.,

1. Analogue Terrestrial Broadcasting and Digital Terrestrial Broadcasting
2. Analogue Cable Broadcasting and Digital Cable Broadcasting
3. Analogue Satellite Broadcasting and Digital Satellite Broadcasting.

---

23 WIPO 30th SCCR on "Current Market and Technology Trends in the Broadcasting Sector", (2015), at p. 7, available at http://www.wipo.int/edocs/mdocs/copyright/en/sccr_30/sccr_30_5.pdf (last accessed on 28/06/2019).

24 See for the detailed discussion on the same, Martin Peitz, "Content and Advertising in the Media: Pay-TV versus Free-to-Air", available at http://webcache.googleusercontent.com/search?q=cache:http://www3.imperial.ac.uk/pls/portallive/docs/1/21807696.FDF&gws_rd=cr&dcr=0&ei=3P4SWqfoFovgvATW3JWQDA (last accessed on 28/06/2019).

In all these three models, both free to air and pay TV model are available. As on 2009, half of the global viewers had opted for the pay TV model and the residual half remained with the free to air model. However, the data fluctuates from region to region depending on various factors such as individual ability to subscribe and country's economic condition to promote such models.

As of 2009, North America topped among the countries which had pay TV subscribers with 90% of the total population and the remaining 10% was with the free to air model followed by Western Europe with 52% pay TV subscribers. It was projected that worldwide, the pay TV model would reach 59% by 2013. Out of this, 52% to 60% is with cable TV and 30% is with satellite TV and the remaining 10% is with terrestrial and IPTV.[25] As far as, India is concerned, as on 2009, cable remained the most preferred mode of TV reception than terrestrial broadcasting and it was forecasted that by 2013, 2/3 of the Indian households would be a part of pay TV subscribers.[26]

As of 2011, 50% households of the globe had either subscribed to cable TV or satellite TV which comprises of 900 million subscriptions with 2.6 billion viewers.[27] Among the industrial world's households, 64% had the pay TV subscription which comprises of 670 million viewers. But in the case of developing world, pay TV subscription comes down to 35% of the households which covers 55% of the digital divide population.[28] Interestingly, radio broadcasting, which was perceived as an outdated technology, has a considerable number of audience as similar to that of TV viewers across the world. Among the industrial world households, 480 million households have 2.6 billion radio receivers. However, in the emerging world, only 1.43 billion households have radio receivers with an audience of 3.14 billion. In general, across the world, 4 billion radio receivers are with 1.43 billion households which covers 4.2 billion audience.[29]

As of 2015, the pay TV subscription is at 97% in the USA.[30] Western Europe and the Central & Eastern Europe are also witnessing substantial growth

25 WIPO 19th SCCR "Study on the Socio-Economic Dimension of the Unauthorized Use of Signals: Part I: Current Market and Technology Trends in the Broadcasting Sector", (2009–2010), at p. 19, available at http://www.wipo.int/meetings/en/doc_details.jsp?doc_id=142819 (last accessed on 28/06/2019).

26 *Ibid.*

27 "Digital Divide: Global Household Penetration Rates for Technology", available at http://vrworld.com/2011/01/26/digital-divide-global-household-penetration-rates-for-technology/ (last accessed on 28/06/2019).

28 *Ibid.*

29 *Ibid.*

30 WIPO 30th SCCR on "Current Market and Technology trends in the Broadcasting Sector", (2015), at p. 64, available at http://www.wipo.int/edocs/mdocs/copyright/en/sccr_30/sccr_30_5.pdf (last accessed on 28/06/2019).

in the pay TV model. Pay TV model has substantially penetrated into Indian market i.e., 80% of total TV households.[31] With respect to TV platforms, terrestrial broadcasting is the predominant model[32] being used in the Sub-Saharan Africa[33] then followed by satellite. However, the cable TV penetration is almost Zero in this region.[34] In the Asia Pacific region,[35] all three platforms are widely used. Terrestrial broadcasting does not have any pay TV model in most of the countries. Among these three, cable broadcasting is the most preferred by many of the households in this region then followed by satellite broadcasting.[36]

Terrestrial broadcasting is still preferred in Central and South America,[37] Western Europe[38] and Central and Eastern Europe[39] due to the strong presence of public broadcasting entities but satellite broadcasting has an edge over terrestrial broadcasting.[40] Even in the Middle East and North African[41] region, terrestrial broadcasting model is prominent. However, satellite broadcasting is preferred over cable broadcasting which has almost negligible presence.[42] As far as India is concerned, cable broadcasting is the top most platform followed by satellite and terrestrial broadcasting respectively. Cable broadcasting covers almost 50% TV households whereas the satellite covers 32% with 100% digital broadcasting. The remaining is with

31 *Id.*, p. 48.

32 WIPO 30th SCCR on "Current Market and Technology trends in the Broadcasting Sector", (2015), at pp. 40–45, available at http://www.wipo.int/edocs/mdocs/copyright/en/sccr_30/sccr_30_5.pdf (last accessed on 28/06/2019).

33 Sub-Saharan region refers and includes South Africa, Nigeria, Senegal and Kenya.

34 WIPO 30th SCCR on "Current Market and Technology trends in the Broadcasting Sector", (2015), at pp. 40–45, available at http://www.wipo.int/edocs/mdocs/copyright/en/sccr_30/sccr_30_5.pdf (last accessed on 28/06/2019).

35 Asia Pacific region refers and includes China, India, Japan, Australia and Vietnam.

36 WIPO 30th SCCR on "Current Market and Technology trends in the Broadcasting Sector", (2015), at pp. 46–53, available at http://www.wipo.int/edocs/mdocs/copyright/en/sccr_30/sccr_30_5.pdf (last accessed on 28/06/2019).

37 Central and South America refers and includes Brazil, Mexico, Argentina and Colombia.

38 Western Europe refers and includes Netherlands, Finland, Austria, Italy and UK.

39 Central and Eastern Europe refers and includes Russia, Poland, Estonia and Croatia.

40 WIPO 30th SCCR on "Current Market and Technology trends in the Broadcasting Sector", (2015), at pp. 54–79, available at http://www.wipo.int/edocs/mdocs/copyright/en/sccr_30/sccr_30_5.pdf (last accessed on 28/06/2019).

41 Middle East and North Africa refers and includes Egypt, Saudi Arabia, Morocco and Kuwait.

42 WIPO 30th SCCR on "Current Market and Technology trends in the Broadcasting Sector", (2015), at pp. 60–63, available at http://www.wipo.int/edocs/mdocs/copyright/en/sccr_30/sccr_30_5.pdf (last accessed on 28/06/2019).

TABLE 3 TV platform: an overview

Country		Terrestrial		Satellite			Cable			IPTV		
Pay subs ('000)		Free subs ('000)	Platform digitiza-tion (%)	Pay subs ('000)	Free subs ('000)	Plat-form digiti-zation (%)	Pay subs ('000)	Free subs ('000)	Platform digitization (%)	Pay subs ('000)	Free subs ('000)	Platform digitization (%)
Sub-Saharan Africa												
South Africa	0	5,573	9	5,581	849	100	0	0	0	0	0	100
Nigeria	2,612	2,466	52	960	9,858	100	0	0	0	0	0	0
Senegal	0	1,035	0	63	52	0	0	0	0	0	0	0
Kenya	275	2,725	34	295	205	100	0	0	0	0	0	0
Asia Pacific												
China	0	24,814	20	0	136,500	100	234,000	0	79	34,400	0	100
India	0	30,458	0	50,764	3,120	100	84,210	0	49	203	0	100
Japan	0	6,629	100	5,981	9,473	100	26,323	0	100	3,785	0	100
Australia	0	6,096	100	1,727	111	100	907	0	100	222	0	100
Vietnam	0	11,300	9	2,260	448	100	4,420	4,580	28	0	0	0
Central & South America												
Brazil	0	20,840	23	12,371	19,000	100	7,545	0	97	191	0	100
Mexico	0	11,599	54	8,873	0	100	7,281	0	73	163	0	100
Argentina	350	2,983	90	2,475	0	100	6,210	0	45	0	0	100
Colombia	0	7,259	65	1,420	1,580	100	3,631	47	0	0	0	0

Middle East and North Africa												
Egypt	0	1,017	65	497	18,288	100	0	0	0	0	0	100
Saudi Arabia	0	190	100	1,219	3,429	98	0	0	0	164	0	100
Morocco	0	1,893	36	198	4,094	100	0	0	0	54	0	100
Kuwait	0	16	84	263	80	100	0	0	0	0	0	100
North America												
USA	0	19,407	100	34,330	100	100	54,041	0	91	12,677	0	100
Western Europe												
Netherlands	441	54	100	673	53	100	4,448	0	81	1,755	0	100
Finland	225	347	100	63	48	100	1,481	0	100	270	0	100
Austria	12	164	100	101	1,805	100	1,270	0	56	278	0	100
Italy	2,805	15,639	100	4,734	2,003	100	0	0	0	81	0	100
UK	0	10,303	100	10,079	2,051	100	3,770	0	100	2,190	0	100
Central and Eastern Europe												
Russia	0	13,048	68	14,313	5,600	99	17,480	0	20	4,187	0	100
Poland	135	1,858	100	6,331	386	100	4,364	0	55	326	0	100
Estonia	56	61	100	37	18	100	208	0	70	174	0	100
Croatia	48	898	100	111	39	100	154	0	69	394	0	100

terrestrial broadcasting.[43] Table 3[44] depicts the current status of the TV platforms region wise.

3.2.4 *Economics of the Broadcasting Industry*

Worldwide, revenue of the broadcasting industry has reached £366 billion in 2016 which includes TV advertisement revenue, pay TV subscription and public license fee.[45] Out of this total revenue, £200 billion was derived out of pay TV subscription alone which is just above the half of total revenue. The TV advertisement revenue was £138 billion and the public license fee revenue stood £29 billion.

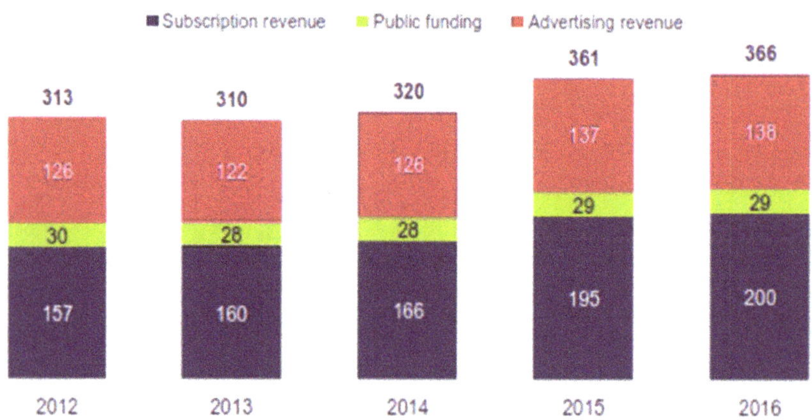

FIGURE 9 Global TV industry revenue[46]

When the 2016 revenue is compared with 2012, the advertisement revenue stood £126 billion while the subscription stood at £157 billion. The revenue progress shows that there is around 20% hike in the total revenue.[47] It

43 WIPO 30th SCCR on "Current Market and Technology trends in the Broadcasting Sector", (2015), at pp. 48–49, available at http://www.wipo.int/edocs/mdocs/copyright/en/sccr_30/sccr_30_5.pdf (last accessed on 28/06/2019).

44 Data is taken from the WIPO 30th SCCR on "Current Market and Technology trends in the Broadcasting Sector", (2015), available at http://www.wipo.int/edocs/mdocs/copyright/en/sccr_30/sccr_30_5.pdf (last accessed on 28/06/2019).

45 Ofcom, "International Communication Market Report, 2017 on Television and audio-visual", available at https://www.ofcom.org.uk/__data/assets/pdf_file/0032/108896/icmr-2017.pdf (last accessed on 28/06/2019).

46 *Ibid.*

47 WIPO 30th SCCR on "Current Market and Technology trends in the Broadcasting Sector", (2015), available at http://www.wipo.int/edocs/mdocs/copyright/en/sccr_30/sccr_30_5.pdf (last accessed on 28/06/2019).

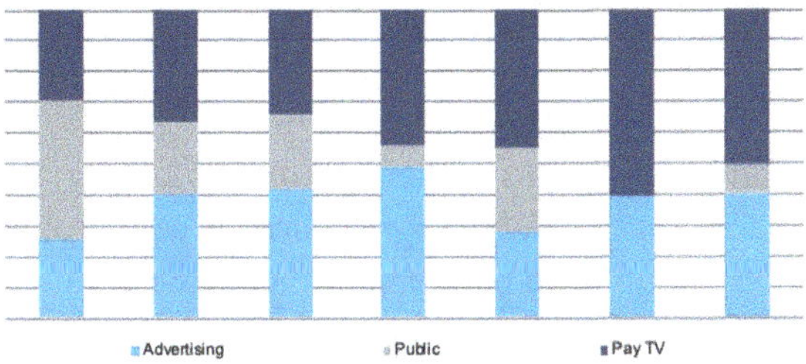

FIGURE 10 The economics of the broadcasting sector[52]

is expected that over a period of time, the revenue out of pay TV will further improve due to the consumer viewing habits with high expectations in terms of content and quality of broadcasting.[48] Therefore, the industry has to satisfy the needs of the consumers.[49] In the beginning of the 21st century, it was found than an adult in USA used to spend 4 hours with TV and 3 hours with radio.[50] It remains the same in the EU as of 2015[51] and even in all developing economies. However, with the increasing internet usage, the users are likely to spend more time with internet than TV. As a result, the broadcasting industry may face revenue losses. Therefore, it is inevitable for them to modify their programming to attract and retain the audiences for its survival. Figure 10 explains the source of this industry's income. Table 4 shows the SWOT analysis of the current trends in the broadcasting industry in a nutshell.

Due to the digitalization of broadcasting, quality of the content and number of channels have considerably increased which may help in retaining the viewers. As mandated by the international telecommunication union

48 WIPO 30th SCCR on "Current Market and Technology trends in the Broadcasting Sector", (2015), at pp. 7–8, available at http://www.wipo.int/edocs/mdocs/copyright/en/sccr_30/sccr_30_5.pdf (last accessed on 28/06/2019).

49 Artur Lugmayr, "Current Issues in Broadcasting from a Market Perspective", available at https://www.researchgate.net/publication/228843649_Current_issues_in_broadcasting_from_a_market_perspective (last accessed on 28/06/2019).

50 S. Anderson and S. Coate, "Market Provision of Broadcasting: A Welfare Analysis," 72 *Review of Economic Studies*, (2005), pp. 947–972, at p. 947.

51 Artur Lugmayr, "Current Issues in Broadcasting from a Market Perspective", at p.2, available at https://www.researchgate.net/publication/228843649_Current_issues_in_broadcasting_from_a_market_perspective (last accessed on 28/06/2019).

52 WIPO 30th SCCR on "Current Market and Technology trends in the Broadcasting Sector", (2015), available at http://www.wipo.int/edocs/mdocs/copyright/en/sccr_30/sccr_30_5.pdf (last accessed on 28/06/2019).

TABLE 4 SWOT analysis of current trends in the broadcasting industry[a]

STRENGTH	WEAKNESS
– High entry barriers and capital investment – Additional revenue streams through multi-channel and mutli-format distribution – TV is still a well accepted mass medium – Well established advertising models – New distribution channels allow content re-engineering and enable new revenue streams	– Non-sufficient payment offers – Lack of program formats coping with participatory consumers – Strong regulatory framework and diverse governmental policies – Internet takes attention of consumers away from TV – Rivalry between advertising platforms on the Internet – Lack of program formats suitable for multi-platform and interactivity
OPPORTUNITIES	**THREATS**
– Internet as additional distribution channel – Content diversification through new technologies – Premium content offerings (e.g. HD, 3D) – Broadband as additional competition to existing TV distributors – Consumers are prepared to pay for online – Merger and cooperation between both, traditional and new value chain partners – Fragmentation of value chain eases entry barriers	– Internet with service offerings substituting TV services – Advertising budgets are spent on the medium Internet – Young audiences prefer other media – Lack of adequate advertisement platforms – Demand side advertising platforms determining pricing for advertising – Participatory content models are not adaptable in a TV environment – 'Internet services are free' mentality difficult to adapt for established media companies

[a] Artur Lugmayr,: "Current Issues in Broadcasting from a Market Perspective", at p. 4, available at https://www.researchgate.net/publication/228843649_Current_issues_in_broadcasting_from_a_market_perspective (last accessed on 28/06/2019).

(ITU),[53] the digital switchover should be completed by 2020. Many countries have commenced the process. Some of the countries have already completed the process. The digital switchover will help in the following ways:[54]

- Expanded services
- Higher quality video and audio
- Greater variety and faster rates of data transmission
- Consistency of data flows over long distances
- More spectrum efficiency means more channels

Once the digitalization is completed, the number of channels that would be available would be much higher than analogue broadcasting along with a higher quality content. In case of analogue broadcasting, it would be typically 4 or 5 channels made available but in case of digital terrestrial, it will not be less than 30 channels.[55] Once, the number of channels available for viewers' increases, the viewers would have options to change from one to another. Thus, the viewers' expectations would also be met. By this way, the broadcasting industry would reamin relevant even though the internet penetration is at a much higher level, which may not have a serious impact on the structure of the broadcasting Industry.

3.2.5 *Socio-Economic Relation of Broadcasting Industry (Investment, Access and Piracy)*

Socio-Economic relation of broadcasting industry is examined so as to understand the infrastructure requirements, facilitating access to the content carrying signals, piracy (unauthorized access) to the content carrying signals and economics of such unauthorized access. Though, the economics of the broadcasting industry has been discussed under a single head, due to the advent of technological advancements in broadcasting, it is important to examine the Socio-Economic relation of the broadcasting industry based on the mode of transmission i.e., analogue transmission and digital transmission.

53 "Digital broadcasting set to transform communication landscape by 2015: Accord is major step in implementing World Summit on the Information Society objectives", *International Telecommunication Union*, available at http://www.itu.int/newsarchive/press_releases/2006/11.html (last accessed on 28/06/2019).

54 *Ibid.*

55 WIPO 30th SCCR on "Current Market and Technology Trends in the Broadcasting Sector", (2015), at p. 7, available at http://www.wipo.int/edocs/mdocs/copyright/en/sccr_30/sccr_30_5.pdf (last accessed on 28/06/2019).

3.2.5.1 Analogue Broadcasting

In the international arena, the problems of broadcasters were highlighted and the needs for their protection were emphasized by *Caldwell* in 1930.[56] The problems highlighted at that time were related to radio broadcasting. However, those problems remained the same for TV broadcasting also. At the beginning of an analogue transmission, an intruder could easily access the content carrying signals, on account of the fact that there were no protective measures employed. Since, the prime concern was to deliver the content to the public rather than the security of the content being transmitted. However, during World War II, secured data transmission became an important issue. Therefore, they started with the process of encoding the data. Still, the possibility of content being accessed without authorization in the process of communication by the intruder was omnipresent. However, such unauthorized access required considerable time. Due to technical advancements, unauthorized access of content (content piracy) from the signal became rampant in the analogue transmission. Though TV technology existed during the 1940s and 1950s, it was not commercially employed in the terrestrial broadcasting.

When commercial radio and TV broadcasting were much successful in the developed countries, there was no technological solution for signal piracy in the pre and post broadcasting scenario. Due to this technological limitation, signal piracy was rampant and was considered as a major issue in the copyright context, one which also affected the economic returns of the broadcasters.[57] The piracy problems[58] of the broadcasters can be generally divided into two stages. The first stage is unauthorized use of signal prior to broadcasting by the

---

56 Louis G. Caldwell, "International Protection of Broadcasters against Commercial Uses of their Programs", 2 *Journal of Radio Law*, (1932), pp. 479–527 and also see Shyam Balganesh, "The Social Costs of Property Rights in Broadcast (and Cable) Signals," 22 *Berkeley Technology Law Journal*, (2007), pp.1303 – –1387.

57 According to Govt. of India, for running a terrestrial channel through *Doordarshan* was estimated in 2007 that it would be around Rs.139.28 crores. Even for running a community radio station, it was estimated to have around Rs. 45 lacs at the maximum for 5–10 km surroundings. For the detailed discussion on the same see, Working Group Report of 11th Five Year Plan (2007–12)on Information and Broadcasting Sector, Govt. of India, at pp. 52–53, available at http://planningcommission.nic.in/aboutus/committee/wrkgrp11/wg11_iandb.pdf (last accessed on 28/06/2019). For item wise investment requirement to create broadcasting infrastructure, see "Television Station Construction Cost", available at https://www.ntia.doc.gov/legacy/otiahome/ptfp/application/EquipCost_TV.html (last accessed on 28/06/2019).

58 Though the word 'piracy' is inappropriate terminology to be used for these acts, it is widely known nomenclature at the international level. Thus the author uses the same terminology with the above reservation.

competitors and the second stage is unauthorized use of signal after broadcasting. In case of the first stage, the following are the core issues in the broadcasting i.e., interception by tapping signals which means tapping the wire so that content which is about to be aired can be tapped and then the same is broadcasted simultaneously with the original broadcasting. The second one is having two dimensions; (a) once the signal is released for public reception, prior to the public reception, the same signal is tapped and then broadcasted simultaneously and (b) further, once the signal is tapped and it is, then converted into content, the same content is further rebroadcasted or used for commercial purposes. In both the contexts, due to unauthorized access, there is a loss of revenue to the copyright owner.[59]

Problems of the broadcasters gained international attention, since, the copyrighted works were one of the major components i.e., songs and music to be broadcasted to the public. Since, the copyright works were used by unauthorized persons by way of pre and post broadcasting signal piracy which resulted in considerable economic loss for the copyright owners. The broadcasters' role is very much required in disseminating the copyright works to the public at large by broadcasting. For such dissemination, they have created such massive infrastructure by investing huge money.

Generally, the infrastructure requirement for broadcasting is extremely high. The expenditure includes the setting of a broadcasting station, receiving towers, payment to copyright owners for programme, production of programme carrying signals, spectrum purchase, technical requirements, etc. For setting up cable broadcasting to an area which is not covered by terrestrial broadcast, receivers have to be placed based on the number of subscription. Then, each household should be connected with cable which is a copper cable in case of analogue context for the re-distribution of signals that have been received. Creating this type of transmission requires additional investments for setting up of the above infrastructure in addition to the infrastructure requirements for setting up a broadcasting station. Likewise, in satellite broadcasting, infrastructure requirements for satellite broadcasting are similar to that of terrestrial broadcasting. However, due to technological advancements, the cost has reduced substantially in satellite broadcasting when compared with terrestrial broadcasting.[60]

---

59 Louis G. Caldwell, "International Protection of Broadcasters against Commercial Uses of their Programs", 2 *Journal of Radio Law*, (1932), pp. 479–527 and also see Louis G. Caldwell, "Piracy of Broadcast Programs", 30 *Columbia Law Review*, (1930), pp. 1087–1114.

60 According to Govt. of India, for running a satellite based channel in *Doordarshan* DTH, it was estimated in 2007 that it would be around Rs.32.78 crores. For the detailed discussion on the same see, Working Group Report of 11th Five Year Plan (2007–12) on

The broadcasting organizations recover these investments by broadcasting the programs to the public based on the revenue models explained above. The content carrying signal is live till it is received by the public for viewing on their TV sets. Once, it is viewed, the signal along with the content disappears. The unauthorized access of the signal before it is received by the targeted public and broadcasting it simultaneously will result in economic loss to the broadcasting organization. Similarly, by using devices, it is possible to record the broadcast content which may be further used commercially. In this scenario, the problem comes in the post broadcasting context. Since, the broadcast is completed, the content which has been recorded, if it is further used for broadcasting by competitors, the broadcasting organization will suffer economic loss if they have acquired the copyright for rebroadcasting the programs subsequently. If the broadcasted content is recorded and used without permission for any other purpose by others, then it would very much attract copyright infringement. Therefore, the content creator can very well take care of this problem. Thus, this issue is left without any further deliberation as it has been already addressed by the existing copyright regime.

In the second scenario, once broadcasting is over, the signal is received and simultaneously broadcasted over cable or other means to the public by another broadcasting organization. By this way of simultaneous broadcasting, the broadcasting station faces economic loss which may arise from the new public to whom the simultaneous broadcasting is done. Unlike the previous scenario, here the program carrying signal is accessed without permission and then it is further broadcasted simultaneously to the new group of people which was not covered by the initial broadcasting. Then the issue is whether the content creators' copyright would be sufficient enough to address the issue of unauthorized access to program carrying signal. The answer may be in negative and the same is dealt in detail in the next chapter.

In the third scenario, the pre broadcasting context, where the program carrying signal is intercepted even prior to the broadcasting. In this scenario, like the simultaneous broadcasting, the unauthorized access is to program carrying signal and not to the content alone. As raised above, the issue i.e., whether the content creators' copyright would be sufficient enough to address the issue of unauthorized access to program carrying signal in the pre broadcasting

---

Information and Broadcasting Sector, Govt. of India, at pp. 52–53, available at http://planningcommission.nic.in/aboutus/committee/wrkgrp11/wg11_iandb.pdf (accessed on 28/06/2019). For item wise investment requirement to create broadcasting infrastructure, see "Television Station Construction Cost", available at https://www.ntia.doc.gov/legacy/otiahome/ptfp/application/EquipCost_TV.html (accessed on 28/06/2019).

context. The answer may be in negative and the same is dealt in detail in the next chapter.

If this is the position of signal piracy in the analogue broadcasting, it is imperative to examine whether the issues related to pre and post broadcasting signal piracy associated with analogue broadcasting remain same even in the context of digital broadcasting.

3.2.5.2 Digital Broadcasting

Digitalization of broadcasting has benefited both the broadcasters and the users. From the users' point of view, the number of channels and quality would be much higher than in analogue broadcasting.[61] In addition to this, one of the most important aspects of the digital broadcasting is interactive services.[62] Digital broadcasting, the interactive service which is almost not possible in case of analogue broadcasting, facilitates the consumers or the viewers to interact with the broadcasting stations to provide desired content. As a result of this interactive service, nature of broadcasting service in the digital context when compared with analogue broadcasting, is entirely different due to the technological differences and which opens a new business model for further revenue generation. It provides the option of becoming both signal distributor and content distributor which was not possible in analogue transmission. As a result, a new entrant to the broadcasting service does not require to own spectrum which is otherwise mandatory in analogue transmission.[63] As a result, the cost involved in transmission is also lower than in analogue transmission.[64]

---

61 Totio Filipov, "The Advantages and Disadvantages of Digital Television", available at http://www.sooperarticles.com/shopping-articles/electronics-articles/advantages-disadvantages-digital-television-159751.html (last accessed on 28/06/2019).

62 "The Benefits of Digital TV", available at http://www.digital-tv.co.uk/news-and-features/the-benefits-of-digital-tv (last accessed on 28/06/2019).

63 See for the same in general, Petros Iosifidis, "Digital Switchover in Europe", available at http://citeseerx.ist.psu.edu/viewdoc/download?doi=10.1.1.572.2234&rep=rep1&type=pdf (last accessed on 26/06/2019).

64 See for the detailed discussion on the cost involved in setting up a broadcasting unit, Working Group Report of 11th Five Year Plan (2007–12) on Information and Broadcasting Sector, Govt. of India, pp. 52–53, available at http://planningcommission.nic.in/aboutus/committee/wrkgrp11/wg11_iandb.pdf (last accessed on 28/06/2019). Further, it is understood that with in a limited resource, broadcasters can have more channels that what he would have had under the analogue context. In this way, investment requirement is reduced. For item wise investment requirement to create broadcasting infrastructure, see "Television Station Construction Cost", available at https://www.ntia.doc.gov/legacy/otiahome/ptfp/application/EquipCost_TV.html (last accessed on 28/06/2019).

As digital transmission reduces and regulates the use of spectrum, more players can be in the market. The spectrum, which is occupied by the analogue transmission of a broadcasting channel, can be used to accommodate many channels. It is estimated that up to eight channels can be used by the same spectrum in the digital context. This way the cost involved in the spectrum purchase is substantially reduced when it comes to digital broadcasting.[65] On one side broadcasters' investment requirement is reduced substantially and on the other side, viewers are provided with numerous choices in selecting the channels including the option of even interacting with the service provider which is otherwise widely known as on demand services.

The key benefits of digitalization from both users' and the broadcasters' point of view are summarized as follows:

3.2.5.3 Digitalization of Broadcasting: an Overview

According to a 2015 WIPO study,[66] satellite broadcasting has become digitalized around the world. Except Saudi Arabia which has attained 98% digitalization and Russia which has attained 99% digitalization in the satellite broadcasting, most of the countries have completely switched over to the digital platform. However, as far as cable broadcasting is concerned, North America and Western Europe have been showing the progress of digitalization and leading other regions. In the Asia Pacific region, Japan and Australia have completely digitalized cable broadcasting like Finland and UK in Western Europe. Middle East and the African region have been showing almost nil penetration of digitization in cable broadcasting. The developing economies like China, India and Brazil have achieved 79%, 49% & 97% respectively while the US has achieved only 91% even though it started its digitalization much earlier than other jurisdictions.[67]

As far as terrestrial TV broadcasting (which is operated as public service broadcasting by the respective governments) is concerned USA, Europe, Saudi Arabia, Japan and Australia have achieved 100% digitalization.[68] The

65 See for the same in general, Gregory L. Rosston, "Increasing the Efficiency of Spectrum Allocation", available at https://siepr.stanford.edu/sites/default/files/publications/13-035_0.pdf (last accessed on 28/06/2019).

66 WIPO 30th SCCR on "Current Market and Technology trends in the Broadcasting Sector", (2015), available at http://www.wipo.int/edocs/mdocs/copyright/en/sccr_30/sccr_30_5.pdf (last accessed on 28/06/2019).

67 *Ibid.*

68 *Ibid.*

TABLE 5 Benefits of digital broadcasting[a]

Broadcasting industry benefits	Consumer benefits
Spectrum efficiency gain and increased transmission capacity	Wider choice of programming and services (including additional channels, HD offerings, radio, data services, pay programmes)
Improved signal quality and robustness	Better quality – less likely to experience signal interference and picture quality issues.
Lower energy consumption and maintenance costs	Interactivity – offers a range of interactive applications (games, enhanced teletext), more userfriendly interfaces and better personalization (e.g. mosaic/multiscreen, capability, multi-lingual subtitling, audio-description)
Flexibility and more efficient use of infrastructure	Convenience – video-on-demand/ catch-up services allow viewers to watch programmes at a time of their choosing
Stimulates demand in the consumer electronic market (e.g. STB s, iDTVs, aerials, HDTVs, etc.)	Parental lock setting – gives parents and/or guardians greater control of what their children watch on television via classification of programmes of full channels.

[a]The Compilation is based on the data available in GSMA Report,2014, See for the same GSMA, "Benefits of digital broadcasting (2014)", available at http://www.gsma.com/spectrum/wp-content/uploads/2014/02/Benefits-of-Digital-Broadcasting.-Plum-Consulting.-Jan-2014.pdf (last accessed on 28/06/2019).

remaining jurisdictions have progressed in the switchover. As discussed above, it is hopefully expected that by 2020 digitalization would be completed in all platforms whereby analogue broadcasting would be rolled out from the field. Figure 11–15 give country wise and region wise digitalization status. The data is taken from a WIPO 2015 study.[69]

69 *Ibid.*

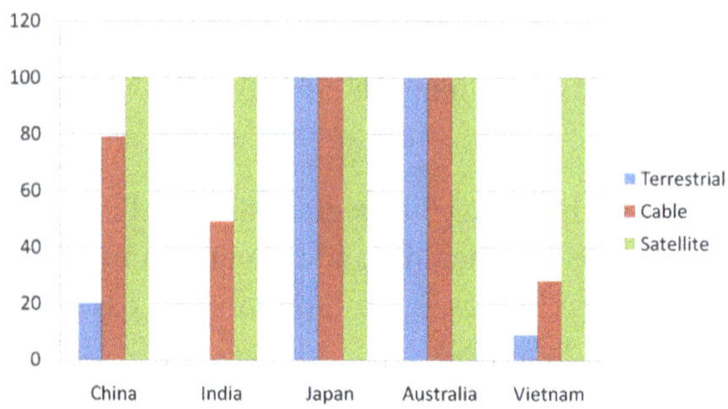

FIGURE 11 Asia Pacific region: digitalization

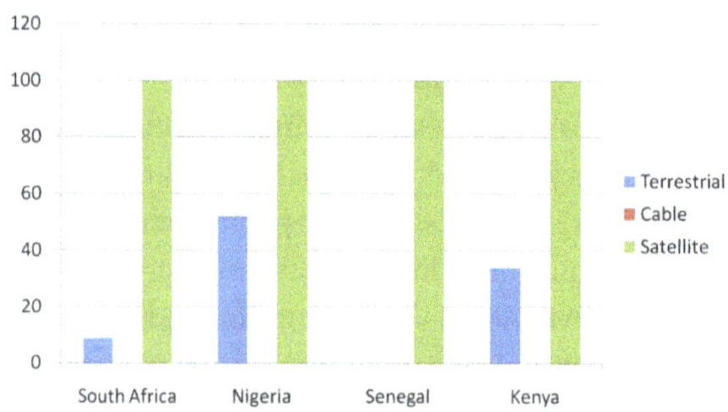

FIGURE 12 Sub-Saharan Africa region: digitalization

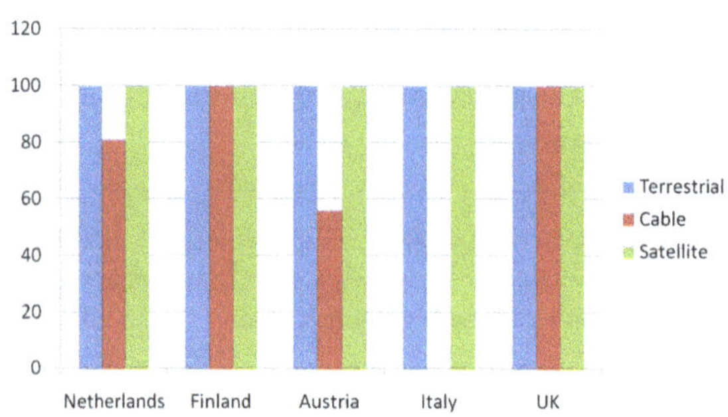

FIGURE 13 Western Europe region: digitalization

3.2.5.4 Signal Piracy: Solution within the Digital Technology?

If the entire broadcasting industry has been progressing towards digitalization, then it is pertinent to examine whether signal piracy during pre and post broadcasting as found in analogue transmission is possible in digital broadcasting. It is also important to examine whether technological solutions are available to prevent this and whether there is a need for any legal (neighbouring rights) intervention. As discussed above, there is a limitation on the part of

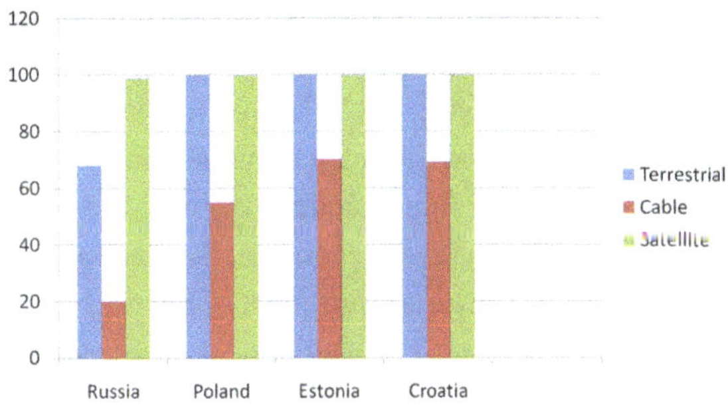

FIGURE 14 Central and Eastern Europe region: digitalization

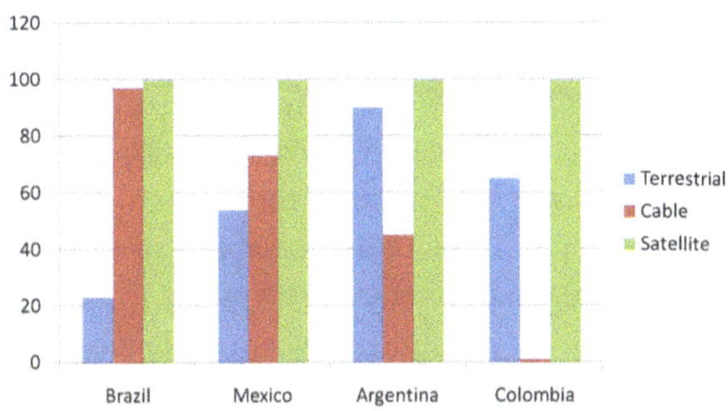

FIGURE 15 Central and South American region: digitalization

the technology to prevent/limit signal piracy which has led to legal regulation i.e., through copyright law. However, with the advancements in digital technology, there are many solutions for signal piracy within the technology itself. This protective measure is widely known as encryption which is used in the digital transmission or scrambling method. The scrambling technology means:

> In telecommunications, a scrambler is a device that transposes or inverts signals or otherwise encodes a message at the senders side to make the message unintelligible at a receiver not equipped with an appropriately set descrambling device. Scrambling is accomplished by the addition of components to the original signal or the changing of some important component of the original signal in order to make extraction of the original signal difficult.[70]

70 See for the same definition, available at http://lists.gnu.org/archive/html/discuss-gnuradio/2017-06/msg00178.html (last accessed on 28/06/2019).

This scrambling method was used in cable broadcasting with the help of set top boxes. When cable broadcasting was introduced in the market, the TVs were not suitable to receive the signal or they were not 'cable ready' TVs. Therefore, they required a device which would enable them to enjoy the content. Set top boxes functioned as the descrambler in cable broadcasting and then enabled the authorized viewers to enjoy the broadcasted content. By this way, set top boxes acted and were used as a tool to prevent unauthorized access of the television signals. However, problems still persist in analogue transmissions. A WIPO study highlights the same as follows:

> Prior to the introduction of digital distribution of broadcast signals, content distributed via analogue terrestrial and analogue cable rarely made use of devices such as set top boxes (STB) or conditional access systems (CAS), despite the fact that early forms of CAS were designed for analogue systems. Unencrypted signals were simply accessed via plugging the coaxial cable from the aerial or cable network directly into the TV set. This lack of signal encryption and lack of addressability of the end subscriber gave rise to widespread unauthorized access of pay TV signals via analogue cable systems, and exists in countries where analogue cable infrastructure is still in existence.[71]

However, this scrambling can be considered as the beginning point of a technological solution developed for content protection in the process of communication. The same scrambling was employed by the satellite broadcasting wherein the set top box has been used since its inception to prevent unauthorized access to the broadcasted signal.[72] This way, the technological solutions not only for the broadcasting but also for all modes of communications have been progressing since 1980s.[73] Even the encryption products which were based on the US encryption standard of 1976 have gained commercial value.[74]

When the encryption technology evolved, it started with very low bits/rate of transmission. It was projected in the 1980s that within few years, the speed

---

71 WIPO 20th SCCR "Study on the Socio-Economic Dimension of the Unauthorized Use of Signals: Part II: Unauthorized Access to Broadcast Content – Cause and Effects: A Global Overview", (2009–2010), at p. 16, available at http://www.wipo.int/meetings/en/doc_details.jsp?doc_id=132819 (last accessed on 28/06/2019).

72 See, Whitfield Diffie and Martin Hellman, "New directions in cryptography", 22 (6) *IEEE Transactions on Information Theory*,(1976), pp. 644–654.

73 *Ibid.*

74 A. Gersho and R. Steele, "Guest Editorial: Encryption of Analog Signals-A Perspective", 2(3) *IEEE Journal on Selected Areas in Communication*, (1984), pp. 423–425.

would increase between 2.4 to 9.6 kbps.[75] Further, it was only for voice protection. However, over a period of time, the entire data such as video, audio, text, images, etc., have been subjected to encryption.

While encoding, the data is converted into redundant data though it might be readable but can not be understood by an intruder. Whereas in encryption, data cannot be read as the data would be converted into algorithm while transmitting. In encryption, different keys are used to encrypt the data. At the beginning of encryption technology, private keys were widely used where it was required to share the keys prior to communication for enjoyment. However, the concept of public key evolved, where the keys were generated by a set of algorithms which would enable the intended receiver to decrypt the data transmitted for enjoyment. If the unintended person received the same, it would not be possible to access the data. Though there was a possibility of the signal being accessed without authorization existed, there would not be any use of such signal due to the access restrictions to the data.

Subsequently, a mixture of public and private key or a hybrid key concept was evolved where in the public key is known to all but the intended users will only possess the private key thereby preventing unauthorized access to communication. In all the above cases, there were some instances in which the intruder could access the signal if they knew the key somehow.[76]

To overcome this problem, authenticated server has been established so as to verify the authenticity of the users whereby unauthorized access is prevented. In this process, the key will be instantaneously generated by the authenticating server on request basis. Once the key is generated, it can be used only for that particular user that too only for that time which is similar to that of OTP in banking transactions. The key difference between the banking and broadcasting encryption is that, smaller keys are used in broadcasting to avoid time delay and reduce the server cost whereas larger keys are used to make more secure transactions in the banking sector.[77] Even the larger keys are used in the broadcasting encryption, the delay may be of micro seconds or nano seconds or even lower than this.[78]

75 *Id.*, at p. 424.

76 James F Kurose and Keith W. Ross, *Computer Networking: A Top Down Approach*, Pearson (7th edn., 2016), Chapter 8.

77 See for the same argument and detailed discussion on the cryptography techniques, B.M. Macq and J.J. Quisquater, "Cryptology for Digital TV Broadcasting", 83(6) *Proceedings of the IEEE*, (1995), available at http://ieeexplore.ieee.org/stamp/stamp.jsp?tp=&arnumber=387094 (last accessed on 28/06/2019).

78 Gerard O'driscoll, *Next Generation IPTV Services and Technologies*, Wiley Publications, (2007), p. 20. Generally, it is understood, internet transmission takes place within seconds and delivers content at the real time.

Along with these developments, the growing advancements in the bits used for the keys have also contributed towards the protection. If less bit key is used, then level of protection is also considerably less. When a higher bit key is used, much stronger protection is offered. As of now, up to 256 bit keys are used. However, in the commercial context, 64 bit/128 bit keys are widely used.[79] If an intruder gets access to the broadcast signal during pre or post broadcasting in the digital context, then it would take years to decode the content. Even with the help of super computers, the encrypted signal would require some years to understand the content.[80] These protections are during the process of transmissions only. Once the received signal is decrypted the access to the content is enabled and the content can be used further for dissemination and not the signal. It means that when the broadcasting is completed i.e., when the decryption is done, there is no life for the digital carrier signal that was transmitted. What would remain is only the content which is also in high quality and that too in a digital format. When the decryption is done and content is enjoyed by the intended users, it is highly possible with the available technological measures such as PVR, DVR etc., or the circumventing devices, the content can be used for retransmission. Even the content is reused/retransmitted after decryption, the unauthorized use/transmission is related to content and not to the signal which is otherwise possible in analogue transmissions. With all these technical advancements in the encryption methods, digital communications including digital broadcasting have been more secure than analogue transmission. In the context of broadcasting, it has moved from the stage of zero protection to defined secured protection. Therefore, the pre and post broadcasting signal piracy issues have been substantially addressed by the much advanced encryption methods. Even when the entire US switched over to the digital terrestrial broadcast, the digital signal piracy was quite common as there was no protection for the signal broadcasted in the free to air model. However, federal communication commission (FCC) came with a technological solution which is widely known as 'broadcast flag'. By this way, piracy of digital signal in US was addressed by the regulating authorities.[81]

If this is the state of digital broadcasting in the world within the context of technology, it is highly pertinent to look into the market trends of piracy so as

79 Behrouz A. Forouzan and Mosharraf, Firouz, *Computer Networks: A Top Down Approach*, McGraw-Hill, (2011), pp. 731–804.

80 See for the same argument and exact details about the circumventing, available at https://crypto.stackexchange.com/questions/48667/how-long-would-it-take-to-brute-force-an-aes-128-key/48685 (last accessed on 28/06/2019).

81 See for the detailed discussion on the same, Shyam Balganesh, "The Social Costs of Property Rights in Broadcast (and Cable) Signals," 22 *Berkeley Technology Law Journal*, (2007), pp. 1303 – –1387.

to understand the possibility of signal piracy in the digital context which is otherwise present in the analogue broadcasting.

With the advancement of technology in broadcasting, as of today the unauthorized uses of broadcast signal have been identified as follows:[82]

- Physical piracy
- Hardware based unauthorized access
- Unauthorized re-broadcasting of signals
- Extra territorial TV access (grey market)

According to a WIPO study, it has been claimed that even with the increasing digitalization process of broadcast, methods of broadcast *'signal' being 'stolen'* for both personal and commercial use has not reduced rather it has helped the pirates to *access and re-distribute better quality content.*[83] From the above discussion about the technological measures and encryption techniques, it can be positively concluded that signal piracy in the digital broadcasting context is highly complex and time consuming. As we discussed above, once decryption is done, what would remain is a content not the signals. Hence, if there is any retransmission, that retransmission is all about the content. If such retransmission is done without authorization, then it would amount to unauthorized use of content received from the signal which could be ideally termed as 'content piracy' if one wish to name it. If the WIPO study claims that signal is being pirated, then it is highly questionable and which is impossible with the above explained technology. It appears what the study means is the stealing of the content received from the signal which it termed as "signal being stolen". The same study has also pointed out that digital broadcasting is a solution for analogue signal piracy which can be gathered from the Argentinian experience:

> In Argentina, it was estimated that there were approximately 1m illegal cable subscribers in 2003. As a result, two of the country's biggest cable operators have since stopped distributing their premium sports and movie channels in analogue, and only offer them to their digital subscribers.[84]

82 WIPO 20th SCCR "Study on the Socio-Economic Dimension of the Unauthorized Use of Signals: Part II: Unauthorized Access to Broadcast Content – Cause and Effects: A Global Overview", (2009–2010), at p. 5, available at http://www.wipo.int/meetings/en/doc_details.jsp?doc_id=132819 (last accessed on 28/06/2019).

83 See for same WIPO 20th SCCR "Study on the Socio-Economic Dimension of the Unauthorized Use of Signals: Part II: Unauthorized Access to Broadcast Content – Cause and Effects: A Global Overview", (2009–2010), pp. 12–16, available at http://www.wipo.int/meetings/en/doc_details.jsp?doc_id=132819 (last accessed on 28/06/2019).

84 *Id.*, at p. 7.

As explained, once the broadcasting is over, the signal does not remain. If so, the hardware based unauthorized access is all about content that is transmitted and not the signal. Hardware based access is possible once decryption is done. If decryption is completed, the signal is no more in existence or it disappears. Since the signal does not exist once the decryption is done, the hardware based access is onlyabout content. If the signal does not exist after decryption, the rebroadcasting of the signal is also impossible. Even the content remains same and the rebroadcasting is done within few seconds/minutes, it is all about rebroadcasting of the received content by converting it into new signals and not the original signal because every rebroadcast requires new signal generation for carrying the content. Hence, each transmission would constitute a new transmission rather than retransmission. With the advancement of technology, there are many less expensive/economically viable tools available for such retransmissions. Therefore, it would be more appropriate to discuss in detail the concept of internet TV or Streaming TV.

From these discussions, it may be well concluded that most of the piracy issues in digital broadcasting and the unauthorized access issues are related to content received from the signal and not on the digital signal. While examining the piracy of content/unauthorized use of content simultaneously, it would also constitute revenue loss to the broadcasters as well as the copyright owners. The solutions to these types of problems lie on the nature of the copyright license agreement between the copyright owners and the broadcasters. The following extracted points from WIPO study also corroborate the above conclusions.

> While copying of legally obtained broadcast signals for personal use by the legal viewer has been generally approved under most national/international copyright regulations, copying of broadcast signals (including movies) and content onto optical disks/storage devices for commercial purposes has been a concern for all elements of the TV value chain.[85]
>
> Digitization of content and growing internet penetration has resulted in online piracy starting to become a much more serious threat than other forms of piracy in many developed markets. Peer-to-peer (P2P) file-sharing remains popular due to the availability of a wide range of content; however, browser-based services such as YouTube have simplified the way content can be watched online, enabling a larger proportion of the population to gain access to video content online. Moreover, viewers

85 *Id.*, at p. 13.

> are often unaware that the content they are watching is infringing copyright laws, and further feeds into the belief that online content is free.[86]

Throughout the WIPO study, the word 'signal' is mentioned at many places,[87] however, nowhere they have established/highlighted/showed the problem of digital signal being accessed without authorization in the stage of pre-broadcast or before it is decrypted after broadcast. The study itself has confessed that the problem of signal piracy has been substantially tackled by digital broadcast.[88] Obviously, it is the result of technological developments. The South American experience is an apt illustration to prove that there can be no chance of signal piracy in the pre-broadcast context. Though the North American data has given a different impression:

> Unauthorized access of broadcast signals in North America has its origins in the theft of analogue cable signals – known as 'splicing'. Digital cable and satellite TV theft in the US and Canada are known to primarily take place through the use of cable 'black boxes' and modified FTA boxes which circumvent CAS. Canada's CASST (Coalition Against Satellite Signal Theft) estimated that that there were close to 750,000 illegal pay-TV users in Canada in 2004 – costing the industry approximately $400m in lost revenues.[89]

The North American data as studied by the WIPO is a decade old which is related to analogue signal, which cannot be acceptable because, as of 2015, penetration of digital broadcast is in more than 90% total households. Moreover, the WIPO Study of 2015 does not talk of this signal piracy issue at all, rather, it focuses only on the online model of piracy i.e., use of broadcasted content online.[90] From the above discussion, it is possible to observe that even the WIPO study has corroborated this conclusion i.e., pre and post broadcasting signal piracy is not feasible with digital broadcasting due to technological advancements in the methods of transmission. Thus, it may be safely concluded that digital broadcasting industry is substantially free from pre and post

86 *Id.*, at p. 6.

87 See the whole document of WIPO 20th SCCR "Study on the Socio-Economic Dimension of the Unauthorized Use of Signals: Part II: Unauthorized Access to Broadcast Content – Cause and Effects: A Global Overview", (2009–2010), available at http://www.wipo.int/meetings/en/doc_details.jsp?doc_id=132819 (last accessed on 28/06/2019).

88 *Id.*, at p. 12.

89 *Id.*, at p. 30.

90 *Ibid.*

broadcasting signal piracy. However, the industry is trying to project the piracy of the content received from their signal as signal piracy by making a claim to recognize post fixation rights. It is worth examining whether broadcasters deserve a layer of protection on the unauthorized retransmission of content received from the signal.

Since the Rome Convention provides signal based approach protection to broadcasting organizations to prevent unauthorized use of their post broadcasting signal, in the digital broadcasting context, due to the technological advancements, the Rome Convention model of protection to the broadcasting organizations becomes redundant, as there is no signal piracy. Therefore, it may be concluded based on the technological advancements and the current trends in the market that digital broadcasting does not require any protection i.e., signal based protection as envisaged under the Rome Convention. Due to lack of signal piracy, the investment protection or the economic logic which has been used for accommodating the traditional broadcasting organizations is not required in the digital context not only due to the lack of signal piracy but also due to economic implications in digital broadcasting i.e., the investment required for digital broadcasting is substantially low when compared with traditional broadcasting.

In addition to the above points, digital broadcasting provides an alternative business model i.e., provides on-demand service which is not present in analogue broadcasting. Due to this interactive feature, digital broadcasting can be considered as one of the different modes of communication rather than terming it as a broadcasting. Thus the content creators' rights would take care of the remaining issue.

The remaining issue in digital broadcasting is unauthorized distribution over internet of the content being broadcasted. It is projected as major issue for the broadcasting industry as of now. Since digital broadcasting employs high quality compression techniques such as MPEG-4, the content used in most cases is of the same quality i.e., high definition (HD). If these broadcasted content is distributed over internet, then the core issue would be on the 'unauthorized use of content' received from the signal and not the signal being redistributed. When the broadcasted content is used and distributed over internet without prior permission, then it would be a violation of the content creators' rights if the content is copyrightable in nature. Then, it is pertinent to examine whether the broadcasting organizations have any legitimate interest (both in terms of economical and technical) to regulate the retransmission of content which was received through their signal. It is also important to examine whether the economic loss which would occur due to this retransmission of content could be well addressed by the content creators' copyright. As far as the content is concerned, the content creators' right will take care of the unauthorized use of the content.[91]

As we discussed in the previous chapter, though IPTV and the streaming TV function on internet protocol, due to the nature of IPTV which is completely closed network, if the content is distributed without permission, it is possible to find out either during the transmission or post transmission whether the content has been transmitted or not. Hence, if the unauthorized content distribution happens over IPTV, it would be easily identified by the authors. The only possibility of unauthorized use of content is the reuse of the content by distributing it over the internet. Even the WIPO 2015 study, only talks about the usage of broadcasted content over internet. Neither the 2010[92] study nor the 2015 study could prove that there was any substantial problem with respect to unauthorized distribution over internet issue. There is no data to show that there is a revenue loss out of the unauthorized distribution over internet. However, there is data about the economics of such unauthorized distribution over internet. Most of them are related to sports content. Since, there is a serious debate going on about the copyrightability of such sports content, it is impossible to reach to a conclusion based on this data. However, the issue of unauthorized distribution of content received from broadcast signal over internet transmission cannot be merely rejected because of the non-availability of data. The problem remains even today. Lack of corroborative data leaves a vacuum in understanding the economics of such unauthorized distribution of content over internet. Let us look into these issues of redistribution of the content received from broadcast signal over internet without permission and the nature of content being distributed etc., in detail.

3.2.5.5 Issue of Unauthorized Distribution of Content Received from Broadcast Signal over Computer Networks: a Critical Analysis

As concluded above, most of the content received from broadcast signal that is reused over internet are sports. In addition to sports, some entertainment content such as reality shows and some musical concerts etc., are the most desired and wanted content over the world. Though all entertainment related content received from broadcast signal could be subjected to unauthorized distribution over internet, sports content is most vulnerable to illegal

91 For the detailed discussion on the copyright issues, see the next chapter.

92 WIPO 20th SCCR "Study on the Socio-Economic Dimension of the Unauthorized Use of Signals: Part II: Unauthorized Access to Broadcast Content – Cause and Effects: A Global Overview", (2009–2010), available at http://www.wipo.int/meetings/en/doc_details.jsp?doc_id=132819 (last accessed on 28/06/2019).

streaming because of its real time value. Moreover, the entertainment related content is already available over the peer to peer file sharing methods like torrent, bit torrent etc., Since, the high quality well compressed entertainment content is available via these P2P file sharing modes, retransmitting it after receiving it from broadcast signal is not going to be profitable. In addition to this, the content that is captured from the broadcast would be definitely of a lower quality than the one available in a P2P file sharing model. Thus, the P2P file sharing has been widely preferred over P2P streaming for entertainment content. However, in the context of sport content, information is the primary concern rather than the quality as it would not be used further unlike the entertainment content. One of the main reasons for the high demand of sports content is to know the result and some of the memorable movements/ performances of the players during the game. As most of the world population expects to have first hand information while watching the games or shows, the sports content has been the subject matter of unauthorized uses over internet because, each one wants to personally realize the happenings/sequence of the game. The commercial value associated with the sports content last as long as there is a market demand. As a result, the market demand/common man's interest over the sports will remain only till the game is over. Once the result is out, it won't have much demand in the market. It would change into the nature of news item rather than remaining as a high commercial value content.[93] Therefore, demand for the sports content is based on real time i.e., at the time of happening of the event and not after the game. Thereby, the streaming technology enables the content received from broadcast signal to be redistributed over the internet. Thus, a large number of people around the world are provided with access to sports content over internet protocol. This is the reason why, the P2P is preferred over other mode of online file sharing for sports content.

With respect to the technology in the process of unauthorized use of content over internet, as explained above, it is possible to be distributed through both IPTV and Web TV due to commonality of the internet protocol based technology. As IPTV deploys a closed network model, the service provider can only distribute the content to the viewers who are connected by the deployed network and not to all. It means content has to flow from the service provider to the subscriber. If the service provider distributes the content received from

93 Though it is stated that there is no economic value once the game is over, it has been noticed that there is a market/niche market for the broadcasted sports content. However, this market model is not within the purview of this research work since it is based on on-demand services rather than live.

broadcast signal in an unauthorized manner to its IPTV subscriber, it would be obvious to all that the content has been distributed over this service provider path. Once such unauthorized distribution is done, it would make the service provider liable for such unauthorized content distribution and not the signal of the broadcasting organization. Due to the nature of the technology, though the sports content can be transmitted over IPTV network, it has not been used for other content so far. This is very clear from the current market trend of this unauthorized distribution of content over internet.[94]

Unlike IPTV which is a closed network model, live streaming/ web TV which is based on the open internet model, enables the content received from broadcast signal to be distributed over internet to all. Therefore, it may be preliminarily stated here that sports content received from broadcast signal is available on the websites only either by the unicast streaming or multicast streaming.[95]

Current market practice of the sports in general is that transmission of the sports content is authorized by the sports content owners based on the regions and this is also given platform wise. It means broadcasting over free to air, satellite and internet are considered as separate medium/platform and thus the broadcasting rights are given separately and exclusively for that medium only. Therefore, the authorization or license is given to a particular jurisdiction and the same is given to only one broadcasting entity.[96] When there are multiple broadcastings taking place simultaneously around the world, from any part of the world, one can upload and then transmit the content they have accessed over internet by using the streaming technology.

It is worth to recollect that when the broadcast signal is decrypted, signal disappears and then, only content remains that will also disappear once it is

94 See the whole document of WIPO 20th SCCR "Study on the Socio-Economic Dimension of the Unauthorized Use of Signals: Part II: Unauthorized Access to Broadcast Content – Cause and Effects: A Global Overview", (2009–2010), available at https://www.wipo.int/edocs/mdocs/copyright/en/sccr_20/sccr_20_2_rev.pdf (last accessed on 28/06/2019) and also see OECD working Paper on "Piracy of the Digital Content", available at https://www.oecd-ilibrary.org/science-and-technology/piracy-of-digital-content_9789264065437-en (last accessed on 28/06/2019) and also see Netresult on "Update on Digital Piracy of Sporting Events 2011", available at https://www.wipo.int/export/sites/www/ip-sport/en/pdf/piracy_report_2011.pdf (last accessed on 28/06/2019).

95 See for the detailed discussion on the same, Michael J Mellis, "Internet Piracy of Live Sports Telecasts", 18 *Marquette Sports Law Review*, (2007), pp. 259–284, at p. 261.

96 It is very common with respect to many of the international sporting events such as Olympic, Football League, Cricket, etc. were the licenses are granted/auctioned on the basis of communication platforms.

enjoyed by the subscriber/public. If the subscriber uses much sophisticated digital recording device which is commonly available in the market, the content can be recorded. Such reordered content can be redistributed over internet with or without commercial gains. Since, the signal disappeared during the encryption process, there is no question of using the same signal in this process. Therefore, the unauthorized redistribution over internet is all about the content received from broadcast signal only. It may be remembered that the possibility of taking the content from live streaming would be extremely difficult when compared with digital broadcasting and IPTV. Though there are a few circumventing software available through which access and distribution of content derived out of live streaming is possible, the quality of the content would be extremely low as of today due to technological limitations. Thus, the access to content is preferred over digital broadcasting than streaming due to the quality of content. Let us look into the nature of these unauthorized uses and the current practices in detail.

Generally, the content received from broadcast signal has been redistributed, as discussed above, not only through the commercial websites but also the users who can also upload the content in a website or social network platform in a live manner without expecting any commercial gain. As per various studies[97] on the sports content issues, it has been unanimously pointed out that the following two modes of pirated content received from broadcast signal are being retransmitted over internet.

1. Live streams transmission via peer to peer television services or streamed directly from a web server
2. Highlights placed on UGC sites like YouTube or uploaded to file sharing networks.

As a result of these modes of unauthorized transmission over the internet, the OECD's 2008 study projected that the number of paid subscriptions have decreased and the number of illegal peer to peer streaming sites have increased, accordingly.[98] Though the reports have highlighted the level of piracy of sports content, it has been stated that there are some successful steps including

97 See Envisional Ltd and NetResult Ltd on "Background Report on Digital Piracy of Sporting Events" available at http://ininet.org/background-report-on-digital-piracy-of-sporting-events.html (last accessed on 28/06/2019), OECD working Paper on "Piracy of the Digital Content", at p. 15, available at http://www.ifap.ru/library/book443.pdf (last accessed on 28/06/2019) and also see Netresult on "Update on Digital Piracy of Sporting Events 2011", available at http://www.wipo.int/export/sites/www/ip-sport/en/pdf/piracy_report_2011.pdf (last accessed on 28/06/2019).

98 See OECD working Paper on "Piracy of the Digital Content", at p. 101, available at http://www.ifap.ru/library/book443.pdf, (last accessed on 28/06/2019).

legislative measures to combat piracy however, due to technology problems, it remains a challenge. The following observation is pertinent:

> Legislation to counter piracy has had a direct impact, as well as allowing for the 'management' of illegal activity. With many thousands of illegal streams being removed, ISPs blocking access to illegitimate content providing sites and also with legitimate websites becoming increasingly co-operative or prideful of protecting content IP there has been a sizeable success in the promotion of legitimate, monetized content. Although sites have been closed and even some major players in online piracy have been incarcerated, it still remains possible to bypass restrictions…[99]

From the above discussions, it may be possible to conclude that the issue of unauthorized retransmission of sports content received from broadcast signal over internet by using streaming technology is the burning issue. However, the solution to this issue is subject to the following points.

If sports content is given to the service providers (including radio, television, internet, mobile etc.,) as discussed above based on the platforms, then the right to transmit the content over each platform would be with the respective platform rights licensee ideally. If this is the case, the sports content received from broadcast signal is redistributed over internet without permission, then it will be a violation of the holder of right to transmit over internet platform as internet is a separate medium of communication.

As far as the copyright works are concerned other than the sports content, the position of the authors would remain the same. Generally, the right to communicate the works is given based on the mediums through which it could be done. For each mode of exploitation, separate specific permission from the authors is required. As stated in the sport content context, if the works received from broadcast signal are redistributed over internet without permission, then it will be a violation of the holder of right to transmit over internet platform because internet is a separate medium of communication.

In both the scenarios, the subscription of the authorized streamer would go down because of the works otherwise made available at free of cost or at reduced subscription fee. Thus, there could be an economic loss for the streaming right holder. Though the studies are not available on these economic losses incurred out of illegal retransmission of content over internet, it is

---

99 WIPO 30th SCCR on "Current Market and Technology trends in the Broadcasting Sector", (2015), at p. 30, available at http://www.wipo.int/edocs/mdocs/copyright/en/sccr_30/sccr_30_5.pdf (last accessed on 28/06/2019).

very pertinent to examine whether the existing copyright regime is adequate enough to address this economic loss issue arising out of content piracy and the same is discussed in the next chapter.

3.3 4G P2P Streaming Technology: Penetration, Market Structure and Justification for Protection

3.3.1 *Introduction*

As streaming technology is on the internet platform, it is essential for us to first look at the penetration of internet at the global level and the extent to which it will be useful to further understand and analyze the problems associated with streaming.

3.3.2 *Penetration of Internet: a Global Outlook*

The tremendous increase in global internet users have substantially escalated since 1991.[100] In 1991, it was just 4.4 million population of the world who had internet access.[101] In 1995, it was even less than 1% of the global population.[102] In 1997, it was just 2% and 7% in 2000.[103] With 888 million internet users in 2004, it was estimated that the figure will touch 1.35 billion by 2007.[104] In 2011, it was around 30% of the world population.[105] As of today, the figure is around 56%.[106]

The substantial increase in the number of internet users is the result of an increase in the number of mobile internet users. It was estimated that by 2018, mobile based internet users would be around 50% of the total internet users.[107]

---

100 Prior to 1990, it was nil as per the World Bank Data on Internet Users, available at http://data.worldbank.org/indicator/IT.NET.USER.P2 (last accessed on 05/09/2017) and also see for the same, OECD on Understanding of Digital Dive, available at https://www.oecd.org/sti/1888451.pdf (last accessed on 28/06/2019).

101 Barry Wellman and Wenhong Chen, "The Global Digital Divide —Within and Between Countries," 7 (1) *IT & Society*, (2004), pp. 39–45.

102 See for the same, OECD on Understanding of Digital Dive, available at https://www.oecd.org/sti/1888451.pdf (last accessed on 28/06/2019) and also available at http://www.internetlivestats.com/internet-users/ (last accessed on 05/09/2017).

103 Barry Wellman and Wenhong Chen, "The Global Digital Divide —Within and Between Countries," 7 (1) *IT & Society*, (2004), pp. 39–45.

104 Wen Gong Zhan and Li Rodney L. Stump, "Global Internet Use and Access: Cultural Considerations", 19 (1) *Asia Pacific Journal of Marketing and Logistics*, (2007), pp. 57–74.

105 M. Sakthivel, "Webcasters' Protection under Copyright – A Comparative Study", 27 (5) *Computer Law & Security Review*, (2011), pp. 479–496, at p. 484.

106 See as of June, 2017, available at http://www.internetworldstats.com/stats.htm (last accessed on 28/06/2019).

107 See J. Clement, "Mobile Internet – Statistics & Facts", (As on 2018), available at https://www.statista.com/topics/779/mobile-internet/ (last accessed on 28/06/2019).

Though internet penetration is around 56% of the world population, it is important to note that quality internet connections are considerably low among the total number of users. A broadband connection with good bandwidth is an essential requirement for the streaming technology. Therefore, broadband connection (may be a dial up connection) or 4G LTE is inevitable for the users to enjoy the streaming service and even for IPTV. Thus, the use of IPTV and live streaming is directly proportionate to the high quality internet/broadband connection. Let us examine the penetration of internet based transmissions such as IPTV and live streaming at the global level in detail.

3.3.3 *Penetration of Internet Based Transmissions and Their Socio-Economic Relation (Investment, Access and Piracy)*

3.3.3.1 IPTV

IPTV is one of the potential alternative platforms for broadcasting organizations including cable and satellite. Unlike traditional broadcasters, people who are actively involved in IPTV's roll out throughout the world, are telecom companies. Since, IPTV is based on broadband which is related to spectrum management, the telecom companies enter into TV market. Only the developed countries and the countries which lead in ICT have introduced IPTV. Since many countries are still lagging behind in internet penetration, IPTV services have not been successful. Let us examine the market structure of IPTV first.

IPTV service was first launched in UK at the end of last century. It was provided by Kingston communications TV and Home choice TV, which is now widely known as Tiscali TV, in a small scale at the end of 1999.[108] By 2006, most of the IPTV services were launched in Europe. In 2007, Arqiva, Red Bee Media, and Siemens Business Services were providing IPTV services in UK.[109] It was launched in France during 2003–2004. Since then, the country has witnessed tremendous growth in IPTV. During 2009, it was estimated that the country had around 7 million households with IPTV which was 28% of total TV households. When compared with France, other parts of Europe had even less than 5%.[110]

---

108 WIPO 19th SCCR "Study on the Socio-Economic Dimension of the Unauthorized Use of Signals: Part I: Current Market and Technology Trends in the Broadcasting Sector", (2009–2010), at p. 25, available at http://www.wipo.int/meetings/en/doc_details.jsp?doc_id=142819 (last accessed on 28/06/2019).

109 Ofcom, "Pay TV Market Overview: Annex 8 to Pay TV market Investigation Consultation", available at https://www.ofcom.org.uk/__data/assets/pdf_file/0020/46145/a8.pdf (last accessed on 28/06/2019).

110 WIPO 19th SCCR "Study on the Socio-Economic Dimension of the Unauthorized Use of Signals: Part I: Current Market and Technology Trends in the Broadcasting Sector", (2009–2010), at p. 26, available at http://www.wipo.int/meetings/en/doc_details.jsp?doc_id=142819 (last accessed on 28/06/2019).

As per P*oint Topic* 2013 study,[111] the IPTV subscriptions increased from 65.6 million in 2012 to 79.3 million in 2013. The number further increased to 110 million in 2014 and to around 135 million at the end of 2015.[112] As per the report, as on 2013, out of 79.3 million subscriptions, North America had 15%, East Asia had 42.8% and Europe was with 32.9%. Due to the high penetration of broadband among the East Asian countries, number of subscribers is substantially high in that region.[113] Even *Point Topic* 2015 study data substantially matches *Satista.com's* report of 2015.[114] Both are given in Figure 16–18:

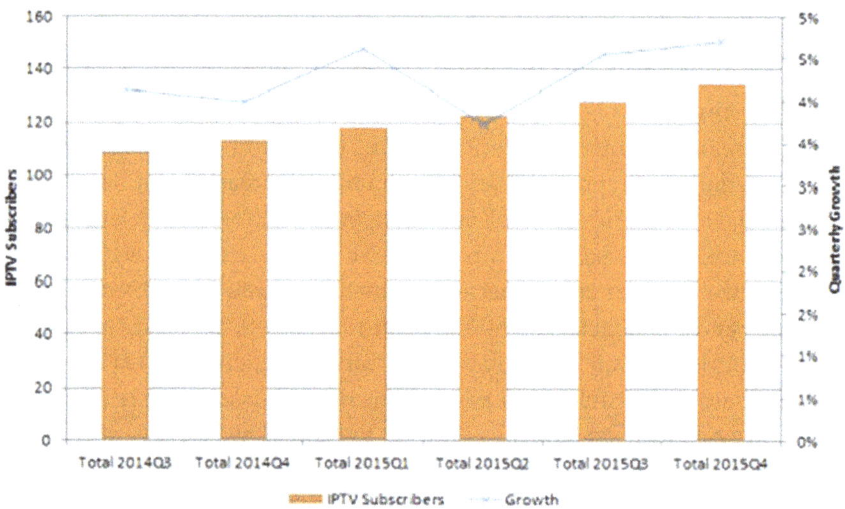

FIGURE 16 World IPTV subscribers and quarterly growth (2015)[115]

111 Point topic, "IPTV Statistics – Market Analysis: Q1 2013", at p. 3 available at http://point-topic.com/wp-content/uploads/2013/02/Point-Topic-Global-IPTV-Statistics-Q1-2013.pdf (last accessed on 28/06/2019).

112 Point topic, "IPTV Statistics – Market Analysis: Q4 2015", available at http://point-topic.com/free-analysis/iptv-subscribers-market-analysis-q4-2015/ (last accessed on 28/06/2019).

113 Point topic, "IPTV Statistics – Market Analysis: Q1 2013", at p. 5 available at http://point-topic.com/wp-content/uploads/2013/02/Point-Topic-Global-IPTV-Statistics-Q1-2013.pdf (last accessed on 28/06/2019).

114 Satista, "Number of IPTV Subscriptions Worldwide from 2009 to 2015 (in millions)", available at http://www.statista.com/statistics/274021/number-of-iptv-subscriptions-worldwide-since-2009/ (last accessed on 28/06/2019).

115 Point topic, "IPTV Statistics – Market Analysis: Q4 2015", available at http://point-topic.com/free-analysis/iptv-subscribers-market-analysis-q4-2015/ (last accessed on 28/06/2019).

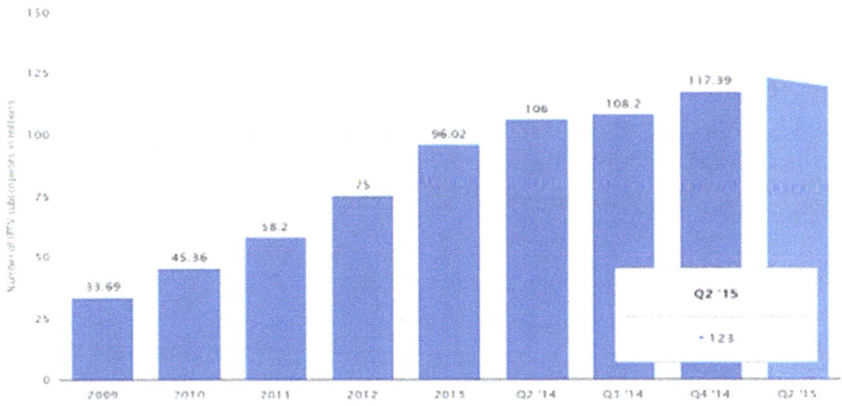

FIGURE 17 World IPTV subscribers growth[116]

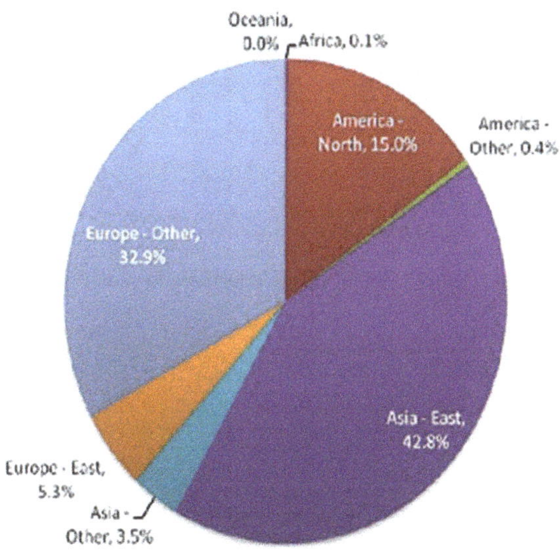

FIGURE 18 Regional overview of IPTV penetration (2013)[117]

116 Satista, "Number of IPTV Subscriptions Worldwide from 2009 to 2015 (in millions)", available at http://www.statista.com/statistics/274021/number-of-iptv-subscriptions-worldwide-since-2009/ (last accessed on 28/06/2019).

117 Point topic, "IPTV Statistics – Market Analysis: Q1 2013", at p. 5 available at http://point-topic.com/wp-content/uploads/2013/02/Point-Topic-Global-IPTV-Statistics-Q1-2013.pdf (last accessed on 28/06/2019).

Since, there has been a tremendous growth in IPTV penetration; it is believed that it is a potential threat to the traditional broadcasting models.[118] It has been projected that by 2020, around 68% of total TV households in Iceland would be with IPTV subscription and would lead among all other nations. Most of the East Asian countries would be having IPTV subscriptions (around 40% to 50% total TV households) by 2020.[119] Figure 19 clearly indicates the same.

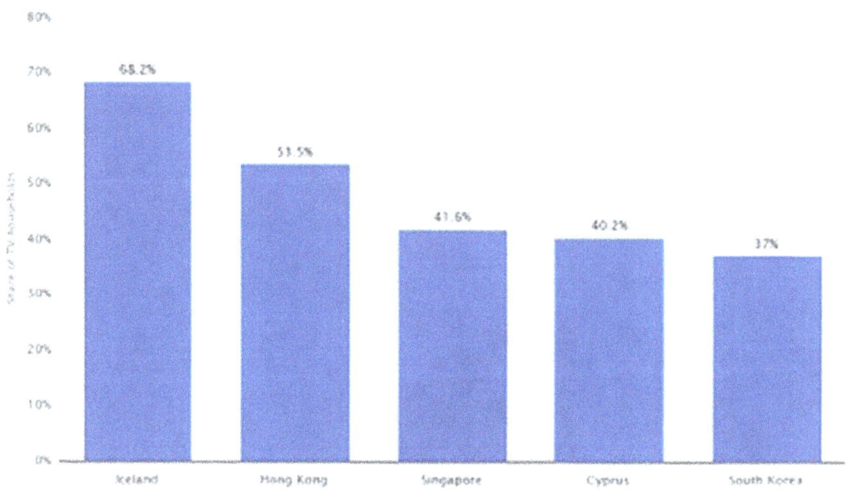

FIGURE 19 Countries with the highest projected IPTV penetration worldwide (2020)[120]

Important factors which help in such a global switchover from traditional mode of broadcasting to IPTV can be summarized as follows:[121]

---

118 WIPO 19th SCCR "Study on the Socio-Economic Dimension of the Unauthorized Use of Signals: Part I: Current Market and Technology Trends in the Broadcasting Sector", (2009–2010), at p. 26 available at http://www.wipo.int/meetings/en/doc_details.jsp?doc_id=142819 (last accessed on 28/06/2019).

119 Satista, "Countries with the Highest IPTV Penetration Worldwide in 2020", available at http://www.statista.com/statistics/322763/iptv-penetration/ (last accessed on 28/06/2019).

120 Satista, "Countries with the Highest IPTV Penetration Worldwide in 2020", available at http://www.statista.com/statistics/322763/iptv-penetration/ (last accessed on 28/06/2019).

121 See, Dong Hee Shin, "Retracted: Potential User Factors Driving Adoption of IPTV. What are Customers Expecting from IPTV?", 74 *Technological Forecasting & Social Change*, (2007), pp. 1446–1464 and also see TC Lin, S Wu, JSC Hsu and YC Chou, "The Integration of Value-based Adoption and Expectation–Confirmation Models: An Example of IPTV Continuance Intention", 54 (1) *Decision Support Systems*, (2012), pp. 63–75.

1. MPEG mode of content compression which results in higher resolution
2. High quality content delivery
3. Speedier than other traditional digital broadcasting models
4. More channel options than other traditional digital broadcasting
5. Some advanced software/technology can deliver content even with less bandwidth. As a result, even modern electronics through which IPTV can be accessed without any trouble, when compared to Internet TV.[122]

When compared with traditional broadcasting, the IPTV model of transmission is successful for various reasons. In traditional broadcasting, the content is broadcasted with the help of carrier waves which is otherwise known as content carrying signal. However, in digital traditional broadcasting, the content is redistributed based on the transfer control protocol (TCP) model which is much similar to that of IPTV/Web TV as both are based on TCP/UDP model. Since, the content production would be in digital form, it would be quite easy to use the same content in the same form if they are transmitted over IP network which is not possible in the case of analogue transmission.

As far as the investment requirement is concerned, it is similar to that of digital cable broadcasting since both are closed network models and and based on a similar structure.[123] The only difference between digital cable and IPTV transmission is about the investment in cable and the type of cable used in the communication. In digital broadcasting,the ordinary copper cable or the coax copper cable which is commonly used would be sufficient, whereas in IPTV, the basic requirement is to connect every household with optical fiber cable (OFC) which is quite expensive compared to a coaxial copper cable. Even creating the OFC infrastructure network is also comparatively expensive. In most of the countries around the world, broadband connections for connecting every household is done by the telecommunication companies. As they have already established OFC nationwide pathways for data communication, it would be easy for such telecommunication companies to provide IPTV services as IPTV is based on OFC. Since, the telecommunication companies have access to OFC pathway; they can make use of the OFC for the following purposes:

- To provide internet connection
- To provide telephone connection
- To provide IPTV connection

---

122 Dong Hee Shin, "Retracted: Potential User Factors Driving Adoption of IPTV. What are Customers Expecting from IPTV?", 74 *Technological Forecasting & Social Change*, (2007), pp. 1446–1464.

123 David Clark, "Economics of IPTV", available at https://www.curvedview.com/economics-iptv/ (last accessed on 28/06/2019).

Thus, IPTV has become a cost effective model for the companies who have established or are licensed to use the OFC pathway. Even in many countries including in India,[124] this 3 in 1 model has been implemented. The only requirement for the service provider is to place the appropriate modem at the subscribers' place. It means if Mr. A is interested to have a broadband connection, a broadband modem which will restrict the voice and IPTV services needs to be installed. If Mr. B is interested in all three services, then a suitable modem needs to be placed. These modems streamline the services based on IP address thereby the access is limited to the identified subscribers only.[125] As the same OFC is being used for multiple purposes, IPTV has become a cost effective model for the companies who have established or are licensed to use the OFC pathway.

In addition to the above, another important feature of the OFC pathway is to provide interactive service in a full-fledged manner. Though, the interactive service is very much possible in most of the digital traditional broadcasting platform, there are some limitations. As a result, the digital traditional broadcasting platform can provide only limited interactive service when compared to the OFC model. Thus, IPTV platform is being widely used for on-demand services as per the subscribers' choice in addition to the television channels being provided. Therefore, the revenue model in IPTV is entirely different from both traditional and digital traditional broadcasting. In both the broadcastings, revenue is generated out of TV advertisements or the viewers' subscription for channels. In the case of IPTV, the revenue is generated out of providing interactive services, telephone connection and internet services in addition to the advertisement revenues and users' subscription fee for the channels.

Table 6 summarizes the key characteristics of all forms of transmissions.

From the above discussion, it may be well concluded that the business model and the business environment in IPTV context is completely different which cannot be compared or equated with any form of broadcasting from the investment and revenue point of view. Let us look into the problems of IPTV market in detail.

---

124 Telecom operators such as BSNL, Airtel have been providing IPTV services since the beginning of this decade.

125 For the detailed discussion on the same, see Mirko Škrbić, Nerma Šečić and Mirza Varatanović, "A Unicast-based IPTV Service Control", *IEEE Xplore*, (2010), available at http://ieeexplore.ieee.org/stamp/stamp.jsp?arnumber=5635284 (last accessed on 28/06/2019).

TABLE 6 Characteristics comparison of analogue, digital and internet transmissions

Category	Analogue transmission			Digital Transmission			Internet Transmission	
	Terrestrial	Cable	Satellite	Terrestrial	Cable	Satellite	IPTV	Web Live TV
Quality of the contents	Low	Low	Better	Good	Good	Good	Good	Good
Nature of transmission	Free and Pay TV	Free and Pay TV	Free and Pay TV	Free and Pay TV	Free and Pay TV	Free and Pay TV	Free and Pay TV	Free and Pay TV
No of channels available	Very Few	Very Few	Very Few	High	High	High/ Unlimited	Unlimited	Unlimited
Type of the programs	Scheduled	Scheduled	Scheduled	Scheduled	Scheduled	Scheduled/ Viewer Choice	Scheduled/ Viewer Choice	Scheduled
Interactive option	No	No	No	No/Limited	No/Limited	Limited	Yes	No
On-demand service	No	No	No	No/Limited	No/Limited	Limited	Yes	No
Security of signals while transmission	Nil/ Low	Low	Low	Protected	Protected	Protected	Protected	Protected

TABLE 6 Characteristics comparison of analogue, digital and internet transmissions (*cont.*)

Category	Analogue transmission			Digital Transmission			Internet Transmission	
	Terrestrial	**Cable**	**Satellite**	**Terrestrial**	**Cable**	**Satellite**	**IPTV**	**Web Live TV**
Spectrum conception	High	High	High	Medium/Low	Medium/ Low	Medium/ Low	Low	Low
Boundaries of transmission	Limited by territory	Limited by territory	Limited by territory	Limited by territory	Limited by territory	Limited by territory	Limited by territory	World wide
User centric approach	No	Limited	No	No	Limited	May be limited	Yes	No/ Limited
Simultaneous/ selected channel transmission	Simultaneous	Simultaneous	Simultaneous	Hybrid	Hybrid	Hybrid	Selected	Selected
Devices Required for Enjoyment of Contents	Antenna and TV	Analog Set top box and TV / TV only	Dish, Set top box and TV	Receiver, Set top box and TV	Set top box and TV	Dish, Set top box, TV	Modem and TV	Internet Connection and PC

3.3.3.2 IPTV Issues and Challenges

The problems of IPTV transmission are distinct in nature as the content is transmitted over internet protocol.[126] If any copyright work has to be exploited over IPTV, at first, the work has to be authorized by the copyright owner as the copyright owner will be having the right of exploiting it over IPTV. Because of the authorization, the right of exploiting the work over IPTV is given to the IPTV provider. However, due to the authors' right of broadcasting through which the broadcasting organizations gets permission to broadcast, the broadcasters have been demanding simultaneous transmission right of the broadcast content over IPTV as well. Therefore, a direct conflict emerges at the start of this IPTV transmission. Detailed position of this conflict is discussed in the next chapter.

Due to the technological difference in transmission, unlike the analogue broadcasting, there is no possibility of the transmitted streams/packets being accessed without authorization either at the pre transmission or at the post transmission stage. The entire transmission would be completed within a fraction of seconds. During this time period, the access to stream and decrypting for accessing the content would be highly difficult. Even for the pirates attempting to access the streams; it would require longer time to decrypt one packet or stream. Thus, illegal decryption is not a viable proposition for the pirates in the digital context in general and IPTV in particular.[127]

As discussed in the digital broadcasting part of this chapter, it would be very easy for the service provider to authenticate and verify the subscriber before allowing a channel to be accessed due to the advancements of technology. It means, when a subscriber wants to see a news channel i.e, X, when the same channel number is typed by using the set top box/modem remote, then the channel will not appear immediately. It would take some time to verify your subscription status and will find out whether the desired channel is within your selected monthly package. If you have already subscribed and paid the monthly pack, then the service provider will enable you to enjoy the channel X based on your IP address. Though, there may be a delay in accessing the channel, it is not a time consuming process; it requires only a fraction of a second to verify the authenticity of the subscriber. Therefore, the illegal access

---

126 Jan Loskowski, "IPTV Services and Technologies", available at https://www.tu-braunschweig.de/Medien-DB/ida-kn/seminar_komm_syst/laskowski_ws09.pdf (last accessed on 28/06/2019).

127 See for the same in general, for all transmission technology, Whitfield Diffie and Martin Hellman, "New Directions in Cryptography", 22(6) *IEEE transactions on Information Theory,* (1976), pp. 644–654.

to packets/streams is not a concern as the technology addresses the issue of the security of the content and the accessibility of the same. The same server based authentication process is very much in practice in an IPTV transmission, thereby, the illegal access is restricted.

As a result of these technological advancements, the access to stream/packets during the course of transmission is not possible for further use.[128] However, similar to that of digital broadcasting, the content that has been transmitted can be accessed after the enjoyment i.e., after the decryption of the transmitted packets. The transmitted content would be of a much higher quality than digital broadcasting as most of the IPTV services use MPEG-4 model of compression for data transmission.[129] Once, this content is accessed, the same can be further used/transmitted without any authorization over the open internet by using live streaming so as to enable the outsiders of the IPTV community, who have access to internet to enjoy the content without any entry fee or at a substantially lower rate. As discussed above, under the digital traditional broadcasting, the cost for doing such an unauthorized retransmission is extremely low due to the tools required for such transmissions which are widely available. Due to these unauthorized retransmissions over the web, as the platforms are licensed separately, there is a revenue loss to the live streaming right holders as well as to the content owner. However, it is to be noted that due to the said unauthorized retransmission over web, the IPTV provider is not affected. As discussed above, in most of the cases, the retransmission has been taking place only in the context of entertainment, reality shows and sports as they enjoy a huge demand among the audience at the instance of live action. Since, the people would like to see the event as it is happening, it would be an option for the people who do not have any other source of enjoying the content.[130] This issue can be also addressed as pointed above. The unauthorized retransmission out of the IPTV transmission is all about the content. As the content gets transmitted via open internet in unauthorized modes, the content creators' right would be sufficient to address the issue.

---

128 William D. Hong, "IPTV Technology, Trends and Challenges", available at http://www-inst.eecs.berkeley.edu/~ee233/sp06/student_presentations/EE233_IPTV.pdf (last accessed on 28/06/2019).

129 Nate Anderson, "An Introduction to IPTV", available at http://arstechnica.com/business/2006/03/iptv/1/ (last accessed on 28/06/2019).

130 See for the same argument, M. Sakthivel, "Webcasters' Protection under Copyright – A Comparative Study", 27 (5) *Computer Law & Security Review,* (2011), pp. 479–496 and also see M. Sakthivel, "Copyrightability of Sports Content: Indian Scenario", *Entertainment Law Review,* (2012), pp. 91–95.

Issues related to live streaming in both IPTV and Internet TV are very unique due to the very nature of the technology in which it is working. In addition to that, the entire transmission takes place over the internet platform. IPTV transmissions in many countries around the world transmit the same channels that are being broadcasted in analogue and digital broadcasting mode. As a result, the consumers have now one more option to enjoy the content via IPTV in addition to analogue and digital broadcasting models.[131]

3.3.3.3 Is there any Need for Intervention?

In the light of above discussion, while examining the possibility of stream/ packets being accessed without authorization similar to that of traditional broadcasters either prior to the streaming or post streaming in IPTV, it has been found that such problems do not persist in IPTV due to the advanced encryption techniques. Due to the inbuilt technological solution, revenue loss resulting out of stream piracy has been addressed at the very beginning itself. Even WIPO's studies on the broadcasting industry is silent on the stream piracy issue arising out of IPTV, if any, as there is no such problem while practicing the IPTV. If stream piracy is not feasible either in the pre or post streaming era, then it is pertinent to examine, whether there is any gap in law to protect investment of the IPTV provider.

As concluded above, since the possibility of streams/ packets being accessed without authorization either pre or post streaming in the IPTV context has been ruled out, there is no question of gap in law to be filled so as to protect the investment of the IPTV provider. When there is no threat to their investment, then it is highly unwarranted to interfere in the commercial exploitation of IPTV for communicating the copyright works. Then, the only remaining issue is unauthorized use of content of the IPTV transmission. As discussed and concluded, the unauthorized use of the content could be only over the open internet by using live streaming not on the IPTV, such unauthorized uses do not conflict with the normal exploitation of the IPTV service provider rather it would affect the revenue flow of the live streaming license holder. Even if there is any issue, it could be based only on the content which could be effectively and sufficiently addressed by the authors' right of communication to public by using IPTV. Therefore, it can be concluded that there is no compelling reason for the law to step in and regulate the current position of the exploitation of works by using IPTV.

131 WIPO 30th SCCR on "Current Market and Technology trends in the Broadcasting Sector", (2015), at p. 18, available at http://www.wipo.int/edocs/mdocs/copyright/en/sccr_30/sccr_30_5.pdf (last accessed on 28/06/2019).

3.3.3.4 Internet TV

Live streaming/internet television model has been widely used since the very beginning of the 21st century.[132] However, due to low bandwidth/speed of the internet connection, there were many issues like; the stream packets would take time to be delivered, loss of packets etc., equipping the service provider by himself was required so as to accommodate a higher number of streaming audience.[133] However, simultaneously, IPTV model was developed as a closed network internet transmission against this open network transmission model so as to overcome from the above said shortcomings.[134] Nevertheless, internet TV has been continuously used since then and it has been projected that in the near future, the use of live streaming will be at an increased level and will gain much popularity.[135]

The real time streaming has been an attractive mode of communication due to its speedy manner of content delivery. Since, multiple electronic gadgets have been equipped with browsers and player applications, it has become a highly sophisticated mode of content delivery in real time. Right from the last decade, many important events including sports such as world cup football and cricket, Olympic Games, news reporting, celebrities' performances, historical events are being streamed in real time. Even the *Michael Jackson* memorial service was also live streamed.[136] The eagerness of people to know the status of events in real time is the key component which boosts this technology among the global viewers. This group of peoples completely rely on real time internet information. This reliability factor clubbed with other factors like increased speed, penetration etc., help the streaming technology in its rapid expansion.[137] Key features of the Internet TV [over the top] (both Live Streaming and on-demand streaming) and the IPTV are highlighted in Table 7.

---

132 Tim Siglin, "The Economics of Live Events", available at http://www.streamingmedia.com/Articles/Editorial/Featured-Articles/The-Economics-of-Live-Events-66648.aspx (last accessed on 28/06/2019).

133 See, Dong Hee Shin, "Retracted: Potential User Factors Driving Adoption of IPTV. What are Customers Expecting from IPTV?", 74 *Technological Forecasting & Social Change*, (2007), pp. 1446–1464.

134 *Ibid.*

135 Jason Mander, "The Rise of Live Streaming", available at https://blog.globalwebindex.com/chart-of-the-day/the-rise-of-live-streaming-2/ (last accessed on 28/06/2019) and also see Shirley Pelts, "The Rising Trend of Online Streaming", available at http://marketrealist.com/2015/08/rising-trend-online-streaming/ (last accessed on 28/06/2019).

136 Tim Siglin, "The Economics of Live Events", available at http://www.streamingmedia.com/Articles/Editorial/Featured-Articles/The-Economics-of-Live-Events-66648.aspx (last accessed on 28/06/2019).

137 See "Netflix's View: Internet TV is Replacing Linear TV", available at https://hackerfall.com/story/netflix-long-term-view (last accessed on 28/06/2019).

TABLE 7 Differences between OTT and IPTV

	OTT(Over-the top)	IPTV(Internet Protocal TV)
Content delivery	Uses open internet, unmanaged network "open ecosystem"	Uses dedicated, managed network "Walled Garden ecosystem"
Network type	Deliverd from the provider/ content aggregator to the viewer using open network	Closed, Proprietary network, accessed via a specific internet service provider
Network ownership	Without the need for intervening carriage negotiations, or infrastructure investments	Services are optimized and customized to suit the network and end-device capability
Quality of service(QOS)	Not guaranteed, works under best effort conditions	Enable control over quality of delivery
Examples	Popular Video on demand services like YouTube, Netflix, Amazon Lovefilm, BBC iPlayer, Hulu etc.	Service Example includes U-verse (AT&T), Prism Tv (Century Link)
Protocol	Delivered using HTTP (TCP), a connected transport protocal. Emerging trends using adaptive streaming technologies like HLS (Apple), Smooth Streaming (Microsoft) and HDS (Adobe)	Traditional IPTV uses TS (transport stream) transmission technology. Delivers content over UDP, connectionless protocol
Content catalog	Widely usrd for freemium and economical VOD delivery models	Used primarily for premium content and real time content delivery like broadcasting TV
Content type	Generally not premium due to security DRM Concerns	Premium Content
Routing topology	Unicast (Based on HTTP)	Multicast, Unicast burst during channel change leading multicast join
Category	Complementary Service	Parallel service category to Cable/Satellite

TABLE 7 Differences between OTT and IPTV (*cont.*)

	OTT(Over-the top)	**IPTV(Internet Protocal TV)**
Major players	OVP (Kaltura. Brightcove), CDN Players (Akamai, L3, Limelight) and Content Aggregators	TSP and IPTV Platform vendors – Microsoft Mediaroom (Ericsson), ALU, Cisco..
Key challenges	Low Quality, Non Premium Content, No Live Broadcast, Unicast Model	Expensive, Competition from Cable/DTH industry, Bandwidth and infrastructure
Key benefits	Low cost, Flexibility of content consumption across devices	Interactive Service, Quality of Service and Quality of Experience

According to a study, among the content being streamed, the following are most popular in descending order.[138]

- News
- Sports
- Live Concerts
- Corporate Events
- Public Events/Govt. functions
- Press Conferences
- Entertainment Content

The above given items are the content that is commonly used in live streaming. In case of on demand streaming, the entertainment content would be at the top. Access to real time would be either by paying access fee or free. If it is publicly funded event, in most of the cases, it would be free. In case of live streaming, due to its high demand, sports content is being preferred by many streaming service providers.

While analyzing the market of the IPTV, it was made to understand that the telecom companies are into IPTV services. However, in case of live streaming, it is interesting to note that not only the technology giants *Google, Apple* &

138 Tim Siglin, "The Economics of Live Events", available at http://www.streamingmedia.com/Articles/Editorial/Featured-Articles/The-Economics-of-Live-Events-66648.aspx (last accessed on 28/06/2019).

e-commerce business site *Amazon*,[139] even the social networking giants *Facebook* and *Twitter* have also shown their keen interest in buying sports right for real-time streaming through their own applications such as *Facebook Live and Periscope.*[140]

In US, a channel named *Pluto TV*, a streaming service provider, offers free television over internet with channels that are available in traditional broadcasting, since the viewers would like to watch the same.[141] Even some entertainment and news channels all over the world, including some Indian channels are also available online.[142]

Data related to streaming industry is not available at the global level. Even, as per the European Union's study of 2015,[143] it has been clearly stated that no statistics is available on streaming.

> As such there is no real market on its own for streaming of sports events and EU and global market data is scarce; As of June 2015 there were no publicly available studies or data regarding market size of streaming of sports events.
>
> However, based on the DSM consumer survey from 2014, ICF estimates that around 58 per cent of European internet users watch live events (e.g. sports, concerts) online. The number of online consumers in EU28 in 2015 is estimated to 148 million.[144]

It is believed that streaming activity has yet to become an industry due to its nature and lack of strong presence of multinational players in this regard. Due to the diversity of viewers, language preferences etc., the most popular content wanted by streaming services are sports and music concerts. As stated above, according to a 2014 survey about the streaming users, it has been projected

139 The Economist on "Changing the Channel: A Startup seeks to keep the Conventional TV Station Alive in the Digital Era", available at http://www.scoreandchange.com/live-video-streaming-changes-sports-market/ (last accessed on 28/06/2019).

140 See for the same, "Live Video Streaming Changes the Sports Market", available at http://www.scoreandchange.com/live-video-streaming-changes-sports-market/ (last accessed on 28/06/2019).

141 *Ibid.*

142 As of now there is no well known or popular dedicated and exclusive live streaming services available in India. However, the cricket match content and TV content are made available via live streaming by the respective channels in their websites.

143 European Commission, "Study on Consumer Digital Content Products-2015", available at https://ec.europa.eu/info/sites/info/files/study_on_digital_content_products_in_the_eu_en.pdf (last accessed on 28/06/2019).

144 *Id.*, at p. 142.

TABLE 8 Penetration of streaming in EU: an overview

Member State	No. of businesses in 2015	Industry turnover € million	% of online population using product	No. of online consumers million
Austria	Data Not available	Data Not available	47	2
Bulgaria			81	3
Czech Republic			73	4
Denmark			44	1
France			50	17
Germany			51	23
Ireland			61	1
Italy			65	16
Latvia			65	1
Netherlands			36	4
Poland			74	13
Slovenia			71	1
Spain			67	15
Sweden			46	2
United Kingdom			55	20
EU28*			58	148

* The corresponding figure of "% of online population using product" is the average of EU and the "no of online consumers" is the total no of consumers in EU (millions).

that more than half of the internet users watch streaming which is around 148 million in the EU alone. Table 8 clearly gives details about the streaming penetration in EU.[145]

The streaming market is a mixture of both paid and free model.[146] Some are based on the advertisement revenue like free to air model and some are based on pay TV model. Since, there is no other data available on this, let us look into the behavior of the streaming viewers so as to understand whether they would prefer paid streaming or free one. Table 9 gives an insight on this.[147]

145 *Ibid.*
146 *Id.*, at p. 147.
147 *Id.*, at p. 146.

TABLE 9 Preferences of consumers behavior in streaming

Member State	Paid Streaming/Viewing/ Using online	Free Streaming/Viewing/ Using online
Austria	22	80
Bulgaria	15	87
Czech Republic	21	81
Denmark	30	75
France	26	80
Germany	30	75
Ireland	30	75
Italy	30	73
Latvia	9	92
Netherlands	28	78
Poland	27	80
Slovenia	20	84
Spain	34	72
Sweden	34	74
United Kingdom	39	68
EU28	28	77

According to this table, it is very clear that most of the streaming viewers would prefer free streaming model than the paid one irrespective of the fact that whether the free one is legal or illegal. As discussed above, according to the sports market, the content is sold based on the territorial market and that is also based on the platforms.[148] It means, that channel X and company Y have purchased the sports rights for Live TV broadcast and Live streaming respectively from the organizer of sport event and the same is being broadcasted. Assume that Mr. A, who is an authorized subscriber who has accessed the content by circumventing device and streaming the same over internet. In this context, Mr. A's action would be considered as unauthorized one from the company Y's point of view. If the company Y does the live streaming of the same sports event, it would be an authorized one. Thus at a time, there would be two streaming services of the same sport. Therefore, there may be many

148 *Id.*, at p. 147.

persons involved in streaming or retransmitting the TV broadcast over internet which may be illegal or legal.

As far as the future of the industry is concerned, an EU study has projected that there will be tremendous growth in streaming services and its viewership.[149] However, sports content owners' association[150] has expressed its reservation on this view. As stated above, due to the lack of a multinational player in the streaming service, sports content owners' association does not show its willingness to give international license rather it prefers region wise permission only.[151] From the above discussion, since Google, Facebook, Amazon, Twitter etc., have shown their interest in streaming especially in the sports content, it may be expected that a couple of years down the line, there will be an industry in this context too due to the huge investment possibilities that are being developed. Let us examine the issues related to streaming in detail.

3.3.3.5 Internet TV: Issues and Challenges

Neither the IPTV service providers nor the internet TV service providers have reported any piracy related problems similar to that of their peers in the traditional broadcasting who are facing the signal piracy and unauthorized retransmission issues etc., Even WIPO's studies conducted in 2009–2010[152] and 2015[153] on the broadcasting industry, wherein the IPTV has also been discussed, remain silent on the stream piracy issue and unauthorized retransmission issue arising out of IPTV, if any. Since, there is no active presence of an industry; the problems of live streaming have not been identified. As of now, even the small scale live streaming service providers have not reported any of the issues related to their commercial activity. So far, there is no case which is reported regarding stream/packet being accessed without authorization either prior to the streaming or after the streaming for further transmission over internet. It is also believed that there is no possibility of stream or packet being accessed without authorization due to the nature of technology i.e., the streaming is completed within fraction

149 *Ibid.*

150 The Sports Rights Owners Coalition ("SROC") is a forum of over 50 international and national sports bodies and competition organisers with a particular focus on rights issues. See for further details, available at https://www.sroc.info (last accessed on 28/06/2019).

151 European Commission, "Study on Consumer Digital Content Products-2015", at p.147, available at https://ec.europa.eu/info/sites/info/files/study-consumer-digital-content-products_en.pdf (last accessed on 28/06/2019).

152 See WIPO's "Study on the Socio-Economic Dimension of the Unauthorized Use of Signals": Part I, Part II & Part III.

153 WIPO 30th SCCR on "Current Market and Technology trends in the Broadcasting Sector", (2015), available at http://www.wipo.int/edocs/mdocs/copyright/en/sccr_30/sccr_30_5.pdf (last accessed on 28/06/2019).

of seconds.[154] In fact, it would be highly difficult to understand and monitor that, when the streams are generated and when do the streams disappear once the streaming is completed. At the end, nothing remains with the viewers since live streaming makes them passive viewers.[155] However, with the help of circumventing tools, even the live streamed content could be accessed once the streaming is enjoyed. If the quality of content is extremely good, then such content would also be used for retransmission. As of now the content transmitted out of live streaming would not be at the highest of quality due to technological reasons i.e., high end techniques are not used, availability of bandwidth etc. However, there is no such commercial instances reported so far.

As far as the problems of internet TV are concerned, it is distinctive one from all other modes of transmission even from that of IPTV point of view. The main problem is that this platform is being used for the unauthorized retransmission of the content received from broadcasting signal or IPTV. As discussed above, in most of the cases, the sports content is being retransmitted without any permission.

However, one may argue that the issue remains in this platform also by pointing out that the possibility of content that is streamed could be used after the streaming gets over if possible or by circumventing methods. As of now, the live streaming technology is widely used only in sports, music concerts, news etc. As discussed in the previous part, the viewers have been switching over to the streaming service due to its real time delivery. Therefore, live streaming is gaining popularity among global viewers.[156] Even if we presume that there is a possibility of post streaming use, the content would be old and lose its demand and may be considered as outdated.[157] The viewership of the streaming services is there to know/to access the content at first in real time. Once it is consumed, the content loses part of its relevance.[158] Even if someone wishes to see the old content/past content; they will go to sites/platforms

---

154 Gerard O'driscoll, *Next Generation IPTV Services and Technologies*, Wiley Publications, (2007), at p. 20, where it has been stated that high speed distribution. Generally, it is understood, internet transmission takes place within seconds and delivers content at the real time.

155 See Nate Anderson, "An Introduction to IPTV", available at http://arstechnica.com/business/2006/03/iptv/1/ (last accessed on 28/06/2019).

156 M. Sakthivel, "Webcasters' Protection under Copyright – A Comparative Study", 27 (5) *Computer Law & Security Review*, (2011), pp. 479–496, at p.484.

157 M. Sakthivel, "Copyrightability of Sports Content: Indian Scenario", *Entertainment Law Review*, (2012), at p.91.

158 See OECD working Paper on "Piracy of the Digital Content", at p. 15, available at http://www.ifap.ru/library/book443.pdf (last accessed on 28/06/2019).

like *YouTube*[159] for their enjoyment in an exceptionally higher quality. Therefore, they may not prefer this content in the retransmission mode. Therefore, instances of retransmission are extremely low in case of live streaming. As a result, it may be preliminarily concluded by saying that the issues with traditional broadcasting do not have their presence in the internet based platform.

3.3.3.6 Is there a Need for Intervention?

In the light of the above discussion, similar to the inquiry which was done on IPTV, while examining the possibility of stream/packets being accessed without authorization similar to that of traditional broadcasters either prior to the streaming or post streaming in Internet IPTV, it has been found that such problems do not persist in internet TV due to advanced encryption techniques. Due to the inbuilt technological solution, revenue loss resulting out of stream piracy has been addressed at the very beginning point itself. Even WIPO's studies on the broadcasting industry are silent on the stream piracy issue arising out of internet TV. In this context, it is pertinent to examine that whether there is any gap in law to protect investment on internet TV service provider.

As concluded above, since the possibility of streams/ packets being accessed without authorization either prior to the streaming or post streaming in the internet TV context have been ruled out, there is no question of a gap in law to be filled so as to protect the investment of the internet TV provider like IPTV scenario. When there is no threat for their investment, then it is highly unwarranted to interfere in the commercial exploitation of internet TV for communicating the copyright works. The only remaining issue is unauthorized use of content of the IPTV transmission over internet TV, which is obviously a major concern and such unauthorized uses usually conflict with the normal exploitation of the internet TV service provider as well. However, as the unauthorized use of content is within the authors' circle of rights which could be addressed by the authors' right of communication to public. Therefore, it can be well concluded that there is no compelling reason for the law to step in and regulate the current position of the exploitation of works by using internet TV similar to that of IPTV.

3.4 Conclusion

From the overall discussion on the socio-economic relations of the various modes of transmission, the following general conclusions could be derived as summarized at the respective sub headings.

159 YouTube is a global video-sharing website owned by Google.

As traditional broadcasting is signal based, the problem of signal piracy has been very much present in both pre and post broadcasting context. So as to protect the investment of broadcasting organizations in signal generation and diffusion of the same, the signal piracy issue has been addressed by copyright through neighbouring rights. As the entire world will be moving towards digital broadcasting within another five years from now, we could find that as the signal is digital signal which is encrypted with high end keys for decryption, access to digital signal is too complex thus the possibility of signal piracy is going to be almost nil. Thus, there is no signal piracy issue in digital broadcasting as is persistant in traditional analogue broadcasting. However, the content received out of digital broadcasting could be retransmitted over internet, due to which the internet TV streamer and content owners would face revenue loss out of the illegal transmission of content. Hence, the issue in the digital broadcasting is all about content, it is better that the content piracy issue is addressed by the content owners rather than addressing through broadcasters. Thus, the legal aspects are further discussed in the next chapter.

In the light of above discussion, while examining the possibility of stream/packets being accessed without authorization similar to that of traditional broadcasters' right either prior to the streaming or post streaming in internet TV and IPTV, it has been found that such problems do not persist in the internet TV due to the advanced encryption techniques. If the stream piracy is not feasible either in the pre or post streaming stage in both internet TV and the IPTV, then, there is no question of a gap in law to be filled so as to protect the investment. Further, it has been concluded that as the issues, if any is on content, the same could be addressed by the authors' right of communication to public by using internet TV and IPTV. Therefore, it can be well concluded that there is no compelling reason for the law to step in and regulate the current position of the exploitation of works by using internet TV and IPTV. The scope of the right of communication to public of the author and the rights given to broadcasting organizations are discussed in the next chapter to find out whether there is any need to further expand the rights to protect their interests in the face of an emergence of a new technology like streaming.

CHAPTER 4

Evolution of the Authors' Right of Communication to Public: Implications to Broadcasters in the Context of Live Streaming

4.1 Introduction

Technological advancements in the field of communication have changed the modes of exploitation of the works of author. In order to meet the new demands of enjoyment of works, the international copyright system and domestic copyright laws recognized new rights for the authors to exploit their works through new mediums. In this context, evolution of broadcasting and streaming has seriously influenced not only the mode of communication of the works but also changed the mode of enjoyment of works. While exploiting the authors' work using the traditional analogue broadcasting, the broadcasters faced the problem of unauthorized access and use of content carrying signal resulting in financial losses. This problem was due to the technological limitations of the then existing broadcasting techniques. This is also associated with the limitation of authors' right of broadcasting to protect the unauthorized use of signal of the broadcasting organizations. In order to protect the broadcasters' investment, the broadcasters' protection originated.

However, due to the progress of technology in broadcasting and the development of associated tools such as encryption techniques, technological solutions emerged to prevent unauthorized use of signal of the broadcasting organizations. Similarly, in case of live streaming technology used to transmit the work over the internet, due to sophisticated technological encryption tools, it is practically impossible to access the streams during transmission. As a result of the development of inbuilt technological solutions in the digital context, the socio-economic analysis has revealed that the economic concerns/problems of broadcasting organizations as a result of the signal piracy have been adequately addressed. In this technological and socio-economic background, it is important to find out whether the right of communication to public of the author is adequate to address the new challenges of unauthorized use of content received from the broadcast signal through streaming and simultaneous retransmission of content received from live streaming. In this chapter, the evolution and scope of the authors' right of communication to public from broadcasting to live streaming at the international level has been

 | DOI:10.1163/9789004419155_005

traced followed by the evolution of the broadcasters' protection and the new demand for its extension to simultaneous live streaming.

4.2 Evolution of the Authors' Right of Broadcasting

With the evolution of radio broadcasting in the US, there emerged a direct market conflict between the authors' public performances right[1] in their musical work and the broadcasting of the same by radio broadcasters. By the mid 1920s, radio broadcasting had flourished and there existed a strong competition between many radio stations.[2] As a result, radio stations broadcasted new & popular copyrighted music of the time without permission and paying any royalty to the authors. In short the radio broadcasting stations operated out of content piracy i.e., songs of authors broadcasted without permission and without paying any royalty to the authors. Thus, the use of this technology for the copyright works substantially affected the authors' public performances and their existing market causing considerable economic loss. However, the new technology had huge economic implications, provided wide publicity to musical works and created a wide spectrum of market.[3] The authors and the composers decided to reap the fruit of this new technology within the copyright regime and thus demanded to bring broadcasting under the public performance right of copyright in the US.[4]

When the broadcasters were sued by the composers for copyright infringement i.e., infringement of public performance right, it was strongly contented that radio broadcasting was neither public performance and nor for profit and thus there was no question of violation of public performance right as per the US 1909 Code. Though the same contention was accepted by the Lower Court[5]

1 Jane C. Ginsburg, "Copyright and Control over New Technologies of Dissemination", 101 (7) *Columbia Law Review*, (2001), pp. 1613–1647, at p. 1621.

2 Makeen Fouad Makeen, *Copyright in a Global Information Society: The Scope of Copyright Protection under International, US, UK and French Law*, Kluwer Law International, London (2000), p. 35.

3 M. Sakthivel, "Communication to the Public under Copyright Law and the Impact of Information and Communication Technologies – An Analysis", in B.C. Nirmal, *Contemporary Issues in International Law*. 2014, Satyam Law International, (2014), pp. 349–354 and also see Makeen Fouad Makeen, *Copyright in a Global Information Society: The Scope of Copyright Protection under International, US, UK and French Law*, Kluwer Law International, London (2000), at p. 35.

4 *Id.*, at p. 36.

5 See Leo L. Linck, "Copyright Law Applied to Radio Broadcasting", 19 *Notre Dame Law Review*, (1943), pp. 13–30, at p. 18.

and held that radio broadcasting was not a public performance as it was not performed before an audience,[6] the Circuit Court of Appeal reversed the decision and held radio broadcasting was public performance.[7] The explanation offered by the Court reads thus:

> A performance, in our judgment, is no less public because the listeners are unable to communicate with one another or are not assembled within an enclosure or gathered together in some open stadium or park or other public place. Nor can a performance, in our judgment, be deemed private because each listener may enjoy it alone in the privacy of his home. Radio broadcasting is intended to and in fact does reach a very much larger number of the public at the moment of the rendition than any other medium of performance. The artist is consciously addressing a great though unseen and widely scattered audience and is therefore participating in a public performance.[8]

By this interpretation the authors' right over new technology was recognised by expanding the existing right.[9] This judgement resulted in preventing the piracy of the composers' work by the broadcasting organizations and the authors' right over the new technology was also ascertained enabling them to enjoy economic benefits from the new medium for their works.[10]

The developments in broadcasting also resulted in bringing the issue as an agenda item of the Berne Revision and was discussed and accepted in the Rome Conference, 1928.[11] As per Article 11 *bis* of the Rome Act of Berne Convention, the authors' right of diffusion over the radio technology was specifically recognized based on the then existing technology.[12] The same kind of

---

6 See Jack C. Hynes, "Radio v. Royalties", 15 *Notre Dame Lawyer*, (1940), pp. 290–306, at p. 294.

7 See *Jerome H. Remick & Co.* v. *American Automobile Accessories, Co.*, 5 F.2d 411(6th Cir., 1925).

8 See *Jerome H. Remick & Co.* v. *American Automobile Accessories, Co.*, 5 F.2d 411(6th Cir., 1925), at p. 412.

9 Stanley Rothenberg, *Copyright and Public Performance of Music*, Martinus Nijhoff, The Hague, (1954), at pp. 24–25.

10 Lawrence P. Simpson, "The Copyright Situation as Affecting Radio Broadcasting", 9 *New York University Law Quarterly Review*, (1931–1932), pp. 180–197, at p. 191.

11 Rome Act, 1928 of Berne Convention, Art. 11 *bis*: (1) Authors of literary and artistic works shall enjoy the exclusive right of authorizing the communication of their works to the public by radio-diffusion.

12 WIPO, *Guide to the Rome Convention and to the Phonograms Convention*, WIPO Publication No. 617 (E), (Geneva, WIPO, 1981), at p. 8.

right over television was extended by Article 11 *bis* of the Brussels Act, 1948 of Berne Convention.[13] The language of the Article 11 *bis* explicitly covered the new technology that was prevalent in broadcasting at that time. It has been pointed out that through this 1948 Act, not only the radio, even the future technology i.e., TVs have been covered. Such an interpretation is very much possible because of the language of the provision i.e., 'any other means of wireless diffusion of signs, sounds or images'. This is evident from the discussions that have happened during the 1948 Act which read:

> The Brussels Conference felt not only that the exclusive right conferred on authors by the Rome Conference, "to authorize the communication of their works to the public by radio-diffusion" not only ought to remain inviolate, but also that the relevant text ought to be revised so as first to include, beyond all possibility of doubt, all communications to the public by any other method, known or as yet unknown, of wireless diffusion of sounds, signs, or images, thus including television; and secondly to indicate clearly that the mere act of broadcasting, and not that of reception or audition, shall be the determining factor.[14]

---

13 Brussels Act, 1948 of Berne Convention, 1948, Art. 11 *bis*: (1) Authors of literary and artistic works shall have the exclusive right of authorizing: (i) the radio-diffusion of their works or the communication thereof to the public by any other means of wireless diffusion of signs, sounds or images; (ii) any communication to the public, whether over wires or not, of the radio diffusion of the work, when this communication is made by a body other than the original one; (iii) the communication to the public by loudspeaker or any other similar instrument transmitting, by signs, sounds or images, the radio-diffusion of the work.

(2) It shall be a matter for legislation in the countries of the Union to determine the conditions under which the rights mentioned in the preceding paragraph may be exercised, but these conditions shall apply only in the countries where they have been prescribed. They shall not in any circumstances be prejudicial to the moral right of the author, nor to his right to obtain just remuneration which, in the absence of agreement, shall be fixed by competent authority.

(3) Except where otherwise provided, permission granted in accordance with paragraph (1) of this Article shall not imply permission to record the radio-diffused work by means of instruments recording sounds or images. It shall, however, be a matter for legislation in the countries of the Union to determine the regulations for ephemeral recordings made by a broadcasting body by means of its own facilities and used for its own emissions. The preservation of these recordings in official archives may, on the ground of their exceptional documentary character, be authorized by such legislation.

14 Arthur Fisher, "The 1948 Revision of the Berne Convention", 10 *Fed. Comm. B.J.*, (1949), pp. 53–58, at p. 55.

Therefore, it is clear from the above discussion that though TV broadcasting was at an infant stage, the right has been extended by the Brussels Act, 1948. The use of the words "wireless diffusion" also refers to the signal based technology developed for broadcasting during that period.

4.3 Authors' Right of Broadcasting: Scope & Limitations

The authors' right of broadcasting means the right of communicating the songs/works by using radio broadcasting/diffusion/emission.[15] Though the terminologies are multiple and different, in essence, all these three i.e., broadcasting, diffusion, emission could mean the same. As discussed in the second chapter, from a technological point of view, it means the essential requirement of the signal being diffused for mass reception by the public at the same time at a place of reception as per the receivers' choice. However, the terminology of diffusion is closely associated and often used only with the radio, and the term broadcasting is often used with TV and the word emission with satellite. In all these cases, it is the content carrying signal generated by the broadcasting organization with the permission of the owner of the work that is diffused to the public for reception.

In the initial stage of the development of radio and TV broadcasting, it was not imagined that the content carrying signal could be captured and used without permission, which, later became a new business model. Thus, there were no technological measures available for preventing the unauthorized capturing of the signal for its further diffusion to the unintended audience for commercial gains. Due to heavy competition in the US market, the signal of one of the broadcasting organizations was intercepted by another broadcasting organization without permission and broadcasted the same again to the new audience simultaneously causing huge revenue loss.[16]

Since the problem is with the content carrying signal which is the sole property of the broadcasting organization, the protection of signal from unauthorized reception/interception either prior to or before the broadcasting is completed (the content is received by the public) become a necessity. This content carrying signal is commonly understood as "broadcast" in the

15 See for the detailed discussion on the broadcast and broadcasting under the copyright, M. Sakthivel, "Is it Broadcast or Broadcasting?", 16 (1) *Journal of Intellectual Property Rights*, (2011), pp. 23–26.

16 See for the detailed discussion on the same, Louis G. Caldwell, "The Broadcasting of Copyrighted Works", 1 *J. Air L*, (1930), pp. 584–598.

copyright context.[17] Though, it seems to be the sole problem of broadcasting organizations, it is also connected with the authors' right of broadcasting. The broadcasting right of author can be enjoyed only if the content carrying signal is being generated by the broadcasters and diffused to the public for reception. If the same is intercepted and used without permission, both the author and the broadcasting organization will have economic loss. It is well understood that the copyright of the author protects only the content (expression) that is fixed in any tangible medium. This created the problem of protecting the content that is carried by the signal within the broadcasting right of the author. So the content carrying signal was left with no protection from unauthorized use.[18] Though it seems to be the problem of the radio broadcasting technology, the problem remains even with television broadcasting technology since both radio and TV are based on diffusion of content carrying signal.

As far as the problem is concerned, copyright did not have any solution for signal piracy as signal could not be protected within it. Even though there could be a contractual arrangement between the authors and the broadcasting organizations, the intended result could not be achieved because the contractual arrangement is only for the broadcasting (transmission) of the content. Since the interception is only with the signal, there cannot be any remedy under the contract. As a result of this obvious gap in the authors' right of broadcasting, the broadcasters initiated their demand to find a solution within the copyright regime.[19]

---

17 See WIPO 8th SCCR " Protection Of Broadcasting Organizations: Terms And Concepts", at p. 3, available at www.wipo.int/edocs/mdocs/copyright/en/sccr_8/sccr_8_inf_1.doc (last accessed on 25/09/2017) and also see for the detailed discussion on the broadcast and broadcasting under the copyright, M. Sakthivel, "Is it Broadcast or Broadcasting?", 16 (1) *JIPR* (2011), pp. 23–26.

18 One can infer from the model of protection and subject matter of protection demanded. See Louis G. Caldwell, "Piracy of Broadcast Programs", 30 (8) *Columbia Law Review*, (1930), pp. 1087–1114.

19 While demanding for the protection of broadcasting organizations, it was stated that the protection sought is only for the piracy of the program. Further it was made obvious that the authors' right would also have an edge and the protection sought would not conflict with the authors' right. Further, the broadcasters' position was made clear that they were committed to pay for content being exploited. Based on all these points, the author assumes that the protection sought for the broadcasting organization was only for the signal which has been left out by the authors' right of public performance. For the detailed discussion on the same, see Louis G. Caldwell, "The Copyright Problems of Broadcasters", 2 *J. Radio L.*, (1932), pp. 287–314 and also see for the piracy of the broadcast program and instances, Louis G. Caldwell, "Piracy of Broadcast Programs", 30 (8) *Columbia Law Review*, (1930), pp. 1087–1114. Based on the above cited two articles, the researchers infers that

Though, on the one hand the broadcasting organizations had been using the works of authors' without permission, on the other hand their broadcast was used without their permission by other competitors in the market. When the introduction of the authors' right of broadcasting had been considered as a major setback for the broadcasting organizations in terms of economic returns because they had built their entire business model without paying anything to the creators of the works, the unauthorized use of their broadcast by another broadcasting organizations had resulted in another economic setback. This forced the broadcasting organizations to demand protection for their broadcast (signals) from unauthorized use. As the US was the one which witnessed major problem due to over reach of the radio technology, in 1930's the following demand for protection of broadcasters in US was raised:[20]

1. Due to lack of availability of legal protection under any legislation of US, by considering the nature of the activities involved in the course of broadcasting, it was demanded that a set of civil rights and remedies may be provided under the Radio Act, 1927.[21] Further, it was also suggested to make suitable modifications in the International Radiotelegraph Convention, 1927[22] so as to accommodate the same.
2. So as to enforce the exclusive right of the authors of copyright, the broadcasters might be given rights under the Copyright Act, 1909. However, there was no reference placed in the modality in which the protection under copyright would be given. At the same time, it might be possible to understand that the nature of protection demanded is merely for the enforcement of the authors' right and not for a separate right at par with authors'.
3. Development of the protection under the common principles of law of unfair competition.

---

as the copyright protects the content and the protection sought in this case is for the program which is understood as signal.

20 See for the same arguments, Louis G. Caldwell, "International Protection of Broadcasters against Commercial uses of their Programs", 2 J. *Radio L.*, (1932), pp. 479–527, at p. 527.

21 United States Radio Act of 1927, Public Law 632, 69th Congress, February 23, 1927. As stated in the preamble, "it is intended to regulate all forms of interstate and foreign radio transmissions and communications within the United States, its Territories and possessions; to maintain the control of the United States over all the channels of interstate and foreign radio transmission; and to provide for the use of such channels, but not the ownership thereof, by individuals, firms, or corporations, for limited periods of time, under licenses granted by Federal authority, and no such license shall be construed to create any right, beyond the terms, conditions, and periods of the license."

22 International Radiotelegraph Convention and General and Supplementary Regulations, signed at Washington, 25th November, 1927.

However, there was no response from the US on the issue of unauthorized use of the signal of broadcasting organizations. In the meantime, with the help of International Labour Organisation (ILO) which actually intended to help the performers due to the evolution of technology, the broadcasting organizations' demand gained international attention.

4.4 Evolution of the Protection of Broadcasting Organizations

Discussion on the protection of broadcasting organizations along with the performers commenced internationally at the beginning of 20th century. Issues related to emerging technologies including radio was discussed at first in the International Literary and Artistic Association's Congress held in 1903.[23] Since the issues had somehow been connected with employment opportunities of the performers', ILO highlighted the economic issues associated with performers and sought international attention. It highlighted that due to the technological advancements such as radio and television broadcasting, the opportunities for the performers had been reduced substantially. In 1926, the international musicians' union highlighted the unemployment issue of performers resulting out of records and broadcast and it was referred to ILO seeking protection against the 'technological unemployment of performers'.[24] Since then, the international community started its discourse on the same at various occasions. Even, initiatives were taken to address the issue of broadcasting at the Berne Convention Revision Conference of Rome.[25] However, the issue i.e., rights of the broadcasting organizations were not taken for discussion rather the authors' rights of broadcasting was discussed.[26]

In continuation of the Berne Convention Revision Conference in Rome held in 1928, wherein the performers' rights issue was discussed along with the authors' right of broadcasting, a preliminary consultation on the "international agreement on the rights of performing artists, producers of phonograms and broadcasting organizations" was held at *Samaden* (Switzerland) in 1939 to

23 WIPO, *Guide to the Rome Convention and to the Phonograms Convention*, WIPO Publication No. 617 (E), (Geneva, WIPO, 1981), at p. 7.

24 Pierre Chesnais, "The Communication of Phonograms to the Public: Remuneration of Performers and Producers", *Working Paper of the Salaried Employees and Professional Workers' Branch, ILO*, (1991), at p. 3.

25 Berne Convention for the Protection of Literary and Artistic Works, 1886 revised at Rome on June 2, 1928.

26 WIPO, *Guide to the Rome Convention and to the Phonograms Convention*, WIPO Publication No. 617 (E), (Geneva, WIPO, 1981), at p. 8.

provide independent protections for each of them.[27] The International Bureau of the Berne Union and the International Institute of Rome for the unification of Private law jointly convened the Samedan meeting wherein four independent drafts were prepared.[28] The details of the same are as follows:

1. Draft on performers and the producers of phonograms
2. Draft on broadcasters
3. Draft on information by the press
4. Draft on *droit de suite*

These four drafts were prepared with an aim of presenting it to the Berne Union meeting supposed to be held at Brussels in 1939 which could not take place.[29] Combining the performers and the producers into one category had been done to offer higher degree of protection to the producers rather than performers.[30] In the meantime, Italy which was ruled by the fascist, introduced a new model of protection for these three stakeholders in its Copyright Act, 1941 where the producers of musical records, broadcasters and performers were protected under the neighbouring right category based on the *Sameden* model. The 1941 Act combined the performers and producers into one category and provided a hierarchy of protection i.e., producers of the records were provided more economic incentives when the music was played or used elsewhere. Thus, the producer was provided with economic incentive similar to that of the performers. Likewise, the broadcasters who broadcasted their music/performances were also given with higher degree of protection than the performers. Though the protection was given, it is completely based on the fascist's economic and political model.[31] As a result

27 Eugen Ulmer. "The Rome Convention for the Protection of Performers, Producers of Phonograms and Broadcasting Organizations", 10 *Bull. Copyright Soc'y* USA, (1962), pp. 90–101, at p.91 and also see Pierre Chesnais, "The Communication of Phonograms to the Public: Remuneration of Performers and Producers", *Working Paper of the Salaried Employees and Professional Workers' Branch*, ILO, (1991), at p. 3.

28 Arpad Bogsch, *The First Hundred Years of the Berne Convention for the Protection of Literary and Artistic Works*, WIPO (1986), at p. 323.

29 Arpad Bogsch, *The First Hundred Years of the Berne Convention for the Protection of Literary and Artistic Works*, WIPO, (1986), at p. 323. The Berne Convention, Brussels meeting held in 1948.

30 Arnold Kohler, "Performers' Rights with regard to Broadcasting and Mechanical Reproduction", 73 *International Labour Review*, (1956), pp. 643–665, at p. 659 and also see Rasmus Fleisher, "Protecting the Musicians and /or the Record Industry? On the History of 'Neighbouring Rights' and the Role of Fascist Italy", 5(3) *Queen Mary Journal of Intellectual Property*, pp. 327–343, at p. 336.

31 For the detailed discussion on the neighbouring rights protection in Fascist Italy, see Rasmus Fleisher, " Protecting the Musicians and /or the Record Industry? On the History

of the Second World War, there was no development at the international level until 1948.[32]

The Brussels Revision of Berne Convention which was supposed to be held in 1935 got postponed many times and finally it was held in 1948 wherein the discussions were resumed at the international level by *Voeux*.[33] Though the ILO initiated discussions on the protection of performers few decades ago, it also stood at an impasse for various reasons. Since the ILO considered the performers' issues as employment related issues, it had shown its desire to develop a model agreement at the international level.[34] In addition to that, even the Berne Union held in 1928 at the Berne Convention Revision Conference in Rome wherein the performers' rights issue was only discussed along with the authors' right of broadcasting. However, the remaining issues were left untouched. The reason for the same could be that the rational and the justification of protecting performers might fit into the rational of protecting creativity under copyright whereas the protection of producers of records and broadcasting organization is not based on creativity involved but on economic justifications.[35]

From the above discussion on the evolution of the neighbouring rights, it may be summarized that the broadcasters' had no valid reason or justification to be protected under the copyright regime so far, like producers of records. It is further very clear from the following explanation of the rationale for the protection given by *Prof. Eugen Ulmar*:[36]

---

of 'Neighbouring Rights' and the Role of Fascist Italy", 5(3) *Queen Mary Journal of Intellectual Property*, pp. 327–343, at p. 336.

32 Eugen Ulmer, "The Rome Convention for the Protection of Performers, Producers of Phonograms and Broadcasting Organizations" , 10 *Bulletin of the Copyright Society of the U.S.A.*, (1962), pp. 90–101, at p. 91.

33 See Arpad Bogsch, *The First Hundred Years of the Berne Convention for the Protection of Literary and Artistic Works*, WIPO (1986), at p. 323 and also see Eugen Ulmer, "The Rome Convention for the Protection of Performers, Producers of Phonograms and Broadcasting Organizations", 10 *Bulletin of the Copyright Society of the U.S.A.*, (1962), pp. 90–101, at p. 91.

34 See for the detailed discussion on the ILO and the Performers rights, Arnold Kohler, "Performers' Rights with regard to Broadcasting and Mechanical Reproduction", 21 *International Labour Review*, (1930), pp. 643–665.

35 See for the same justification of performers, producers of records and broadcasters, Eugen Ulmer, "The Rome Convention for the Protection of Performers, Producers of Phonograms and Broadcasting Organizations", 10 *Bulletin of the Copyright Society of the U.S.A.*, (1962), pp. 90–101, at p. 99.

36 He was the German delegate to the Rome Diplomatic Conference who headed the working group II. See Eugen Ulmer, "The Rome Convention for the Protection of Performers, Producers of Phonograms and Broadcasting Organizations" , 10 *Bulletin of the Copyright Society of the U.S.A.*, (1962), pp. 90–101, at p. 99.

> In the case of performers' rights there is a mixture -in a way similar to copyright-of elements of moral and property rights. But in the case of the rights of producers of phonograms and broadcasting organizations, it is solely a matter of protecting property interests; as far as its juridical nature is concerned, this protection is close to the protection granted by the law of unfair competition. These differences in their legal nature do not, however, rule out regulation in the same convention, since there is a close relationship among the protected objects, phonograms and broadcasts being the media whereby the artists' performances are recorded or broadcast, and since there is a need for harmonizing the rights of the three groups concerned. It is a well-known fact that the Paris Convention, too, deals not only with patent and design law, but also with the law of unfair competition. Between the rights of performers and those of producers of phonograms and broadcasting organizations, there is no greater difference than that between, say, the protection of authors of designs and the protection of business enterprises against unfair competition.

Further he equated the protection being offered for the producers of the records and the broadcasters to protection against unfair competition provided under the Paris Convention. Thus, it is obvious that there is no copyright rationale for broadcasters' protection. Only their property interest is protected like protection against unfair competition.[37] It is further clear that protection to broadcasting organizations was initiated because of the problems confronted by the performers due to technological developments i.e., production of musical records and broadcasting of live and recorded performances of music. It may also be noted that except from the US, no jurisdictions had pointed out the unauthorized use of signal or the problems related to broadcasting until Rome Convention. In all the discussions, the broadcasting organizations had been considered as a stake holder in the performers' rights issues.

During the initial stages, due to lack of wide penetration of technology, issue of unauthorized uses of broadcast was not visualized in most of the

37 The authors' right over the radio diffusion was given at the Rome Act, 1928 but the authors' right over the television broadcast was recognized only during Stockholm Act, 1967. It was proposed by the sub-committee at the Brussels Revision about the inclusion of television to the authors' rights. See for detailed discussion on the same, Text proposed by the sub-committee on Broadcasting and Mechanical Instruments on Art. 11 *bis*, 15th June, 1948, available at http://keionline.org/sites/default/files/Records_of_the_Conference_1948_Brussels_Revisions.pdf (last accessed on 28/06/2019).

jurisdictions and hence there was no reason and urgency in examining the issue of protection to broadcasting organization. At a later stage, with the increased penetration of technology, issues cropped up. Many live broadcasting of the works were simultaneously broadcasted without any permission from the broadcasting organizations and thus resulting in substantial economic losses not only to the broadcasters but also to the authors.[38] Due to this socio-economic factor, with lots of reservations on broadcasting organizations' protections under the copyright regimes, the international community showed their inclination towards the issues of protecting the signals of broadcasting organizations. One among the major concerns was that whether the protection to broadcasting organizations would undermine the authors' right of broadcasting.

4.5 Rome Convention: Internationalization of Neighbouring Rights – an Overview

During the beginning of internationalization of the neighbouring rights, as discussed above, ILO was proactive from the very beginning of the 20th century itself and then the Berne Union also joined in the process. Though both the entities were working together on this issue, the ILO took a lead on this aspect and thus it came out with a draft in 1951 for the protection of broadcasters along with the other two entities. However, the draft did not form part of the ILO subcommittee report on performers and further it was only for the information and internal discussion. Hence, it did not create any substantial impact on the progress of the protection though it set the foundation for the internationalization of the neighbouring rights protection. With the joining of the UNESCO in the process of protecting broadcasting organizations along with the performers and producers of records after the establishment of Universal Copyright Convention in 1952, the preliminary draft of 1951 was further discussed and debated at various levels. As there were some differences of opinion about the composition of the committee, all these three intergovernmental organizations decided to depart from working jointly on this issue. Thus, UNESCO and the Berne Union on the one side and the ILO on the

38 This is the inference of the author based on the reason that the authors' bargaining power would go down, if the problem of signal piracy is so rampant and used unauthorized manner. Thus, it has been stated that it affects the economic returns of the authors in addition to the broadcasters.

other side were working on the same issue differently.[39] Therefore, ILO constituted committee to work on the draft model treaty for the neighbouring rights which met at Geneva came with a draft[40] which is known as the Geneva draft, 1956.[41] At the same time, and the Berne Union were also involved in preparing a draft simultaneously which is widely known as the Monaco draft, 1957.[42]

So as to remove the differences between the Geneva draft, 1956 and Monaco draft, 1957, there was an immediate need to have an integrated approach among all three intergovernmental organizations. Finally the three intergovernmental organizations joined together and came up with the new draft to have unanimous approach on the protection of these three entities. As all the stake holders joined together along with the three intergovernmental organizations, the comprehensive model draft was formulated and the same was the basic document on which the Rome Convention was developed. There were three documents before the expert committee of the three intergovernmental organization based on which the Hague Draft, 1960[43] was prepared. They were:

1. The Geneva Draft, 1956
2. The Monaco Draft, 1957
3. The observation of the certain Governments on both the drafts.

During The Hague discussion for finalizing the draft text for the diplomatic conference, both the drafts were discussed extensively and then the texts were

---

39 Eugen Ulmer, "The Rome Convention for the Protection of Performers, Producers of Phonograms and Broadcasting Organizations" , 10 *Bulletin of the Copyright Society of the U.S.A.*, (1962), pp. 90–101, at p. 92.

40 See Preliminary Draft International Convention regarding the Protection of Performers Manufacturers of Phonographic Records and Broadcasting Organisations was prepared by the Mixed Committee of Experts of the Berne Union. The same was adopted on 17 November, 1951). See for further details, "Summary Record of the 2nd session of the Advisory Committee on Salaried Employees and Professional Workers", *ILO, Geneva*, 1952, pp. 48–55. Hereinafter, it is referred as Geneva draft, 1956.

41 ILO, "Advisory Committee on Salaried Employees and Professional Workers, 4th meeting, 1956", *ILO, Geneva*, at p. 126–135 and also see '*Annex: Draft Convention of the Committee of Experts of ILO*' X *UNESCO Copyright Bulletin*, (1957), at p. 32.

42 Draft Agreement on the Protection of certain Rights called Neighbouring on Copyrights was adopted by the Committee of Experts which met at Monaco from 4 to 13 March, 1957. Hereinafter, it is referred as Monaco Draft, 1957.

43 The Draft International Convention Concerning the Protection of Performers, Makers of Phonograms and broadcasters, 1960 (The Hague Draft) was adopted by the Committee of Experts, which met at The Hague from 9–21 May, 1960. The same can be accessed from: "Conventions, Treaties and Proclamations." 8(1) *Bulletin of the Copyright Society of the U.S.A.*, (1960–1961), pp. 31–46. Hereinafter, it is referred as The Hague Draft, 1961.

adopted based on the majorities' viewpoints. While having deliberations on the scope of the draft convention, it was pointed out by the experts from Poland and Yugoslavia that it would be wrong to treat the rights of the performers in the same instrument as that of record producers and the broadcasting organizations. It was also further corroborated by citing that the performers would be related/neighbouring to copyright, however, the record producers and the broadcasters would not be. It was observed:

> ...it was a mistake to treat the rights of performers in the same instrument as that of record producers and broadcasting organisations. In the latter's view, the first was akin to copyright and the others were sui generis property rights.[44]

With regard to the nature of rights provided under The Hague Draft as the progress was leading towards a diplomatic conference, the International Confederation of Authors and Composers Societies (CISAC) and the International Literary and Artistic Association (ALAI) felt that the communication to the public of television broadcast right could be given to the broadcasters only when sports events would be broadcasted and the same was agreed. Many of the experts felt that this would be an unnecessary one. However, it was further decided to limit its application.[45] From this discussion, it would be very much evident that CISAC and ALAI had agreed to give communication right only when sports would be broadcasted and not in the case of works for which the right is with the author. As both the entities have been working to protect the interest of the authors and creators since the beginning of the 20th century, they strongly opposed a separate treaty of neighbouring rights and also protection for broadcasting organization under the copyright. However, their stand in case of sports could very well be appreciated since there is no creativity in sport content to consider this as a work for protection under copyright. Thus they did not bother much about giving communication right of broadcast of sports to the broadcasting organizations.[46] At the same time, CISAC and ALAI had been constantly striving to stall this neighbouring rights protection getting developed at the international level. The authors' associations even went to

44 "Conventions, Treaties and Proclamations." 8(1) *Bulletin of the Copyright Society of the U.S.A.*, (1960–1961), pp. 31–46, at p. 35.

45 "Conventions, Treaties and Proclamations." 8(1) *Bulletin of the Copyright Society of the U.S.A.* (1960–1961), pp. 31–46, at p. 42.

46 *Ibid.*

the extent of lobbying with the countries and secured their support to prevent the finalization of this international agreement.[47]

Further, during the Brussels Act 1948, it was discussed in detail about the change of terminology from diffusion to broadcasting or transmission. This was because of the fact that the authors raised concerns about the extension of right to the new technology i.e., signal authorization would lead to exploitation in multiple technologies. To address this concern, it was decided that the nature of exploitation could be determined by the contractual arrangements between the authors and broadcasting organizations. However, it was emphasized that the change of word to broadcasting/transmission would address the issues and thus single authorization would be sufficient for multiple exploitations.[48] This created another problem because, a new set of rights were introduced to the broadcasters. The single authorization for multiple exploitations would even cover the rebroadcast of the content. Ultimately, it was rightly sensed by the authors that the new rights would be economically detrimental to them and it would ultimately affect the contractual practices that were existing prior to the introduction of broadcasters' rights.[49]

CISAC in its Tel Aviv Conference, 1961 pointed out that as the performers, producers of records and broadcasters had been already addressed either by general legal principles or by contract, and their protection should be called off. The following observation is pertinent:

> ...that an international agreement on neighboring rights was unnecessary, since the protection of the legitimate interests of performers, producers of phonograms, and broadcasting organizations was already safeguarded by general legal principles and, in particular, by the possibility of concluding contractual arrangements.[50]

Similarly ALAI also demanded in its Florence Conference, 1961 that the same development should be put on hold and passed the following resolution:

47 Eugen Ulmer, "The Rome Convention for the Protection of Performers, Producers of Phonograms and Broadcasting Organizations" , 10 *Bulletin of the Copyright Society of the U.S.A.*, (1962), pp. 90–101, at p. 92.

48 Arthur Fisher, "The 1948 Revision of the Berne Convention", 10 *Fed. Comm. B.J.*, (1949), pp. 53–58, at p. 55.

49 Eugen Ulmer, "The Rome Convention for the Protection of Performers, Producers of Phonograms and Broadcasting Organizations" , 10 *Bulletin of the Copyright Society of the U.S.A.*, (1962), pp. 90–101, at p. 95.

50 *Ibid.*

> ...the international agreement envisaged appeared to be uncalled for and useless; at any rate, in view of the existing differences between the views put forward, such an agreement was deemed to be premature at that time...[51]

Even at the Rome Diplomatic Conference, the views expressed by the French delegate were substantially same as that of the views of these authors' associations. Though they had taken a very proactive stand and put their best possible efforts, they could not succeed in the process as the Rome Convention materialized.[52] As stated above, at this stage, TV broadcasting was emerging as a much popular mode in many jurisdictions and became commercially successful.

The Draft International Convention Concerning the Protection of Performers, Makers of Phonograms and Broadcasters, 1960 which was adopted by the Committee of Experts in its meeting held at The Hague from 9–21 May, 1960, had originally contained 17 Articles. During The Hague meeting, it was further decided that the three intergovernmental organizations would draft the final provisions for the diplomatic conference and the same would be reported to the diplomatic conference directly. Thus, after The Hague meeting, the final texts for the diplomatic conference were finalized with 12 Articles along with the originally adopted 17 Articles. As a result, a draft with 29 Articles was finalized and the same was circulated among the countries for their comments prior to the diplomatic conference. The same was compiled and analyzed.[53] Finally the diplomatic conference of Rome Convention was jointly organized by

51 *Ibid.*

52 *Ibid.* The relevant part is extracted here for further understanding about the authors' associations stand on the neighbouring rights and their efforts: "At the Rome Conference it was the French Delegation, more than any other, which made the views of CISAC and ALAI its own. True, State Counsellor Puget expressed readiness, on behalf of France, to take part in the work of the conference, but emphasized that this participation was subject to the most far-reaching reservations and that, as a matter of principle, his Delegation took the view that the conclusion of a convention concerning neighboring rights was uncalled for, useless, and even dangerous, and that the safeguarding of the interest of performers, producers of phonograms, and broadcasting organizations could also be achieved without any special convention, by means of contractual arrangements. These arguments were supplemented by the ALAI observer, Professor Troller, who pointed out organizational considerations allegedly militating against regulation, in the same treaty instrument, of the rights, so different in nature, of performers, producers of phonograms, and broadcasting organizations".

53 "Conventions, Treaties and Proclamations", 8(5) *Bulletin of the Copyright Society of the U.S.A.*, (1960–1961), pp. 306–312.

the three intergovernmental organizations at Rome.[54] There were three working groups formed to study the draft provisions along with the comments of the countries to finalize the texts of the convention to be adopted. With regard to the provisions related to the broadcasting organizations were concerned, though there were definitions for the performer, phonogram, performance, etc., under The Hague draft, there was no definition for broadcast. However, the definition of broadcasting and re-broadcasting was coined and the minimum rights that would be provided to the broadcasting organizations were also finalized. Finally the Rome Convention was adopted with 34 Articles.

Since the focus is on authors' right of communication to public and its enjoyment by broadcasting organization, the discussion on protection of broadcasting organizations could be limited to

- Relationship with copyright;
- Definition;
- Rights and
- Duration.

Therefore, the issue of national treatment[55] and the limitations and exceptions[56] are left out.

54 The diplomatic conference of the Rome convention was held at Rome from 10th to 26th October, 1961.

55 As per the 1951 draft, in case of broadcasting, the country of origin would be the country in which the head office of the broadcasting organization is placed. It was same even under the Geneva draft. At first, the Monaco draft introduced the concept of national treatment to this neighbouring rights protection. It has adopted the same model of Berne Convention as this draft was prepared by the Berne Union and the UNESCO. Due to this national treatment principle makes it clear that each contracting party should treat the broadcasting organizations of another contracting state at par with its own broadcasting organizations and extend the same protection. Though terminology adopted in The Hague draft is country of origin, in essence, the same principle is followed. However, in the final text, Rome has adopted the national treatment as similar to that of Monaco which is same that Berne Convention. From the above discussed provisions, it is evident that the 1951 draft and the Geneva drafts are silent on the issue of national treatment. However, the subsequent documents follow the national treatment and thus extend protection to the foreign broadcasting organizations similar to that of their own broadcasting organizations.

56 Limitations and exceptions could find a place in the drafts from the very first itself. Under the 1951 draft and the Geneva draft, broadcasting organizations would be having following rights/limitations. However, the same would be determined by the member countries at their discretion. They are: (a) With regard to prevention of using loud speakers or other instruments to communicate the sounds to the public (b) Reporting of current events out of the emission by re-emission in short extract (c) If the fixation is done for private use or without any commercial motive. Similarly, the Monaco draft had advocated

4.5.1 *Relationship with Copyright*

Almost all the drafts had a clear stand on the point that the proposed neighbouring protection would no way affect the copyright of the authors over the content. Though the language of the documents were different, the essence was same. In 1951, it was made clear to the member countries that the protection offered to these three, should not prejudice the authors' rights.[57] The Geneva draft also assured that the protection that would be given to these three entities would not affect the authors' rights over literary and artistic works.[58] Unlike, the previous draft, the Monaco draft was accompanied with an explanatory statement where in the basic considerations for the protection of broadcasters' along with other stakeholders were pointed out as follows:[59]

---

for the exceptions which are as follows: Private use of the fixation; Reporting of the current events and exhibition of TV broadcasting for the same purpose for a limited period; Fixation for his own broadcast purposes. However, unlike previous drafts, the Hague draft had introduced a common limitations/exceptions to all these three stakeholders' rights. They were: private use, reporting of current events for a short period, fixation of the broadcast for own broadcast by the broadcaster and for teaching. The Hague draft model was adopted and retained by the Rome. It provides two types of exceptions to the rights given to the all three entities including broadcasting organizations. They are: Specific limitations and Equivalents with Copyright. In the specific limitation category, there are four exceptions provided: (*a*) *private use;* (*b*) *use of short excerpts in connection with the reporting of current events;*(*c*) *Ephemeral fixation by a broadcasting organisation by means of its own facilities and for its own broadcasts;*(*d*) *use solely for the purposes of teaching or scientific research.* With respect to the specific exceptions, except the teaching or scientific research exception, the reaming three were present in the previous drafts. As far as the teaching or scientific research is concerned, it was proposed by India during the diplomatic conference and the same was accepted. With respect to the equivalent with copyright exceptions, it has been introduced only during the diplomatic conference, wherein the members have been given with some exceptions like non-voluntary licenses, etc. From the all 5 documents, it is clear that the reporting of current events, private and research purposes are provided as exceptions to the rights granted to the broadcasters. Likewise, the broadcasters' fixation of their broadcast for their broadcast purpose has also been kept under the exceptions. This clearly indicates that the broadcasters are not provided with the right of fixation of their broadcast and thus they are not provided with any positive right on the post fixation of the broadcast.

57 See Preliminary Draft International Convention regarding the Protection of Performers Manufacturers of Phonographic Records and Broadcasting Organizations', 1951, Art. 1.

58 Proposed International Convention Concerning the Protection of Performers, Manufacturers of Phonographic Records and Broadcasting Organizations, 1956, Art. 1.

59 See for the same explanatory statement associated with the text, "Draft Agreement on the Protection of certain Rights called Neighbouring on Copyrights", *UNESCO*, (1957), at p. 7.

> The legitimate interest of performers, recorders and broadcasters in their creation should be protected by an international agreement. Such agreement will:
> i. Encourage creative activity and the dissemination of artistic works in the public interest;
> ii. Promote the orderly and organic development of the law of copyright and rights neighbouring thereon;
> iii. Foster mutually beneficial co-operation between authors of literary and artistic works and the interpreters and distributors of such works.

From the above statement, it may well be understood, from the broadcasting context, that wider dissemination of artistic work for the larger public through broadcasting and to foster mutually beneficial cooperation between the authors and distributors of such works could be linked with the broadcasters. Even this draft recognized protection based on the fundamental principle that neighbouring rights applied only to works protected under copyright. Therefore, according to *Sam Ricketson* the neighbouring rights are subjected to copyright and thus the broadcasting organizations' protection is considered as social-oriented rational of copyright protection which means the economic aspects/investments and characters of facilitation in attaining social desirables.[60] In addition to this, the Monaco draft emphasized that the Agreement would be effective only among those countries which are either party to the Universal Copyright Convention or the Berne convention.[61] Further, it had clarified that no provisions of the Monaco draft should be interpreted as prejudicing the copyright.[62] Likewise, The Hague draft also emphasized that the protection granted under the draft would not affect the authors' rights and draft provisions should not be interpreted in a prejudicial manner.[63] The final provision of the Rome Convention, like the previous drafts, also emphasized

60 S Ricketson and C Creswell, *The Law of Intellectual Property: Copyright, Designs & Confidential Information*, Sydney Law book Co., (2nd edn., 2001), at p. 130 and also see Megumi Ogawa, *Protection of Broadcasters' Rights*, Martinus Nijhoff Publishers, Boston, (2006), at p. 5.

61 See for the same, "Draft Agreement on the Protection of certain Rights called Neighbouring on Copyrights", *UNESCO*, (1957), Art. 1.

62 See for the same, "Draft Agreement on the Protection of certain Rights called Neighbouring on Copyrights", *UNESCO*, (1957), Art. 1.

63 The Draft International Convention Concerning the Protection of Performers, Makers of Phonograms and Broadcasters, 1960, Art. 2.

that the rights and the protection conferred under this convention shall not in any way affect the rights of the authors.[64]

From the above provisions of the legal documents, it is clear that the neighbouring rights protection would not affect the authors' rights because the neighbouring rights protection is based on copyright and it is subjected to authors' right. Thus, the broadcasters are provided with special protection due to their neighbouring character in getting authors works disseminated. Therefore, it is very evident that the protection given to the broadcasting organizations under the Rome Convention is always subjected to the authors' right.

4.5.2 *Interpretation Clause/Definition Clause*

Prior to the final provisions of the Rome Convention, there was no definition clause/interpretation clause given in any of the previous drafts. Though those drafts had used emission, re-emission, broadcast and rebroadcasting, there were no definitions. When we look into the 1951 draft and the Geneva draft, both used the terms emission and re-emission but without any definition.[65] When we examine provisions with the available technology, it would be possible to conclude that both radio diffusion and TV broadcast are covered under the term emission. Nevertheless, from the very close reading of the 1951 draft, the language was more towards radio diffusion. The same approach has been adopted in the Geneva draft also. It seems, though TV broadcasting penetrated the market, there was no question of television broadcasting to be included due to lack of large scale commercial deployment. Had the committee intended to cover TV broadcasting, they could have used the word broadcast rather than using emission through which the same would have been covered. Therefore, it may be concluded at the preliminary level that technology which was widely available even in 1956 was only radio broadcasting and television broadcasting was still at a nascent stage.

---

64 See International Convention for the Protection of Performers, Producers of Phonograms and Broadcasting Organizations, Rome, 1961, Art. 1. *Safeguard of Copyright Proper*: Protection granted under this Convention shall leave intact and shall in no way affect the protection of copyright in literary and artistic works. Consequently, no provision of this Convention may be interpreted as prejudicing such protection. Though it was demanded by countries like USA and India to include more works under this Art. including musical, dramatic, etc., the same was not considered.

65 See Preliminary Draft International Convention regarding the Protection of Performers Manufacturers of Phonographic Records and Broadcasting Organizations', 1951, Art. 8 and also see Proposed International Convention Concerning the Protection of Performers, Manufacturers of Phonographic Records and Broadcasting Organizations, 1956, Art. 7.

However, in the Monaco draft, TV broadcasting has been clearly and expressly covered. When we compare this with the Geneva draft, it is very clear that though the technology was at an infant stage, they wanted the TV technology to be covered. In addition, the language used in the Monaco draft would be more meaningful in the advanced technological context. Usage of broadcast/broadcasting would address the radio and TV rather than using 'emission' or 'diffusion' which was used in the Geneva draft. Perhaps, it would have been aimed to make it technology neutral as discussed in the Brussels Act, 1948.[66] As the TV technology has been covered already and the terminologies have been changed in the Monaco draft, the changes have been accepted in The Hague draft as well.

The final text of the Rome Convention in Article 3 (f) & (g) defines broadcasting and rebroadcasting which read as follows:

> (f) "broadcasting" means the transmission by wireless means for public reception of sounds or of images and sounds;
> (g) "rebroadcasting" means the simultaneous broadcasting by one broadcasting organisation of the broadcast of another broadcasting organisation.

As per the definition of broadcasting, it is defined to cover both radio and TV broadcast as the language of the definition uses *sounds or of images and sounds.* Though there was no definition for broadcasting given under The Hague draft which was circulated for the diplomatic conference, during the Diplomatic Conference, both the USA[67] and UK[68] advocated for defining 'broadcast' as follows: "*Broadcast means the transmission by wireless means for public reception of sounds or of images and sounds.*" However, the word broadcasting has been defined under the Rome Convention. The term 'rebroadcasting' has been defined as *simultaneous broadcasting by one broadcasting organisation of the*

---

66 This is inference of the author by reading the discussions of the Brussels Act, 1948.

67 *See* "Records of the Diplomatic Conference on the International Protection of Performers, Producers of Phonograms and Broadcasting Organizations", *International Labour Organisation, United Nations Educational, Scientific and Cultural Organization, and the United International Bureaux for the Protection of Intellectual Property*, (1968), at p. 209.

68 *See* "Records of the Diplomatic Conference on the International Protection of Performers, Producers of Phonograms and Broadcasting Organizations", *International Labour Organisation, United Nations Educational, Scientific and Cultural Organization, and the United International Bureaux for the Protection of Intellectual Property*, (1968), at p. 208. UK demanded and it read: "The word 'broadcast' should be defined in this Art. to make it clear that the Convention only grants rights to broadcasting organizations in respect of their transmission by means of Hertzian waves and that no rights are granted in respect of transmissions by means of wires and other paths provided by a material substance."

broadcast of another broadcasting organisation. Though the definition uses the word broadcast, the Convention has not defined the same. In this context, the scope of the definition of 'broadcasting' has to be examined at first. While tracing the authors' right in the Berne Convention, it has been found that the authors' were given with the right of broadcasting i.e., radio diffusion. The authors' right of broadcasting as discussed, it has given the right of communicating the work through wireless diffusion which invariably means the right of transmitting the works by using the diffusion techniques. Even though the word rebroadcasting was not used, the language used in Article 11 *bis* covered rebroadcasting whether it is simultaneous or deferred.[69] However, under the Rome Convention, the broadcasting organizations were given broadcasting right i.e., "transmission by wireless means for public reception of sounds or of images and sounds;" and rebroadcasting right.

Broadcasters' protection was given because of the fact that the authors' works were exploited and the same right was derived out of the authors' right of broadcasting. It means without authorization from the authors', the broadcasting organizations could not exploit the authors' works over their station. The author was conferred with the right of broadcasting i.e., diffusion (transmission) of the work to the public. Based on the detailed discussion on the scope of the authors' right of broadcasting, as observed, the authors' right of broadcasting could not address the signal piracy during the course of diffusion. Hence, it is possible for one to infer that even though the right given to broadcasting organization is for transmission, it is confined to the signal generated to transmit the content if the content is protected by copyright. This interpretation also clarifies that the right of broadcasting organization in no way affect the rights of the author of the content. It will further clarify that there is no co-existence of the right of the author and the broadcasting organization because the term used is broadcasting. They are distinct and different and the right of the broadcasting organization is subjected to the right of the author. The other reason for using the term broadcasting in Rome Convention could be to confer the right of transmission to content that were not protected by the copyright. Since, the subject matter covered are "sounds or of images and sounds", it could very well accommodate content like sports, news etc., that are generally not protected under copyright law. But the rights conferred to broadcasting organizations, as discussed below, make it very clear that they have not only transmission right over the signal carrying content but also on the

69 Art. 11 *bis* (1) (ii) read: "any communication to the public, whether over wires or not, of the radio diffusion of the work, when this communication is made by a body other than the original one."

content once it is fixed. Though the deliberations of Rome Convention is silent on the signal protection approach, the same could be inferred. It is also well established through this book that the need is to fill the gap in the broadcasting right of authors to take care of the economic interest of the broadcasting organization. This is further substantiated based on the signal based approach adopted in the ongoing discussion at the WIPO for protection of broadcasting organizations.

The definition also stated that the transmission is for public reception. This raises a serious concern regarding the nature of public i.e., individual reception or group reception (with entry restrictions) or open to all. This has been discussed during the diplomatic conference and decided that the 'transmission for the public reception' would mean any one from the public could access the same without any restriction which means the broadcast is open to all at free of cost.[70] Further it has been made clear that if the reception is intended by one person or pre-identified group, then the same would not constitute broadcasting. The following observation is pertinent;

> The words 'transmission for public reception' used in the definition should make it clear that broadcasts intended for reception by one person or by a well-defined group-such as ships at sea, planes in the air, taxis circulating in a city, etc. – are not to be considered as broadcasts.[71]

From the above, it can well be understood that if the communication is done for the larger public, only then it would be considered as broadcasting. If the same is done with a well-defined audience, then it would remain as a communication to the public of the works and it would not constitute broadcasting. The clarity may be further brought from the nature of technology covered under the definition i.e., wireless means. In case of wireless broadcasting, the signal would be emitted to all. Then the public can receive the broadcast (content carrying signal), if they have the receiving devices for the enjoyment of content. The content would remain the same and it would be transmitted by wireless means to all. Therefore, the Rome convention definition of broadcasting is aimed to cover group reception and the same should be done only by wireless means. Since the definition gives emphasis to wireless means, the question of

---

70 *See* "Records of the Diplomatic Conference on the International Protection of Performers, Producers of Phonograms and Broadcasting Organizations", *International Labour Organisation, United Nations Educational, Scientific and Cultural Organization, and the United International Bureaux for the Protection of Intellectual Property*, (1968), at p. 40.

71 *Ibid.*

inclusion of wire broadcast does not arise. Even from the records of the diplomatic conference of Rome Convention, it is very much clear that though there were some claims from Australia[72] and Austria[73] to include wire transmissions i.e., cable broadcasting under the definition so as to extend the protection to the same under the Rome Convention, it could not be materialized. This is further clear from the submissions of UK and USA. According to UK, transmission which takes place by Herzian waves should only be covered for protection and the transmissions by wire and other paths provided by a material substance should not be covered.[74] Similarly, USA also envisaged covering wireless transmission only.[75] Therefore, it is very clear even from the negotiating history of the Rome Convention that the drafters had never intended to cover any transmission other than the wireless mode under the definition of broadcasting.

4.5.3 *Nature of the Rights*

According to the 1951 draft, the broadcasting organizations had been provided to authorize the following rights under Article 8 of the draft;[76]

- Re-emission of emission by wire or wireless in whole or part;
- Recording or any other fixation of the emission in whole or part;

---

72 *Ibid.*

73 *Id.*, at p. 209.

74 *See* "Analysis of the Replies: Diplomatic Conference on the International Protection of Performers, Producers of Phonograms and Broadcasting Organizations", *International Labour Organisation, United Nations Educational, Scientific and Cultural Organization, and the United International Bureaux for the Protection of Intellectual Property,* (1961), at p. 11.

75 *See* "Records of the Diplomatic Conference on the International Protection of Performers, Producers of Phonograms and Broadcasting Organizations", *International Labour Organisation, United Nations Educational, Scientific and Cultural Organization, and the United International Bureaux for the Protection of Intellectual Property,* (1968), at p. 209.

76 Preliminary Draft International Convention regarding the Protection of Performers Manufacturers of Phonographic Records and Broadcasting Organisations', 1951, Art. 8:

1. The broadcasting organisations shall enjoy the right to authorise –
   (a) the re-emission, whether over wires or not, of all or a Part of their emission;
   (b) the recording or any other fixation of all or part of their emission or of the re-emission by whatever means;
   (c) the communication to the Public of all or a part of their emission by means of any instrument transmitting images.
2. It is reserved to the legislation of the contracting countries to protect the broadcasting organisations as against third parties who may communicate to the public all or part of their emission by means of loudspeakers or any other instrument transmitting sounds.
3. Recordings of emissions or re-emissions protected by this convention manufactured in a non-contracting country and imported into a contracting country without permission from the broad-casting organisation from which they originate, shall be liable to seizure.

- Communication to the public either in whole or in part by using any instrument transmitting images.

Similarly, the Geneva Draft also provides the same rights to the broadcasting organizations to prevent unauthorized use of signals. The following rights to authors were provided under Article 7 of the proposed international convention:[77]

- Re-emission
- Recording or fixation for commercial purposes or for the communication to the public

---

4. It shall be a matter for the legislation of the contracting countries to determine under which conditions the re-emission, the recording and the communication to the public of short extracts from emissions may be made for the purpose of reporting current events. It shall also be a matter for the same legislation to determine the regulations for ephemeral recordings fixing emissions or re-emissions and made by a broadcasting organisation by means of its own facilities and for its own emissions. The preservation, of these recordings in official archives may, on the ground of their exceptional documentary character, be authorised by the said legislation.
5. It shall be reserved for the legislation of contracting countries to waive the application of paragraph 1 (b) in the case of recordings and other fixations made for private use or without a view to profit.

77 Proposed International Convention Concerning the Protection of Performers, Manufacturers of Phonographic Records and Broadcasting Organisations (1956), Art. 7:
1. The broadcasting organisations shall enjoy the right to authorise:
   (a) the re-emission;
   (b) the recording or any other-fixation for commercial purposes or for communication to the public;
   (c) the communication to the public by means of any instrument transmitting or projecting images;

   of all or part of their emissions or of the re-emissions, whether direct or recorded.
2. It is reserved to the legislation of the contracting countries to protect the broadcasting organisations as against third parties who, may communicate to the public all or part of their emissions by means of loudspeakers or any other instrument transmitting sounds.
3. Recordings of emissions or re-emissions protected by this Convention manufactured in a non-contracting country and imported into a contracting country without permission from the broadcasting organisation from which they originate, shall be liable to seizure.
4. It shall be a matter for the legislation of the contracting countries to determine under which conditions the re-emission, the recording and the communication to the public of short extracts from emissions may be made for the purpose of reporting current events. It shall also be a matter for the same legislation to determine the regulations for the making of ephemeral recordings fixing emissions or re-emissions and made by a broadcasting organisation by means of its own facilities and for its own emissions. The preservation of these recordings in official archives may, on the ground of their exceptional documentary character, be authorised by the said legislation.
5. It is reserved to the legislation of the contracting countries to limit the application of paragraph 1(o) of this Art..

– Communication to the public by using any instrument transmitting or projecting images

When we analysed the technology in the previous part of this book, it is understood that once the signal is communicated and received there is no life/scope for the signal to remain. The gap in the protection is when the content is in the form of signal – pre transmission and during transmission. Once the content reaches the receiver the life of signal is over and the content is expressed in a form to claim copyright protection. Therefore, the protection is needed if the signal is accessed without permission before it is received and re-transmitted to different audience. Hence, the term re-emission is understood as simultaneous broadcasting.

The fixation right and the post fixation right given are self-contradictory to Article 2 and Article 1 of the drafts respectively because the drafts specify the relationship with copyright, wherein, it is pointed out that the neighbouring rights protection would not affect the copyright. However, the fixation and post fixation rights are all about access and use of the broadcasted content further. Generally for every new use, the permission should be obtained from the content owner unless there is a contractual arrangement. If so, then the content owner's right is affected due to the special right given to broadcasting organizations. Therefore, for every post fixation exploitation of the broadcast content, broadcasters should get authorization from the authors. The same is evident from the concept of relationship of this treaty with authors' copyright.

The very purpose of introducing special protection to the broadcasters is to address the signal piracy. If so, providing right beyond the signal i.e., over content like extension of loud speakers and other similar instruments to communicate the works to the public to the broadcasting organization are possible only when the authors' right of communicating the work to public is undermined. Thus, with the co-existence, the authors' right of communication to the public other than broadcasting and the authors' right of broadcasting had been aimed to be diluted.

Under the Monaco draft, Article 5, the following rights were given either to authorize or to prohibit in nature:[78]

– The re-broadcasting of his broadcasts;
– The off-the–air fixation of his broadcasts;
– The public exhibition of his TV broadcast.

---

78 Draft Agreement on the Protection of certain Rights called Neighbouring on Copyrights (1957), Art. 5:

1. Each Contracting State shall accord the same protection to the rights of broadcasters in their broadcasts originating in the territory of another Contracting State, as the former State accords to broadcasts originating on its own territory.

If the broadcast is based on phonograms, this Article would not be applicable. It clearly indicates that the broadcasting organizations did not have any right over the content of the phonograms. Even they did not enjoy any rights over the broadcast on phonograms. It has been further pointed out based on this provision that, it has been intended to protect the content created by the broadcasting organizations only.[79] If so, it is clear that the right of broadcasting organizations would be given to them when their content was broadcasted. If the content was based on phonograms, those rights would be with the phonogram producers. Then, the rationale for the protection of broadcasting organization may be possibly questioned for their content in broadcast. If they create a program and if it is copyrightable, the same could be protected by the copyright. If the same is only performance, the protection would be given to the performers. If the same has been recorded, the protection would be given to them based on the producer of the records. The only possible inference is that the protection is afforded if the programme is not protected either by copyright or performers right. However, the substantial change had been introduced in the 1957 draft on the nature of the rights proposed for the broadcasting organizations. The 1957 draft had proposed either to provide a right to authorize or a right to prohibit when the previous drafts advocated for the right to authorize. This substantial change had secured a permanent place in the subsequent drafts and the final Rome Convention as well. The possible reason for keeping both aspects could be to balance the two conflicting approaches in protecting broadcasting organizations under the copyright.

---

2. Subject to the provisions of paragraph 3 of this article, the protection provided for by the preceding paragraph shall include the recognition of the broadcaster's right to authorize or prohibit:
   (a) the re-broadcasting of his broadcasts;
   (b) the off-the-air fixation of his broadcasts;
   (c) the public exhibition of his television broadcasts.
3. Any Contracting State may, by its domestic law:
   (a) exclude from the application of this article broadcasts of phonograms;
   (b) limit the application of paragraph 2(c) of this article to exhibitions to paying audiences.
4. A Contracting State may provide exceptions to the protection of broadcasters with respect to;
   (a) off-the-air fixation for private use;
   (b) re-broadcasting, off-the-air fixation or public television exhibition within reasonable limits in connexion with the reporting of current events;
   (c) the making of ephemeral off-the-air fixations by a broadcaster for his own broadcasts.

79 See for the same "Draft Agreement on the Protection of certain Rights called Neighbouring on Copyrights", *UNESCO*, 1957, at p. 12.

Similarly, Article 12 of The Hague draft, provides the following rights either to authorize or to prohibit:[80]

- Rebroadcasting of the broadcasts
- Fixation of their broadcasts
- Unlawful reproduction of fixation
- Communication to the public of broadcast against payment.

From the rights provided to the broadcasting organizations under this draft, it is not clear whether the broadcast and the re-broadcast include only by wireless means or by both wire and wireless. As far as this issue of re-broadcast is concerned, except the 1951 draft, none of these drafts could discuss regarding the issue of wire or wireless re-emission or re-broadcast expressly. However, the same had been left to the member countries to be decided at their level.[81] In addition to this, the nature of re-emission/re-broadcast is also not clear from all these drafts. Whether the re-emission/re-broadcast would only mean simultaneous diffusion which was considered as relay transmission or deferred transmission or both? However, it would be clear from the drafts and the text associated, or in the texts associated with the drafts that it is only for simultaneous diffusion.

Under the Rome Convention, the following minimum rights were recognized to the broadcasting organizations:[82]

> Broadcasting organisations shall enjoy the right to authorize or prohibit:
> (a) the rebroadcasting of their broadcasts;
> (b) the fixation of their broadcasts;

---

80 The Draft International Convention Concerning the Protection of Performers, Makers of Phonograms and Broadcasters, 1960, Art. 12: Broadcasters shall enjoy the right to authorise or prohibit:
(a) the rebroadcasting of their broadcasts;
(b) the fixation of their broadcasts;
(c) the reproduction of unlawful fixations or of fixations made in accordance with the provisions of Art. 14, if the reproduction is made for purposes different from those provided for by the above-mentioned provisions;
(d) the communication to the public of their television broadcasts if such communication is made in places accessible to the public against payment of an entrance fee. It shall be left to national legislation to determine the conditions under which this right may be exercised.

81 See "Committee of Experts on the preparation of International Regulation of the Rights of Performers, Producers of Phonographic Records and Broadcasters", *UNESCO*, Monte Carlo, 4th to 13th March, 1957, pp. 26–27.

82 See International Convention for the Protection of Performers, Producers of Phonograms and Broadcasting Organizations, Rome, 1961, Art. 13.

(c) the reproduction:
  (i) of fixations, made without their consent, of their broadcasts;
  (ii) of fixations, made in accordance with the provisions of Article 15, of their broadcasts, if the reproduction is made for purposes different from those referred to in those provisions;

(d) the communication to the public of their television broadcasts if such communication is made in places accessible to the public against payment of an entrance fee; it shall be a matter for the domestic law of the State where protection of this right is claimed to determine the conditions under which it may be exercised.

Just like the 1957 draft and the subsequent drafts, the final provision had also proposed either to provide positive or negative rights. As discussed above, generally the exclusive rights were conferred in the copyright regime only for the creative works and thus the authors had been given with such rights which would enable them to authorize others to exploit those exclusive rights. As the broadcasting organizations activities did not involve any creativity i.e., mere mechanical acts for which intellectual contribution is not required, it could not be justified if they were given with positive rights. Therefore, it was justified that the non-exclusive rights i.e., right to prohibit model for the broadcasters. This is also in tune with the gap that needs to be filled to protect the unauthorized use of content carrying signals. The remedy that requires is to prevent the unauthorized use of the signal by another broadcasting organization. This can be achieved by an injunctive relief against the unauthorized user. There seems to be no demand to facilitate the transfer of content carrying signals by one broadcasting organization to another to create an exclusive right on the content carrying signal i.e., the right to simultaneously show the content through a different broadcasting organization with the permission of the first broadcasting organization who has a right to broadcasting the content. The right to authorize the use of content by another broadcasting organization could only be based on the terms and conditions of the licensing/assignment of the broadcasting right of the author on the content since rebroadcasting right is part of the right of author. This is also in tune with the Article dealing with relationship with copyright. Hence, it is believed that the broadcasting organization can authorize the use of the content by another through the transfer of the content carrying signal only if the contract with the author permits the same. Therefore, the 1957 model has secured a permanent place even in the Rome Convention as well.

As far as these rights are concerned, The Hague draft provision i.e., Article 12 has been retained under Article 13 of the Rome Convention substantially. The broadcasting organizations are given with rebroadcasting rights, fixation rights, reproduction of their fixation and communication to the public of their broadcast. While discussing the right of re-broadcasting, it was made clear that, the word rebroadcasting would mean only simultaneous transmission not the deferred broadcasting or repeated broadcasting.[83]

Regarding post fixation rights, Austria and Switzerland proposed to include a prohibition of taking photos/still pictures to be part of fixation.[84] While addressing this fixation issue, it was decided that the prohibition against fixing in whole or part was covered by this Article but the still picture fixation was left to the member countries.[85] There were some concerns with respect to the communication to the public of the broadcast against payment in places accessible to public included by the US.[86] It was proposed by Austria that irrespective of the entrance fee is charged or not, if the place where the communication occurs is accessible to public, then this right is to be given to the broadcasting organization.[87] However, the provision has been retained with a reservation under Article 16 which enables the members to decide on this issue at the domestic level to provide this right or not. Further, with respect to reproduction of the fixation of broadcast, it was proposed by Austria that the broadcasting organizations should be granted with right to authorize '*putting into circulation copies of their broadcast*'.[88] However, this was not accepted[89] because of the fact that such a move would affect the producers of phonogram and would go against Article 10[90] of Rome Convention.

During that point of time, the musical records were produced and sold based on broadcast due to technical reasons. As this was the market practice to deal with musical records sale, this was also considered at the time of negotiation due to the technical limitation on the authors. In addition to signal piracy, the broadcasted content were recorded and then sold in the market

83 *See* "Records of the Diplomatic Conference on the International Protection of Performers, Producers of Phonograms and Broadcasting Organizations", *International Labour Organisation, United Nations Educational, Scientific and Cultural Organization, and the United International Bureaux for the Protection of Intellectual Property*, (1968), p. 166.

84 *Id.*, at p. 166.

85 *Id.*, at p. 50.

86 *Id.*, at p. 167.

87 *Id.*, at p. 167.

88 *Id.*, at p. 50.

89 *Id.*, at p. 50.

90 International Convention for the Protection of Performers, Producers of Phonograms and Broadcasting Organizations, Rome, 1961, Art. 10 reads: *Right of Reproduction for Phonogram Producers:* Producers of phonograms shall enjoy the right to authorize or prohibit the direct or indirect reproduction of their phonograms.

without any permission from the content owners.[91] Therefore, so as to address the issue of illegal fixation of the broadcast program and sale of those musical records, with a rider (i.e., with copyright owners' permission, any other person other than the broadcasters could go for any kind of economic realization), the broadcasting organizations had been given with the post fixation right only to address the unauthorized uses of the broadcasted program. Thus, it is clear that the post fixation right granted is very limited and narrow only to address certain specific purposes i.e., post broadcast uses of broadcasted programs. As the post fixation rights are subjected to the authors' rights, it only deals with the content of the broadcast and not the signal because the signal does not exist once the broadcasting is over and reception of signal by the consumer. The rights granted to the broadcasters over the broadcast fixation, would invariably affect the authors' right over the content. As discussed above, since these post fixation rights are always subjected to the authors' rights (content creators) or authors' prior permission is required to exploit these rights by broadcasting organizations. Hence, it is clear that the post fixation rights will coexist with the rights of the author and should be enjoyed together provided the fixation of the content is from the signal transmitted by the broadcasting organization. Because of this, the treaty also recognized a minimum of 20 years of protection to broadcasting organizations.[92]

91 Louis G. Caldwell, "Piracy of Broadcast Programs", 30 (8) *Columbia Law Review,* (1930), pp. 1087–1114, at p. 1094.

92 The duration of the protection was initially left to the member countries to decide under the 1951 draft, Geneva draft and Monaco draft. However, The Hague draft was the first one, to come with a common protection provision with a specific period. It provided 20 years protection to the broadcasting organizations at the end of the calendar in which the broadcast took place. Even the Rome also emphasizes to provide at least 20 years protection from the end of the calendar year in which the broadcast took place. If the protection is given for the 20 years duration, it is for what? Is it for signal or for content or for both? The term of protection is for the rights recognized under the Convention. As we have discussed above, these rights include the rights to protect the content carrying signal before it is received by the public and for the content that is fixed from the content carrying signal. It is clear from the provisions that all these rights are subjected to the authors' rights. This means that these rights co-exist with the rights of the author of the content. If the rights are for the signal, the signal would not exist after the broadcasting is completed. In other words, signal does not have any life once it is received for the enjoyment of content. Hence 20 years make no impact as for as the protection of content carrying signal is concerned. Then the term of protection is applicable only to post fixation rights that are to be enjoyed along with the authors. The authors' right of broadcast will continue even after the right of the broadcasting organization expires. During the period of 20 years, the economic return from the context fixed from the signal has to be shared with the author unless contracted out by the author. Whether there is any economic justification for the

From the above detailed discussion on the Rome Convention protection for the broadcasting organizations, it is evident that the nature of protection given is very much restrictive in nature and cannot be extended further to the technological advancements in the area of broadcasting. Thus, it is highly possible to interpret and conclude that one of the objectives of the Rome Convention protection for the broadcasting organizations wass to address signal piracy and the same was restricted to a particular technology which could not be expanded so as to accommodate new emerging technologies in the area of broadcasting.

As far as Rome Convention is concerned, as discussed above, it provides more protection to the broadcasting organizations as compared to the demands. As stated above, there were many parties who strongly objected to the present form of provisions, as it provides more protection to the broadcasters and interferes with the rights of the authors. Due to lack of conceptual clarity in the objectives, nature of technology covered, rights conferred and the reservation clauses, the convention was ratified only by a few countries and it failed to evolve as a minimum international standard for protection. It may be pointed out that India is also not a party to this Convention. This also resulted in the emergence of new international norms to address technologies particularly satellite communication technology developed after the conclusion of Rome Convention. Let us discuss the same in detail in the next part.

4.6 Satellite Convention

As we discussed above, since the Rome Convention only protects the broadcast which is intended for public reception, the satellite transmission cannot be protected under the Rome Convention as it lacks the public reception element in it. Generally, the satellite transmissions, during the 1970s could be divided into two.[93] The first one is 'distribution satellites' which were quiet common and reached many jurisdiction, even at the end of 1960s itself.[94] The second one is 'direct broadcasting satellites' which were still in the pipeline,

same being given to the broadcasting organization is a question that deserves serious consideration particularly in the content of the new technological developments.

93 Barbara Ringer, "Brussels Diplomatic Conference on the Distribution of Programme-Carrying Signals Transmitted by Satellite: Report", 11 *Copyright*, (1974), pp. 267–291, at para 8.

94 Nancy Lowe Henry, "The Convention Relating to the Distribution of Programme-Carrying Signals Transmitted by Satellite: A Potshot at Poaching", 7 *N.Y.U. Journal of International Law and Politics*, (1974), pp. 575–596 at p. 577.

which were not ready for commercial broadcasting until the mid 1970s.[95] With respect to the distribution satellites which were widely used for commercial transmissions, the transmissions have been intended only for the broadcasting organizations which means between the broadcasting organizations or between broadcasting organizations and the cable broadcasting organizations. Thus, there is no public reception option available in the satellite transmissions.

These satellite transmissions waves are generally high frequency waves and are entirely different from the Hertzian waves. As a result of these technological developments, those ground stations which have been equipped with highly sensitive instruments could only receive the transmitted signals by the satellite. Further, for setting up these ground or earth stations for receiving and for the further distribution, huge investment is required as it is highly expensive. Even if someone wants to receive the signal transmitted by the satellites without permission or for further distribution which is otherwise known as 'poaching of satellite signals',[96] they have to make huge investment for setting up the earth receiving stations.[97] During 1970s, in many jurisdictions, not only the broadcasting receiving stations, the entire broadcasting had been in the hands of the governments. Therefore, in most of the countries, the government was the only player in the market even in commercial broadcasting context and thus, poaching or piracy was considered as an occasional phenomenon in the distribution satellite transmissions.[98] Whereas direct broadcasting satellites are concerned, the individuals can receive the satellite signal with the help of receiving device directly from the satellite and therefore, there is no need for any distributor/earth station which is otherwise required in the distribution satellites context. Even in direct satellite transmissions also, public reception would be limited because the receivers are pre-identified subscribers. Therefore, both the satellite transmissions would not be covered by the Rome Convention.

Prior to the satellite transmissions, reach of the broadcasting organizations signal by using the wireless means was very limited. For the expansion of

---

95 *Ibid.*

96 Poaching of satellite signal means unauthorized access to the transmitted signal. Poaching and Piracy are commonly understood as synonyms.

97 Barbara Ringer, "Brussels Diplomatic Conference on the Distribution of Programme-Carrying Signals Transmitted by Satellite: Report", 11 *Copyright*, (1974), pp. 267–291, at para 8 and also see Nancy Lowe Henry, "The Convention Relating to the Distribution of Programme-Carrying Signals Transmitted by Satellite: A Potshot at Poaching", 7 *N.Y.U. Journal of International Law and Politics*, (1974), pp. 575–596 at p. 577.

98 *Ibid.*

coverage area, relay method was used.[99] However, in case of satellite broadcasting, the coverage area could be multiple times higher than the wireless terrestrial broadcasting. It has been pointed out that 1/3 of the earth surface could be covered by these satellite transmissions.[100] Thus, the satellite transmissions created a new issue i.e., intercontinental transmissions.[101] As the coverage area is getting expanded, it was apprehended that the works would be enjoyed without any additional remuneration not only for the creators of the works and the performers but for the broadcasting organizations too. Therefore, it was highly apprehended that the un-authorized reception or poaching would ultimately be detrimental to all.[102]

Since the technology started penetrating rampantly, the broadcasting organizations had been raising their voice that there was an immediate need to address the issue raised out of this satellite transmissions i.e., unintended access or unauthorized access of the programme carrying signal or poaching. Therefore, it was decided to solve this problem internationally.[103]

The intercontinental transmission of television program by satellite was considered as one of the major issues in late 1960s by the UNESCO and the BIRIP.[104] It is worth mentioning here that the satellite convention is aimed to protect the transmissions intended for the broadcasting organizations' reception and not for the public reception.[105] It means the transmissions between broadcasting organizations are the subject matter of protection under this convention.[106] There were four options before the international community:[107]

99 For the detailed discussions on the broadcast relay in the early days, see Jerome S. Berg, *Broadcasting on the Short Waves, 1945 to Today*, McFarland, (2008).

100 Barbara Ringer, "Brussels Diplomatic Conference on the Distribution of Programme-Carrying Signals Transmitted by Satellite: Report", 11 *Copyright*, (1974), pp. 267–291, at para 7.

101 *Id.*, para 5.

102 See Nancy Lowe Henry, "The Convention Relating to the Distribution of Programme-Carrying Signals Transmitted by Satellite: A Potshot at Poaching", 7 *N.Y.U. Journal of International Law and Politic*, (1974), pp. 575–596, at p. 576.

103 Barbara Ringer, "Brussels Diplomatic Conference on the Distribution of Programme-Carrying Signals Transmitted by Satellite: Report", 11 *Copyright* (1974), pp. 267–291, at p. 268.

104 *Id.*, at p. 267.

105 Tom Rivers, "A Broadcasters' treaty?", in Paul Torremans, *Copyright Law: A Handbook of Contemporary Research*, Edward Elgar, UK, (2007), at p. 488.

106 Lucie Guibault and Roy Melzer, "The legal protection of broadcast signals", *IRIS Plus, Legal observations of the European Audiovisual Observatory*, (2004), at p. 3.

107 Barbara Ringer, "Brussels Diplomatic Conference on the Distribution of Programme-Carrying Signals Transmitted by Satellite: Report", 11 *Copyright*, (1974), pp. 267–291, at p.268.

1. Revision of the International Telecommunication Convention or Revision of the Radio Regulations.
2. Revision of the International Convention for the Protection of Performers, Producers of Phonograms and Broadcasting Organisations
3. A new multilateral convention
4. Other methods like passing a simple resolution condemning the satellite signal piracy.

However, it was decided to go-ahead with the new multilateral international convention on this issue. Therefore, initiatives were taken by the intergovernmental organizations since then. There were three drafts during the formulation and finalization of this international convention i.e., the Lausanne Draft, the Paris Draft and the Nairobi Draft. All these draft were discussed in detail at the respective committee of experts meetings.[108]

During the Lausanne draft discussions, most of the members expressed their concerns regarding the nature of protection intended to provide to the broadcasting organizations, that should not be detrimental to the creators and performers and it was demanded that they should support the new international instrument, if the following points would be well addressed.[109]

1. The authors' rights should be safeguarded at first and should ensure that the proposed protection would not affect the authors' rights.
2. The new instrument should not prejudice the future of the Rome Convention.

However, some of the members, particularly Ethiopia advocated that if there are any safeguards for the creators and the performers, it would ultimately affect the efficient functioning of the broadcasting organizations.[110] Therefore, there was a standstill on this issue. During the Paris Draft, the central focus of the discussion was on the nature of protection to be offered for the creators and performers under this convention. It was decided to retain the concept of casting obligations on the states to take measures to stop the poaching of

108 These drafts resulted out of the meeting of the committee of experts held at Lausanne in 1971, at the Paris in 1972 and at Nairobi in 1973 respectively. For the same nomenclature usages, generally see, See Nancy Lowe Henry, "The Convention Relating to the Distribution of Programme-Carrying Signals Transmitted by Satellite: A Potshot at Poaching", 7 *N.Y.U. Journal of International Law and Politics*, (1974), pp. 575–596, at p. 576.

109 See for the same, Barbara Ringer, "Brussels Diplomatic Conference on the Distribution of Programme-Carrying Signals Transmitted by Satellite: Report", 11 *Copyright*, (1974), pp. 267–291, at para 10.

110 See Nancy Lowe Henry, "The Convention Relating to the Distribution of Programme-Carrying Signals Transmitted by Satellite: A Potshot at Poaching", 7 *N.Y.U. Journal of International Law and Politics*, (1974), pp. 575–596, at p. 588.

transmitted programme carrying signals.[111] In addition to this, there was a provision for protecting the creators and neighbouring right holders of copyright[112] which would ultimately affect or reduce the level of protection available to the

111 *Id.*, at p. 589.

112 Paris Draft Art. 4 reads: (1) This Convention shall in no way be interpreted to limit or prejudice the protection, otherwise secured to authors, performers, producers of phonograms, (or) broadcasting organizations (or other contributors to the programmes) under any national legislation or international agreement. (2) Without prejudice to paragraph (1), (a) the originating organization which is a national of a Contracting State and which uses a satellite for the distribution of programme carrying signals made directly by the satellite itself shall be responsible vis-a-vis the authors, performers, producers of phonograms and broadcasting organizations in accordance with the legislation of the State of which the organization is a national, if and to the extent that such legislation grants to them rights in the case of the broadcasting of their works, performances, phonograms, or broadcasts; (b) where the distribution of programme-carrying signals is made on the territory of a Contracting State, the organization making the distribution shall be responsible vis-a-vis the authors, performers, producers of phonograms and broadcasting organizations, in accordance with the legislation of the said State, if and to the extent that such legislation grants to them rights in the case, respectively, of the broadcasting or other distribution of their works, performances, phonograms or broadcasts. (3) Without prejudice to paragraph (1), the authors whose works, protected in the Contracting State of which the originating organization is a national are used in an emission of programme-carrying signals to a satellite, (a) may forbid the originating organization to authorize the distribution of such signals in another Contracting State which is a party to the [UCC] or a member of the [Berne Union] or bound to the State of which the originating organization is a national by a bilateral copyright treaty, where the distribution of these works is not authorized by their authors or is not otherwise lawful under the legislation of that other Contracting State; (b) shall be entitled to claim from the originating organization, for the distribution of such signals, an appropriate remuneration, where the said organization has authorized such distribution in another Contracting State which is neither a party to the [UCC] nor a member of the [Berne Union] nor is bound to the State of which the originating organization is a national by a bilateral copyright treaty, on condition that the distribution does not entitle the said authors to a remuneration under the national legislation of that other Contracting State and that it is not subject to the provisions of Article V. (4) In the cases provided for in paragraph (3). the originating organization is required to inform the authors of works which are intended for use in a distribution of programme-carrying signals before the said distribution and in time to allow them to exercise the prerogatives granted to them in paragraph (3). It shall be a matter for national legislation of each Contracting State to determine the sanction for non-compliance with the preceding provision. (4 bis) Unless otherwise agreed, the originating organization which is a national of a Contracting State is required to inform the performers whose live performances of literary or artistic works it intends to use in a distribution of programme-carrying signals before the said distribution and in time to allow them to exercise any rights they may have. It shall be a matter for national legislation of each Contracting State to determine the sanction for non-compliance with this provision, and each Contracting State may, by its national legislation, specify the man- ner in which performers will be represented for the purpose of the provision, if several of them participate in the same performance.

broadcasting organizations. Thus, there was no consensus on the protection of broadcasting organizations' programme carrying signal even at the end of that meeting.

As we discussed above, until the Nairobi meeting of governmental experts, the two drafts were based on the right based approach and keeping the provisions to envisage the members to provide rights.[113] It was proposed by Australia[114] that as the poaching issue of programme carrying signal is quite common only with respect to sports and current events, there would not be an issue for the creators and performers. Thus, it was demanded that the proposed convention should be divided into two and further, this convention would be limited only to the sports and current events reporting as it would not cause any hurdle for the progress of this convention. The same was rejected as it would ultimately defeat the purpose of the proposed convention. However, a paradigm shift took place due to the proposals submitted by the delegations of Brazil, Morocco, Mexico and India[115] wherein it was proposed to change the very nature of the proposed international convention[116] i.e., from the international private law to the international public law[117] thereby the states would merely ensure that appropriate measures would be taken against the unauthorized distributors.[118] Therefore, it was decided that there is no need for creating new rights for the broadcasting organizations to safeguard their programme carrying signals. Finally, the Convention relating to the distribution of programme carrying signals transmitted via satellite was

113 See Barbara Ringer, "Brussels Diplomatic Conference on the Distribution of Programme-Carrying Signals Transmitted by Satellite: Report", 11 *Copyright*, (1974), pp. 267–291, at p. 268.

114 "Report of the 3rd Committee of the Governmental Experts on Transmissions via Space Satellite, Nairobi, (1973)", *UNESCO/WIPO/SAT.3/23*, p. 5.

115 *Id.*, at p. 12.

116 See "Comments received from intergovernmental and international non-governmental organisations", International Conference of States on the Distribution of Programme Carrying Signals Transmitted by Satellite, Brussels, UNESCO/WIPO/CONFSAT/5, (April, 1974), p. 3.

117 See for the same, Barbara Ringer, "Brussels Diplomatic Conference on the Distribution of Programme-Carrying Signals Transmitted by Satellite: Report", 11 *Copyright* (1974), pp. 267–291, at para 12.

118 See for the same See "Comments received from intergovernmental and international non-governmental organisations", International Conference of States on the Distribution of Programme Carrying Signals Transmitted by Satellite, Brussels, UNESCO/WIPO/CONFSAT/5, (April, 1974), p. 4.

adopted at the international conference of states which was held in Brussels in 1974.[119]

So as to fill the leeway created by the new technological advancement, the Satellite Convention was formulated to protect the broadcasting organizations' satellite transmissions by not conferring any new rights on them. Rather it puts emphasis on the members to initiate adequate measures to prevent the unauthorized use of the 'programme carrying signal'. In this context, this is the first international document, which deals with the signal piracy issue[120] and introduced the innovative concept called 'programme carrying signal'.[121] Due to the introduction of the program carrying signal concept, internationally, it was well accepted that the broadcasters' protection is only for their signal not for the content. Since the convention does not confer any IP based rights to the broadcasters, the examination of the nature of protection given for the broadcasting organizations' 'programme carrying signal' under this convention falls short of the ambit of this book.

Another important development that has taken place internationally is the TRIPS agreement which has set minimum standards and rights with respect to each IPR. It is worth examining the nature of the legal protection given to the broadcasting organizations under the TRIPS Agreement. Before getting into the discussion on TRIPS, it is essential to summarize the legal position of the broadcasting rights of authors based on the Revision of the Berne Convention.

4.7 Authors' Right of Broadcasting: Pre TRIPS and Post Rome Scenario

Article 11 *bis* of the Berne Convention, as revised in Paris, 1971, has expanded the scope of authors' right of broadcasting when compared with the 1948 revision. This Paris revision is after the Rome Convention. Thus, it is extremely important to examine whether the authors' right of broadcasting has been widened compared to the position in 1948. The relevant part of the provision reads:

---

119 The International Conference of States on the Distribution of Programme Carrying Signals Transmitted by Satellite was held at Brussels from 6th -21st, May, 1974.

120 See for the further details, See "Comments received from inter-governmental and international non-governmental organisations", International Conference of States on the Distribution of Programme Carrying Signals Transmitted by Satellite, Brussels, UNESCO/WIPO/CONFSAT/5, (April, 1974), p. 2.

121 See for the same type of argument, Megumi Ogawa, *Protection of Broadcasters' Rights*, Martinus Nijhoff Publishers, Boston, (2006), at p. 48.

1. Broadcasting and other wireless communications, public communication of broadcast by wire or rebroadcast, public communication of broadcast by loudspeaker or analogous instruments; … .

(1) Authors of literary and artistic works shall enjoy the exclusive right of authorizing:
  - (i) the broadcasting of their works or the communication thereof to the public by any other means of wireless diffusion of signs, sounds or images;
  - (ii) any communication to the public by wire or by rebroadcasting of the broadcast of the work, when this communication is made by an organization other than the original one;
  - (iii) the public communication by loudspeaker or any other analogous instrument transmitting, by signs, sounds or images, the broadcast of the work.

This is the first instrument which has used the word broadcasting in the authors' right context. However, it has not defined the same. While understanding the scope of the rights given, it is clear that when compared to 1948, this has extended the right of broadcasting through wire to the authors in addition to the then existed right of radio diffusion by radio or TV. The rights given to the authors also include rebroadcasting right as well.[122] Further, when one examines the nature of rebroadcasting right, it says "rebroadcasting of the broadcast of the work". Then, it is pertinent to note that authors' right of broadcasting as conferred under this provision uses both the term broadcast and broadcasting. However, as stated, both have not been defined.

As per our discussion and conclusion on the Rome Convention based on the signal based approach, if the broadcasters' protection is only for the signal and thus the broadcast would refer to the content carrying signal whereas the broadcasting would refer the authors' right of transmission, then we need to examine the scope of the Berne provision. As both broadcast and broadcasting have been used, it could be possible for one to argue that the Berne Convention has not only given the broadcasting right i.e., transmission right but also the broadcast right i.e., signal right as well to the authors. If such interpretation is accepted, then the entire legal position

---

122 See for the scope of Art. 11 *bis*, Jane C Ginsburg, "The (New?) Right of Making Available to the Public", Columbia Public Law & Legal Theory Working Papers, (2004), available at http://lsr.nellco.org/cgi/viewcontent.cgi?article=1003&context=columbia_pllt (last accessed on 28/06/2019) and also see Silke Von Lewinski, *International Copyright Law and Policy*, Oxford University Press, at pp. 146–147.

of authors' right of broadcasting changes. Assuming that authors' right covers signal as well, then there is no gap after this revision of Berne which was projected and addressed by Rome Convention. If such interpretation is accepted, then there is no need for having neighbouring right protection as the authors' right of broadcasting itself would address the signal piracy issues, if any. However, such interpretation could not be acceptable because for getting protected under the copyright, according to Berne Convention, fixation is required. Then, the only possible interpretation is that broadcast must be understood as broadcasting [used as verb (transmit) to connect it to the noun (transmission)]. But the fact is that the author has a right of re-broadcasting and this will co-exist with the right of the broadcasting organization provided under Rome Convention. Similarly the author is provided with the right of "*public communication by loudspeaker or any other analogous instrument transmitting, by signs, sounds or images, the broadcast of the work*". This is also a right similar to the one provided to the broadcasting organization under Rome Convention. Hence, it may be safely concluded that after the revision of Berne Convention in 1971, all the rights given to the broadcasting organizations under Rome Convention are recognized to the authors also and they will co-exist.[123] This could be the potential reason for the stand taken by the TRIPS with respect to broadcasters' protection and the same is discussed below.[124]

4.8 TRIPS and the Protection of Broadcasting Organizations

Agreement on the Trade Related aspects of Intellectual Property Rights (TRIPS) is the first international multilateral document which is under the governance of World Trade Organization (WTO), which consolidates all the IPR under one umbrella and prescribes some standards with respect to each IP.[125] Though the Berne Convention and the Paris Convention have been successfully adopted,

123 See for the scope of Art. 11 *bis*, Jane C Ginsburg, "The (New?) Right of Making Available to the Public", Columbia Public Law & Legal Theory Working Papers, (2004), available at http://lsr.nellco.org/cgi/viewcontent.cgi?article=1003&context=columbia_pllt (last accessed on 28/06/2019) and also for the contrary view see Silke Von Lewinski, *International Copyright Law and Policy*, Oxford University Press, at pp. 146–156.

124 This is the inference of the author.

125 See for the general discussion about the TRIPS, Jayashree Watal and Antony Taubman, *The Making of the Trips Agreement: Personal Insights from the Uruguay Round Negotiations*, WTO, Geneva, (2015).

much flexibility[126] has been provided with respect to each IP so that members could design their own IP laws in their jurisdictions which ultimately affected the developed countries as they owned most of the IPR.[127] So as to overcome this problem, TRIPS agreement has been a result of the conscious efforts of USA and other developed economies, who, strongly believed that IPR should be linked with GATT[128] for its effective implementation at all the jurisdictions around the world for the maximization of profits.[129] Though the developed economies joined together to push IPR as part of trade under the GATT, they have had differences on some IPR related areas including broadcasting and television rights.[130]

From the jurisprudence point of view, the Berne Convention has been aimed to protect the interest of the authors; thus the author' centric approach was adopted.[131] However, in TRIPS, the owners' interests have been taken care irrespective of the fact that whether the owner is the actual creator of IPR or not. Since our discussion is related to the broadcasting organizations, the focus would be on the provisions related to the same.

Though TRIPS is an entirely new international legal document, it mandates the members to provide the Berne Convention model of protection to copyrights.[132] Even with respect to the Berne Convention, TRIPS mandates only to

126 See for the detailed discussion on the flexibilities under the Berne, Paris and TRIPS, Susan K Sell, *Private Power, Public Law: The Globalization of Intellectual Property Rights*, Cambridge University Press, (2003), p.11 and also see N.S. Goplalakrishnan and T.G. Agitha, *Principles of Intellectual Property*, Eastern Book Company, (2nd edn., 2014), at p. XLI.

127 See for the detailed discussion on the same, Laurence R. Helfer, "Regime Shifting: The TRIPs Agreement and New Dynamics of International Intellectual Property Lawmaking", 29 (1) *Yale Journal of International Law*, (2004), pp. 1–84, at p.20 and also see Frank Emmert, "Intellectual Property in the Uruguay Round – Negotiating Strategies of the Western Industrialized Countries", 11 *Michigan Journal of International Law*, (1989–1990), pp. 1317–1399.

128 General Agreement on Tariffs and Trade.

129 For the detailed discussion about the interfuses of the trade and IPR in the GATT Uruguay round, see Keith E Maskus, "Intellectual Property Rights and Economic Development", 32 *Case Western Reserve Journal of International Law*, (2000), pp. 471–506 and also see Gadbaw, R. Michael, "Intellectual Property and International Trade: Merger or Marriage of Convenience", 22 *Vanderbilt Journal of Transnational Law*, (1989), pp. 223–242.

130 See for the same argument, A.V. Ganesan, "Negotiating for India" in Jayashree Watal and Antony Taubman, *The Making of the Trips Agreement: Personal Insights from the Uruguay Round Negotiations*, WTO, Geneva, (2015), at p. 213.

131 See N.S. Goplalakrishnan and T.G. Agitha, *General Principles of Intellectual Property*, Eastern Book Company, (2nd edn., 2014), at p. XLV.

132 See TRIPS: Agreement on Trade-Related Aspects of Intellectual Property Rights, 1994, Art. 9.

protect Articles 1 to 21 of the same. Further, it does not give any reference to the Rome Convention at all. However, Article 14 of the TRIPS deals with the related rights i.e., protection of performers, producers of phonograms and broadcasting organizations. With respect to the protection of broadcasting organizations, under Article 14 (3),[133] the members are given with two options. The first one is to protect the broadcasting organizations by providing a negative right i.e., right to prevent if any of the following acts are done without authorization. The second one is, if a member does not wish to confer the above given negative right to prevent the following acts; the same should be given to the owners of copyright in the "subject matter of broadcast". According to TRIPS, in both the cases, the 'following acts' means:

1. Fixation
2. Reproduction of fixation
3. Rebroadcasting by wireless means of broadcast
4. Communication of the television broadcast to the public

The reason for giving such an alternative model of protection is entirely based on the differential approaches of the countries towards copyright i.e., civil law approach and the common law approach. So as to accommodate both the views, such an alternative model has been adopted for this Article 14. Further, as discussed in the Berne provision related to broadcasting, it has been found that the position of the authors' right of broadcasting would cover many of the rights identified in Article 14. Thus, TRIPS opted for this approach by leaving to the individual nations to decide.[134]

When we analyze the negotiation history of the TRIPS, it is clear that prior to the Brussels draft of TRIPS agreement, there was a proposal to include in addition to the above mentioned four acts, the possibility of preventing:

- Retransmitting of the broadcast
- Putting on the market, sale and distribution of the copies of the broadcasts.[135]

---

133 TRIPS: Agreement on Trade-Related Aspects of Intellectual Property Rights, 1994, Art. 14: *Protection of Performers, Producers of Phonograms (Sound Recordings) and Broadcasting Organizations;* 3. Broadcasting organizations shall have the right to prohibit the following acts when undertaken without their authorization: the fixation, the reproduction of fixations, and the rebroadcasting by wireless means of broadcasts, as well as the communication to the public of television broadcasts of the same. Where Members do not grant such rights to broadcasting organizations, they shall provide owners of copyright in the subject matter of broadcasts with the possibility of preventing the above acts, subject to the provisions of the Berne Convention (1971).

134 See the previous part discussion on the authors' right of Broadcasting: Pre-TRIPS and Post Rome Context.

135 See Daniel J Gervais, *The TRIPS Agreement: Drafting History and Analysis*, Sweet & Maxwell, (4th edn., 2012), at p. 296.

Though the protection given under this provision covered the broadcasting organizations also, title of this proposed provision was 'protection of performers, producers of phonograms and broadcast'.[136]

Under the Dunkle Draft, however, the above views were altered. The broadcasting organizations were proposed with the right to prohibit or the same would be given to the owners of the copyright of the "subject matter of broadcast". A new condition was added to this provision i.e., while granting the right to prohibit to the broadcasters or to the owners' of the copyright of the "subject matter of broadcast", the same right to prohibit should be subjected to the provisions of the Berne Convention, 1971.[137] The Dunkle Draft has been accepted as the final text of the TRIPS without any change on content of this provision, however, the title of the same has been changed and the broadcast has been replaced with broadcasting.[138]

From the above discussions, it can be clearly established that TRIPS was never intended to provide any positive right to the broadcasting organizations in the advanced technological era. It is still confined to wireless and even not extended to wire. It is also interesting to note that TRIPS recognized limited post fixation rights such as reproduction and communication of the television broadcast to public. These rights are also recognized to the authors under Berne Convention. Hence, it is possible to conclude that TRIPS also envisage the coexistence of these rights. One of the possible reasons for such a model of protection under the TRIPS is because of the nature of the technology and the technological advancements in the broadcasting. By the time of TRIPS negotiation, various modes of broadcasting which existed are:

- Traditional Radio Broadcasting
- Traditional TV Broadcasting
- Cable Broadcasting
- Satellite Broadcasting.

As discussed above, it may be concluded that the problem of signal piracy has been well addressed by the technology itself in the beginning of 1990s except in few jurisdictions. If the technology has substantially addressed the issue of signal piracy, there is no more need of having legal protection under the copyright regime. However, the only model of broadcasting left out in this context was cable broadcasting. Though cable broadcasting was used for copyrighted

---

136 *Id.*, at p. 294.

137 *Id.*, at p. 293.

138 See TRIPS: Agreement on Trade-Related Aspects of Intellectual Property Rights, 1994, Art. 14: *Protection of Performers, Producers of Phonograms (Sound Recordings) and Broadcasting Organizations.*

works in the 1950s itself, it did not penetrate into many jurisdictions in a large scale including countries like India. Thus, the technology was not so common among the countries. Though there were problem of signal piracy and unauthorized retransmission, they remained within their respective jurisdictions. Due to the lack of cable penetration worldwide, many jurisdictions did not have an idea about the technology itself. Hence, the problems of cable broadcasting remained as an issue at the domestic level rather being considered as an international problem. Thus, it seems to be a deliberate omission in the TRIPS Agreement with respect to cable broadcasting due to lack of international issues. Hence, cable broadcasting has been not covered by the TRIPS.

Generally, the right given under the TRIPS for broadcasters is negative in nature. If any one of the above acts is done without the authorization of the broadcasting organizations, then the broadcasting organizations shall have the right of only preventing the same. Since, the right is a negative one and it coexists with the authors' right, then the question arises is whether the broadcasting organizations have any right to transfer the above stated four activities for their realization? The natural answer would be 'no'. If the broadcasting organizations wish to rebroadcast or 'fixation' or reproduce the fixation or communicate to the public, the same would be determined based on the nature of license or agreement which generally exists between the owners of copyright and the broadcasting organizations. This is to ensure that the broadcasting organizations are not going to enjoy any independent right other than based on the rights of the authors of the work. Because of this, TRIPS also recognized[139] the duration of 20 years for the rights conferred to broadcasting organizations.[140]

---

139 From the very beginning of the TRIPS negotiation, the duration of the protection for the broadcasting organizations remained consistently at 25 years. Even the 25 years was kept in Dunkle Draft. However, during the final round out negotiation, it was decided to reduce the same to 20 years. Therefore, according to Art. 14 (3), if a member country decided to provide the negative right to the broadcasting organizations, then the protection would be for 20 years from the end of the calendar year of the broadcast. If the same is given to the owners of the work of broadcast, then the duration would be subjected to Berne Convention as mandated by TRIPS. As there is differential treatment or there is an alternative protection for the broadcasting organizations under the TRIPS, it has been made it clear that most favored nation (MFN) would not be available in TRIPS as the mode of protection would differ with respect to countries. As discussed above, even the 20 years duration for the broadcasters would not be required as such protection would be detrimental to the authors because the post fixation rights would be on the content only. Thus, in this context, though the TRIPS provides very minimal protection to the broadcasters, it has not justified the 20 years protection to the broadcasters.

140 TRIPS: Agreement on Trade-Related Aspects of Intellectual Property Rights, 1994, Art. 14: *Protection of Performers, Producers of Phonograms (Sound Recordings) and Broadcasting Organizations;* 5. The term of the protection available under this Agreement

4.9 Internet Transmission: Expansion of Authors' Right of Communication to Public and its implication for Broadcasting Organizations in the Post TRIPS Scenario: an Analysis

In the post TRIPS context, there are two international treaties concluded within two years after the implementation of TRIPS Agreement under the WIPO's guidance. One of the prime reasons to accede the two treaties is the increasing digital and internet technical advancements that are widely used for the exploitation of copyrighted materials in many jurisdictions.[141] So as to address the technological problems, there was an immediate need for expanding the authors' rights to the extent of those technological advancements since the TRIPS did not address the same. As a result, under the guidance of WIPO, Copyright Treaty (WCT) and Phonograms and Performers' Treaty (WPPT) were negotiated and finalized in 1996. While expanding the rights to the advanced technological context, it has been ensured that adequate measures would be properly placed as limitations and exceptions so as to balance the owners' interests and the users' interests.[142] According to Article 1 of the WCT,[143] it is very clear that the WCT is a special agreement as per Article 20 of the Berne Convention.[144] The principle objective of the WCT is the same as that of the

---

to performers and producers of phonograms shall last at least until the end of a period of 50 years computed from the end of the calendar year in which the fixation was made or the performance took place. The term of protection granted pursuant to paragraph 3 shall last for at least 20 years from the end of the calendar year in which the broadcast took place. For detailed discussion, see Daniel J Gervais, *The TRIPS Agreement: Drafting History and Analysis*, Sweet & Maxwell, (4th edn., 2012), pp. 295–308 and also see Hannu Wager, "Copyright: A Nordic perspective" in Jayashree Watal and Antony Taubman, *The Making Of The Trips Agreement: Personal Insights From the Uruguay Round Negotiations*, WTO, Geneva, (2015), at p. 331.

141 See Jörg Reinbothe and Silke Von Lewinski, *The WIPO Treaties on Copyright: A Commentary on the WCT, the WPPT, and the BTAP*, Oxford University Press, (2015), Chapter 3 and 4.

142 See WCT, 1996, Preamble.

143 It reads: Relation to the Berne Convention: (1) This Treaty is a special agreement within the meaning of Art. 20 of the Berne Convention for the Protection of Literary and Artistic Works, as regards Contracting Parties that are countries of the Union established by that Convention. This Treaty shall not have any connection with treaties other than the Berne Convention, nor shall it prejudice any rights and obligations under any other treaties. (2) Nothing in this Treaty shall derogate from existing obligations that Contracting Parties have to each other under the Berne Convention for the Protection of Literary and Artistic Works.(3) Hereinafter, "Berne Convention" shall refer to the Paris Act of July 24, 1971 of the Berne Convention for the Protection of Literary and Artistic Works.(4) Contracting Parties shall comply with Articles 1 to 21 and the Appendix of the Berne Convention.

144 Art. 20 [Special Agreements Among Countries of the Union]: The Governments of the countries of the Union reserve the right to enter into special agreements among

Berne Convention i.e., the protection of authors' interest and is reflected in the preamble of the WCT.[145]

As our thrust focus is to understand the nature of the current legal protection available at the international level for the internet transmissions using the live streaming (IPTV/ Web TV), the same needs to be examined in detail.

As we discussed in the previous chapter, most of the internet transmissions technologies would be using the same fundamentals though they differ based on the type of protocol that is being used in the internet transmissions. Even though these technologies make substantial differences with respect to end-users' point of view, the fundamental concepts remain the same. As discussed in chapter 3, the content would be travelling through 7 layers and then will be transported as streams/packets. The same would be received and again processed through the layers before the end users could enjoy the content. The stream or packet would be an essential element in every internet transmissions, however the same would be determined by the nature and the type of software used for such internet transmission. As a result, only the software would decide the nature of internet transmissions.

As far as internet transmissions related to authors' rights are concerned, the WCT is the only international document which addresses the same. Under the WCT, the right of communication to the public is broadened in the internet context. Hence, it is important to examine whether authors' rights over internet live transmissions of their content is covered?

4.9.1 *Right of Communication to the Public*

According to Article 8 of the WCT,[146] the authors' right of communication to the public has been further expanded to cover all types of communications by both wire and wireless means. The use of the term by "any communication to public of their works by wire or wireless means" could cover even some form of

---

themselves, in so far as such agreements grant to authors more extensive rights than those granted by the Convention, or contain other provisions not contrary to this Convention. The provisions of existing agreements which satisfy these conditions shall remain applicable.

145 Emphasis added.

146 WIPO Copyright Treaty, 1996, Art. 8: Right of Communication to the Public:- Without prejudice to the provisions of Articles 11(1)(ii), 11bis(1)(i) and (ii),11ter(1)(ii), 14(1)(ii) and 14bis(1) of the Berne Convention, authors of literary and artistic works shall enjoy the exclusive right of authorizing any communication to the public of their works, by wire or wireless means, including the making available to the public of their works in such a way that members of the public may access these works from a place and at a time individually chosen by them.

the internet transmissions as part of the right of communication to the public right. The right also covers on demand transmission based on different platforms. The Article also makes it clear that these rights are without prejudice to the rights recognized under the Berne Convention.

In this context, all types of satellite transmissions including satellite broadcasting have been accommodated by the WCT as the same was left out by Berne Convention even in its 1971 revision. It was because the Berne Convention did not anticipate the technological advancements in the satellite context, thus it covered only wire based broadcasting for the authors. Even TRIPS did not alter the position and thus remained same. Therefore, it can also possibly be concluded that the WCT is aimed to cover the satellite transmissions which were commonly used for commercial purposes of communication either by the direct broadcasting satellites or the distribution satellites.

With respect to wire transmission also, the above discussed aspects would aptly apply. The wire mode of transmissions which were so common during that time was:

- Cable broadcasting
- Dial up- internet connection
- Optical fibre cable (OFC) based broadband connection.

Therefore, in this context, as we discussed above regarding the satellite transmissions which are broadcasting in nature, the same logic applies here i.e., the nature of the cable transmissions. Therefore, the same would remain as authors' rights. As far as the dial up and the OFC based broadband connections, the platform itself is identified as different and a new entrant i.e., internet. Since the communication to the public right over the internet has been extended under the WCT, then existing modes of internet transmissions have also been recognized as possessing authors' rights.

While examining the possibility of live streaming to be covered as authors' rights under the WCT, it is evident that the WCT did not use any technology specific language like the Berne Convention. Since the use of the term "any communication to public of the work by wire or wireless means" is technology neutral it has the potential to cover not only existing technology but also future technologies.[147] A quick reflection of the available records of the Diplomatic Conference of WCT, it has been noticed that Article 8 has been intended to accommodate the on-demand characters of the technology by using all

147 Jorg Reinbothe and Silk Von Lewinski, *The WIPO Treaties on Copyright: A Commentary on the WCT, the WPPT and the BTAP*, Oxford university Press, (2nd edn., 2015), at p. 129.

mediums including Internet.[148] It appears that there has been no discussion regarding inclusion of live streaming technology.[149] It is clear from the following extracted commentary.[150]

> Article 8 of WCT has two main purposes. On the one hand, it aims to complement the fragmentary set of provisions of the Berne Convention concerning the exclusive right of communication to the public and thereby to fill certain gaps, in particular regarding the original cable transmission of works other than literary, dramatic, dramatic-musical, and musical works. On the other hand, it lays down, as a part of the communication right, the minimum right of making available works online.

The possible reason for the absence of discussion of the live streaming technology from the communication to public right could be due to lack of penetration of the same around the world. As the technology was at its infancy at that point of time and that too only in a few jurisdictions, it was never expected to a be commercially viable medium for communication. The possibility of expansion of Article 8 to future technologies is made clear from the 2003 WIPO Guide to the treaty. It reads:

> ...as a result of new technologies – such as through some variants of "webcasting," "simulcasting," "streaming," or any other existing or future techniques – any kind of non-interactive communication to the public took place through the global digital network which might be regarded as being covered by Article 11 bis,.[151]

Therefore, it may be possible to argue that WCT did not envisage to accommodate live streaming transmission under Article 8. However, it may equally be possible for one to argue that authors' right over live streaming was also

---

148 WIPO, "Records of the Diplomatic Conference on Certain Copyright and Neighboring Rights Questions", (1996), at p. 176 available at: ftp://ftp.wipo.int/pub/library/ebooks/wipopublications/wipo_pub_348e_v1.pdf (last accessed on 28/06/2019).

149 *Guide to the Copyright and Related Rights Treaties Administered by WIPO*, WIPO, Geneva, 2003, pp.210–212, available at http://www.wipo.int/edocs/pubdocs/en/copyright/891/wipo_pub_891.pdf (last accessed on 28/06/2019).

150 Jorg Reinbothe and Silk Von Lewinski, *The WIPO Treaties on Copyright: A Commentary on the WCT, the WPPT and the BTAP*, Oxford university Press, (2nd edn., 2015), at p. 129.

151 *Guide to the Copyright and Related Rights Treaties Administered by WIPO*, WIPO, Geneva, 2003, p.211, available at http://www.wipo.int/edocs/pubdocs/en/copyright/891/wipo_pub_891.pdf (last accessed on 28/06/2019).

included under Article 8 since it used "any means of any communication to public wire or wireless means". The same view has been adopted and the right over live streaming has been conferred to the authors in USA and UK which is discussed in detail in the next chapter. In this context, it is important to note that even though WCT has come into force, so far only 96 countries acceded to it when compared to 175 countries which are party to Berne Convention. It may be difficult to argue that an interpretation of the Article 8 to cover live streaming has become an international norm in the above context, it is felt that it is advisable to revisit the Berne Convention to strengthen the authors' rights of communication to public in the emerging new technological environment.

As is evident from the discussion in the previous chapters, since piracy of streams is absent, it is possible to conclude that the authors' right of communication to public including live streaming, if recognized, is adequate to take care of the piracy of content taking place in re-transmission of the content used in the stream, after it is received by the public. In this context, it is also possible to conclude that there is no need for creating any intermediate right in the stream to the persons who are facilitating streaming like broadcasters.

Since the WCT deals with the authors' rights, the related rights aspects are left out. The WPPT was negotiated to address the issues of performers and the producers of sound records[152] and their rights have been updated in the new technological context.[153] However, the broadcasting organizations have been left out even under the WPPT. Due to a lack of consensus among the international community on the protection of broadcasting organizations, they have been singled out from the copyright point of view at the international level while their counterparts of Rome Convention have successfully gained protection in the WPPT, 1996. Their protection at the international level is still limited to the provisions in the TRIPS Agreement.

4.10 WIPO's Proposed Treaty on Broadcasters Protection and Live Streaming

As the TRIPS and WPPT could not provide any scope for the expansion of broadcasters' rights, so as to get a better protection than Rome Convention, the broadcasting organizations mobilized various stakeholders and convinced

152 See WPPT, 1996, Preamble.

153 See Jörg Reinbothe, Silke Von Lewinski, *The WIPO Treaties on Copyright: A Commentary on the WCT, the WPPT, and the BTAP*, Oxford University Press (2015), Chapter 7 and 8, pp. 51–567.

the WIPO to initiate a discussion on the protection of broadcasting organizations. Thus, the present ongoing discussion on the broadcasting organizations' protection was initiated by the WIPO through its World Symposium on 'Broadcasting, New Communication Technologies and Intellectual Property', 1997. In this conference, the impact of modern technology on the broadcasting organizations' rights in the copyright context including the inadequacy of the Rome Convention was pointed out by the broadcasters. Thus, the task was given to the Standing Committee on Copyright and Related Rights (SCCR) in 1998 to deliberate the issues of the broadcasters. Though the technological advancements and its impact was highlighted at the very inception of the discussion, the initial demand was to address the left out issues by the Rome Convention and TRIPS only i.e., cable and satellite broadcasting.[154] Expansion of their rights to the computer network/IP transmissions came later.

It was first brought up in the 8th SCCR 2002, a proposal to expand the broadcasters' rights to the internet world was submitted by the USA.[155] With the support of few jurisdictions especially from the developed world, a non-mandatory proposal for the protection of webcasting along with simulcasting was introduced during the 14th SCCR and became part of the draft basic proposal for the broadcasters' protection. According to the proposal, the definition of webcasting was aimed to cover the live streaming transmission as the technology is non-interactive transmission. It read:

> "webcasting" means the transmission by wire or wireless means over a computer network for the reception by the public, of sounds or of images or of images and sounds or of the representations thereof, by means of a program-carrying signal which is accessible for members of the public at substantially the same time. Such transmissions, when encrypted, shall be considered as "webcasting" where the means for decrypting are provided to the public by the webcasting organization or with its consent.[156]

---

154 WIPO 1st SCCR " Existing International, Regional and National Legislation Concerning The Protection Of The Rights Of Broadcasting Organizations", SCCR/1/3, 1998, at p. 15, available at http://www.wipo.int/edocs/mdocs/copyright/en/sccr_1/sccr_1_3.pdf (last accessed on 28/06/2019).

155 See Proposal submitted by the United States of America on "Protection of the Rights of Broadcasting Organizations", 8th SCCR, Geneva, November 4 to 8, 2002, available at http://www.wipo.int/edocs/mdocs/copyright/en/sccr_8/sccr_8_7.pdf (last accessed on 28/06/2019).

156 WIPO 14th SCCR " Draft Basic Proposal For The WIPO Treaty On The Protection Of Broadcasting Organizations Including A Non-Mandatory Appendix On The Protection

As we examined the technology of live streaming, it has been found that the technology is based on streams not signals. However, the definition of webcasting was that *"transmission by wire or wireless means over computer network by means of a program carrying signal"*. When the concept of program carrying signal is not relevant in the streaming concept, using the same in the definition of webcasting indicates a lack of clarity of the technology itself in 2002.

As the technology was new and so infant even in 2006, the proposal for the protection of webcasting was felt unwarranted by many countries particularly by the developing countries. Therefore, it was decided to take away the proposal regarding webcasting and simulcasting and confine the discussions to the concerns expressed by broadcasters' in the traditional broadcasting.[157] As a result of this, the GA of WIPO decided to exclude the issues relating to webcasting from the ongoing discussions on the broadcasting organizations' protection.[158] However, the provisions to prevent simultaneous transmission of content received from content carrying signal through computer networks (simulcasting) found place in the subsequent drafts/basic documents.

The broadcasters were also exploring the possibilities to get more protection beyond the signal i.e., over the content through the post fixation rights. The efforts of the broadcasters were initially successful and the proposed rights were extended beyond the signal.[159] But many members particularly India[160] insisted to address the unauthorized uses of the broadcasters' signal based on the 'signal based approach' and advocated for very minimal rights to address signal piracy. This effort of India was finally recognized by the WIPO's General Assembly in 2006 and laid down the mandate of 'signal based approach' for the broadcasters' protection. The intervention of India in the WIPO, General Assembly is pertinent and it reads as below:

In Relation To Webcasting", SCCR/14/2, 2006, at p. 75, available at http://www.wipo.int/edocs/mdocs/copyright/en/sccr_14/sccr_14_2.pdf (last accessed on 28/06/2019).

157 Report of the WIPO General Assembly, 18th Session, 2007, p. 56, available at http://www.wipo.int/edocs/mdocs/govbody/en/wo_ga_34/wo_ga_34_16.pdf (last accessed on 28/06/2019).

158 *Ibid.*

159 WIPO 14th SCCR " Draft Basic Proposal for the WIPO Treaty on the protection of Broadcasting Organizations including a Non-Mandatory Appendix on the Protection in Relation to Webcasting", SCCR/14/2, 2006, available at http://www.wipo.int/edocs/mdocs/copyright/en/sccr_14/sccr_14_2.pdf (last accessed on 28/06/2019).

160 Report of the WIPO General Assembly, 18th Session, 2007, at p. 56, available at http://www.wipo.int/edocs/mdocs/govbody/en/wo_ga_34/wo_ga_34_16.pdf (last accessed on 28/06/2019).

> The Delegation of India expressed its disappointment regarding the differences among delegations and lack of agreement on the basic issues. It recalled that US$668 million had already been lost by India due to piracy, and urged Member States to reiterate its earlier mandate to continue discussions on a treaty for the protection of broadcasters in the traditional sense. No protection related to computer networks should be directly or indirectly included in any such treaty. It also stressed the need to prepare impact studies of new layers of protection on the right of creators and other stakeholders, access to knowledge and other issues considered by the PCDA.[161]

As a result of this, the mandate of SCCR was revised by the GA and it reads:

> ...The session of SCCR should aim to agree and finalise, on signal based approach, the objectives, specific scope and objects of protection with a view to submitting to the diplomatic conference a revised basic proposal, which will amend the agreed relevant parts of the revised draft basic proposal RDBP...[162]

Based on the 2006 mandate, during the 15th SCCR, a revised draft basic proposal for the broadcasters' protection was introduced. It introduced the definition of broadcasting and cable casting as follows:

> Broadcasting means the transmission by wireless means for the reception by the public of sounds or of images or of images and sounds or of the representations thereof; such transmission by satellite is also "broadcasting". Wireless transmission of encrypted signals is "broadcasting" where the means for decrypting are provided to the public by the broadcasting organization or with its consent. "Broadcasting" shall not be understood as including transmissions over computer networks.[163]
>
> 'Cablecasting' means the transmission by wire for the reception by the public of sounds or of images or of images and sounds or of the

161 *Ibid.*

162 WIPO, "Report on General Assembly of 33rd session", at p. 38 available at http://www.wipo.int/edocs/mdocs/govbody/en/wo_ga_33/wo_ga_33_10.pdf (last accessed on 28/06/2019).

163 WIPO 15th SCCR "Revised Draft Basic Proposal for the WIPO Treaty on the Protection of Broadcasting Organizations", SCCR/15/2, 2006, at p. 25, available at http://www.wipo.int/edocs/mdocs/copyright/en/sccr_15/sccr_15_2.pdf (last accessed on 28/06/2019).

> representations thereof. Transmission by wire of encrypted signals is "cablecasting" where the means for decrypting are provided to the public by the cablecasting organization or with its consent. "Cablecasting" shall not be understood as including transmissions over computer networks.[164]

As the definitions have made it explicitly clear that the transmissions over the computer networks are not covered, it may be possible to conclude that the definitions have confined only to the traditional broadcasting aspects. However, the definitions have not been linked with the program which the broadcasters transmit rather they focus on sound or images or both. As the protection is based on the copyright, the definition should also focus only on the program which is invariably a copyrightable one. This was highlighted only by the Indian delegates during the SCCR meeting and they advocated for the inclusion of definition for program. Even in the working document formulated as per the 27th SCCR,[165] India had proposed changes to be brought in tune with the 'signal based approach' as mandated by the General Assembly (GA).[166] However, the position remains the same as that of 15th SCCR even today.[167]

Though the GA mandate was to confine the discussion to the traditional platform, keeping the term "any means of transmission" in many provisions has created concerns for many because, the same could be used to cover internet based live streaming transmissions within the scope of traditional broadcasters' right. The definition of 'retransmission' which was meant to explain the retransmission right conferred on the broadcasters in the 15th SCCR[168] and has been retained even in the present working document of 27th SCCR reads:

> (d) "retransmission" means the simultaneous transmission for the reception by the public by any means of a transmission referred to in provisions (a) or (b) of this Article by any other person than the original

164 *Ibid.*

165 WIPO 27th SCCR "Working Document for a Treaty on the Protection of Broadcasting Organizations", SCCR/27/2 REV, 2015, available at http://www.wipo.int/edocs/mdocs/copyright/en/sccr_27/sccr_27_2_rev.pdf (last accessed on 28/06/2019).

166 *Ibid.*

167 *Ibid.*

168 WIPO 15th SCCR "Revised Draft Basic Proposal for the WIPO Treaty on the Protection of Broadcasting Organizations", SCCR/15/2, 2006, at p. 25, available at http://www.wipo.int/edocs/mdocs/copyright/en/sccr_15/sccr_15_2.pdf (last accessed on 28/06/2019).

> broadcasting or cablecasting organization; simultaneous transmission of a retransmission shall be understood as well to be a retransmission;[169]

According to this definition, simultaneous retransmission by 'any means' would provide much wider scope to accommodate each and every mode of transmission including the transmissions over computer network/IP based transmissions. As apprehended, it is evident that the usage of the retransmission has been aimed to cover the simulcasting indirectly and extend the same to the broadcasting organizations. The relevant provision of the 15th SCCR reads:

> Article 9: Right of Retransmission
> Broadcasting organizations shall enjoy the exclusive right of authorizing the retransmission of their broadcasts by any means, including rebroadcasting, retransmission by wire, and retransmission over computer networks.[170]

Likewise, the 27th SCCR provision reads:

> ...the retransmission of their broadcasts by any means, including rebroadcasting, retransmission by wire, and retransmission over computer networks;[171]

The above provision was intended to cover retransmission over computer network under the treaty which was argued as not the mandate of the GA. If the broadcasting and cablecasting do not cover transmission over computer network, then obviously retransmission definition should not go beyond that. If it goes beyond that, then it would affect the authors' right over computer network which is generally considered as a separate medium of communication for which authors' permission is required. Such retransmission right including the transmission over computer network would be beyond the broadcasters'

169 WIPO 27th SCCR "Working Document for a Treaty on the Protection of Broadcasting Organizations", SCCR/27/2 REV, 2015, at p. 5, available at http://www.wipo.int/edocs/mdocs/copyright/en/sccr_27/sccr_27_2_rev.pdf (last accessed on 28/06/2019).

170 WIPO 15th SCCR "Revised Draft Basic Proposal for the WIPO Treaty on the Protection of Broadcasting Organizations", SCCR/15/2, 2006, at p. 41, available at http://www.wipo.int/edocs/mdocs/copyright/en/sccr_15/sccr_15_2.pdf (last accessed on 28/06/2019).

171 WIPO 27th SCCR "Working Document for a Treaty on the Protection of Broadcasting Organizations", SCCR/27/2 REV, 2015, at p. 8, available at: http://www.wipo.int/edocs/mdocs/copyright/en/sccr_27/sccr_27_2_rev.pdf (last accessed on 28/06/2019).

requirement and would amount to intruding into the authors' right over computer network. This was also advocated by the Indian delegates.[172]

Further, India rightly advocated that once the broadcast is fixed, there is no life for the signals transmitted and there is no need for post fixation rights. If there is no more signal, then there is no need for giving any post fixation rights to the broadcaster based on the signal based approach and it found a place in the document.[173] However, the alternative provided goes beyond the signal protection approach.[174] Thus, the important area of difference of opinion among the members of WIPO that prevented the finalization of the treaty is all about the extension of the right of broadcasting organizations to retransmission of the content received from their signal through computer network.

4.11 Critical Analysis of the Proposed WIPO Treaty on Broadcasters' Protection

When WIPO initiated discussions on the protection of the broadcasting organizations, the only technology which was left out from copyright protection even under the TRIPS was cable broadcasting. As discussed above, cable broadcasting was deliberately left from TRIPS protection, due to the fact that the problems of cable broadcasting remained as an issue at the domestic level rather than being considered as an international problem. Thus, when the problems emerged internationally, WIPO decided to address the issue by bringing a new treaty by which all forms of broadcasting would be covered including the cable broadcasting.

However, simultaneously, there was a technological development that changed the very nature of the cable broadcasting i.e., digitization of cable broadcasting. With the introduction of digitization, as discussed, not only the quality of content improved but also the issue of unauthorized use of signal has also been well taken care of by the technological advancements used in broadcasting. Thus, the possibility of unauthorized use of signal is almost nil due to the technological changes in cable broadcasting using digital signals. As mandated by the ITU, the entire word is moving towards digitalization of cable broadcasting with major jurisdictions already completing the process. According to WIPO's study, this will eliminate the unauthorized use of signal. By 2020, most of the jurisdictions including the Asian and African Countries would be

172 *Id.*, Annex.
173 *Ibid.*
174 *Id.*, at p.10.

part of the digital broadcasting not only in cable but also in all forms of broadcasting. If not by 2020 due to practical difficulties in changing to digital transmission, at least by 2025, the entire world would be using digital broadcasting and analogue broadcasting would be completely abandoned.

If the whole world is moving towards digital broadcasting and that is going to govern the entire broadcasting industry and if possible in the technological advancing environment, there is no scope for signal piracy. The prevailing gap under the Rome Convention has been addressed by the technological advancements. The existing technological gap in the analogue transmission could be well addressed by the TRIPS Agreement itself. If so, even the discussion in WIPO or a treaty based on the present 'signal based approach' is of no value.

As far as the expansion of broadcasters rights to the live internet streaming is concerned, as explained in the previous part of this text, it is mere transmission not broadcasting as the nature of the technology differs substantially. It is also clear that streaming technology is substantially free from unauthorized use of streams. The only possibility is the unauthorized use of content received from signals of the broadcasting organizations. In this context, the question is whether there is any justification to extend the right to simulcasting i.e., streams created from the content received out of the broadcasting organization. As substantiated in chapter 3, there is no socio-economic justification for the same and it will be an encroachment on the authors' right of internet transmission which should be part of authors' right of communication to the public. Even if there is any issue, it would be only on the content which could very well be taken care of by the authors' internet transmission right. In this context, it would be interesting to find out how the developed countries addressed this issue in their respective domestic jurisdictions and the same is discussed in the next chapter.

4.12 Conclusion

From the above detailed discussions on the historical evolution of the right of communication to public from broadcasting to live streaming and the broadcasting organizations' protection, based on Berne Convention, Rome Convention, Satellite Convention, TRIPS Agreement and WIPO Internet Treaties of 1996, it can very well be concluded that the authors' right in the context of live streaming seems to have been addressed but the protection of broadcasting organizations in the modern digital context is still under consideration. One possible reason could be that the authors' right over the content is adequate enough to address the issues arising out of retransmission of work based on broadcasting.

As far as live streaming is concerned, it is true that authors' right of internet transmission as recognized under the WCT, 1996 has not been expressly covered. However, based on technology neutral language used in Article 8 of WCT, it is possible to argue that any technological advancements in future is covered under this provision. Based on this, individual jurisdictions have extended the same to the authors through judicial interpretations based on the technology neutral language of the right of communication to public in their domestic laws. Assuming that the authors' right of live streaming has been recognized, then the remaining issue would be whether there is any need for creating a special right to the live streaming service provider similar to that of broadcasters. As we concluded, due to technological and socio-economic justifications, there is no rationale to create such special intermediate right in the live streaming context. Such creation would seriously undermine the authors' right.

Regarding the protection of broadcasting orgnaistions in the digital context, the right of author as recognized in Article 8 of WCT and interpreted by developed countries seems to be adequate. The reason being, the possibility of signal piracy in the advanced technological environment is substantially lower or even nil. Therefore, the international developments that have taken place after the Rome Convention on copyright, have only expanded and strengthened the authors' rights over the emerging technological environment and have not provided any additional rights i.e., neighbouring rights especially to the broadcasters. As of today, there is no international mandate to protect the broadcasting organizations beyond the scope of TRIPS Agreement.

With respect to WIPO's proposed treaty for the broadcasters is concerned, as concluded above, the extension of the broadcasters' right to the cable broadcasting which is left out of TRIPS is unwarranted today as digitalization has taken care of the piracy issue in this mode of broadcasting. Even digitalization has addressed the issue of signal piracy in terrestrial broadcasting too. Due to encryption techniques, signal piracy has become highly complicated. It can be stated even that it is almost nil due to technological advancements. If so, it is questionable even to continue with the TRIPS model of protection in the years to come.

Even in the context of simulcasting, automatic extension of live streaming to the traditional broadcasting organizations would go against the authors' right. Thus, there is no need of any further expansion of traditional broadcasters' rights to the internet, since they could not clearly establish any economic loss due to simultaneous transmission of content received from their signal.

Streaming is a separate mode of transmission and is a new market for the author. Since there is no possibility of piracy of the signal in the digital context, there seems to be no economic justification for extending the rights of broadcasters on the signal to simulcasting. The legal position of live streaming technology addressed in USA, UK and EU is discussed in the next chapter.

CHAPTER 5

Copyright Works and Live Streaming: a Comparative Analysis of the Copyright Protection in US, EU and UK

5.1 Introduction

The origin and growth of live streaming technology in the developed markets such as USA, EU including UK, etc., has resulted in the adaptation of the technology for communication purposes on a large scale. Use of copyright works for communication through live streaming raised the issue whether permission of copyright owner is required or not? For understanding this issue, we need to explore whether the copyright law of these jurisdictions have recognized authors 'right over the new medium/platform/technology'. Though the authors' right over the new technology has been recognized in a limited way internationally through the WIPO Copyright Treaty, it would be more appropriate to examine the response of copyright law in individual jurisdictions especially developed markets towards this new technology. In addition to examining the rights of authors of work it is also important to find out whether the person facilitating live streaming has been recognized a right similar to the right of traditional broadcasting organizations to prevent unauthorized simultaneous streaming of the content. Similarly it is also necessary to examine whether the right of broadcasting organization is also expanded to prevent unauthorized simultaneous retransmission of the content received from the signal of TV broadcast over this new platform. In this chapter, at first, authors' right over the live streaming technology in USA is examined and then followed by the broadcasters' protection in the same jurisdiction. The same inquiry is undertaken in the EU context which is followed by the UK. The copyright law in UK is studied to find out as an example how the EU Directives are implemented.

5.2 US Copyright and Live Streaming

The US copyright law from the very beginning of the 20th century has been accommodating the new technological modes through which copyright works

 | DOI:10.1163/9789004419155_006

are exploited under the public performance right of the author.[1] When radio broadcasting was commercially used, the communication of copyright works over the same without prior authorization was held as an infringement of authors' public performance right.[2] In a way historically, it is the practice that as and when, there is a technological advancement in the communication of the works, the same was considered as part of authors' public performance right.[3] Therefore, it may be safe to conclude that the public performance right is the one which widely covered all forms of communication of works to the public in USA.

In USA whenever any new technological advancements relating to the exploitation of copyright works were challenged, the judiciary rightly expanded the scope and ambit of the public performance right, and thus decided that such techno logical advancements would form part of authors' public performance right under the Copyright Act, 1909.[4] However, when the retransmission of over the air broadcasting via cable broadcasting *i.e.,* CATV without prior authorization was challenged before the Court for the infringement under the public performance right as the subsequent transmission through cable without any valid permission of copyright holders of the broadcast content, courts took a different approach.[5]

In CATV, the service provider had been merely receiving the signals of the over the air broadcasting and facilitated the people who were living in the remote area by extending the availability of the signal through cable. It is to be noted that the CATV service provider neither created the content nor edited content of the broadcast but it just retransmitted the content carrying signal to the unintended public of the broadcasting organization. In *Fortnightly Corporation* v. *United Artists Television, Inc.*,[6] as the local CATV service providers were

1 See for detailed discussion on the US Copyright Act and New communication technologies of the early stages, Makeen Fouad Makeen, *Copyright in a Global Information Society: The Scope of Copyright Protection under International, US, UK and French Law*, Kluwer Law International, London, (2000), p.35 and also see Lawrence P Simpson, "The Copyright Situation as Affecting Radio Broadcasting", 9 *N.Y. University Law Quarterly Rev.*, (1931), pp. 180–197.

2 *Remick & Co.* v. *Auotomobile Accessories Co,* 5 F.(2d) 411 (C.C. A. 6th,1925).

3 See Jane C. Ginsburg, "Copyright and control over new technologies of dissemination." *Columbia Law Review,* (2001), pp. 1613–1647.

4 See for detailed discussion on the same, Lawrence P Simpson, "The Copyright Situation as Affecting Radio Broadcasting", 9 *N.Y. University Law Quarterly Rev.*, (1931), pp. 180–197 and also See Jane C. Ginsburg, "Copyright and control over new technologies of dissemination." *Columbia Law Review,* (2001), pp. 1613–1647.

5 See for detailed discussion on the CATV litigation and its evolution, S.A Gold, "Television Broadcasting and Copyright Law: The Community Antenna Television Controversy", 41 *St. John's L. Rev.,* (1966–1967), pp. 225–238.

6 *Fortnightly Corporation* v. *United Artists Television, Inc.*, 392 U.S. 390 (1968).

making unauthorized transmission, the issue which was highlighted before the court was: whether the mere retransmission of signal via the cable would amount to infringement of copyright holders' public performance right or not? The Court opined thus:

> Essentially, a CATV system no more than enhances the viewer's capacity to receive the broadcaster's signals; it provides a well-located antenna with an efficient connection to the viewer's television set … … If an individual erected an antenna on a hill, strung a cable to his house, and installed the necessary amplifying equipment, he would not be "performing" the programs he received on his television set. The result would be no different if several people combined to erect a cooperative antenna for the same purpose. The only difference in the case of CATV is that the antenna system is erected and owned not by its users but by an entrepreneur.
>
> The function of CATV systems has little in common with the function of broadcasters. CATV systems do not in fact broadcast or rebroadcast. Broadcasters select the programs to be viewed; CATV systems simply carry, without editing, whatever programs they receive. Broadcasters procure programs and propagate them to the public; CATV systems receive programs that have been released to the public and carry them by private channels to additional viewers. We hold that CATV operators, like viewers and unlike broadcasters, do not perform the programs that they receive and carry.[7]

Therefore, it was decided that the CATV did not perform the copyrighted works publicly at all rather it enhanced the ability of the signal to be received in remote locations. However, the dissenting opinion of the same court highlighted how the CATV system's retransmission does not merely enhances the capacity of the viewers to receive the signal, but actually performs the work. The dissenting Judge, Mr. Justice *Blackmun* observed thus:

> … CATV has picked up the signals of a licensed broadcaster and carried them beyond the area – however that area be defined – which the broadcaster normally serves. In such a case the CATV is performing a function different from a simple antenna for, by hypothesis, the antenna could not pick up the signals of the licensed broadcaster and enable CATV

7 *Id.,* at pp. 400–401.

> patrons to receive them in their homes a CATV system does "perform" the material...[8]

As the dissenting judge rightly pointed out, the right holder/authorized person of the right holder can very well decide the geographical location of the reception of signal and make the same available to the public for reception. If so, the initial broadcaster has already intended to cover only geographical location which could be covered by the free to air broadcast and not otherwise. Therefore, any act of covering the left over geographical location by CATV would amount to performance and thus it would be an infringement of broadcasting right of copyright holder. As this was the dissenting opinion, the majority view i.e., CATV system does not perform was the interpretation given to the public performance definition.

The *Fortnightly's*[9] majority view was accepted and corroborated in *Teleprompter Corp.* v. *Columbia Broad. Sys., Inc.,*.[10] It further discussed the economic aspects of the retransmission and held:[11]

> By extending the range of viewability of a broadcast program, CATV systems thus do not interfere in any traditional sense with the copyright holders' means of extracting recompense for their creativity or labor. When a broadcaster transmits a program under license from the copyright holder he has no control over the segment of the population which may view the program the broadcaster cannot beam the program exclusively to the young or to the old, only to women or only to men but rather he gets paid by advertisers on the basis of all viewers who watch the program. The use of CATV does not significantly alter this situation. Instead of basing advertising fees on the number of viewers within the range of direct transmission plus those who may receive "local signals" via a CATV system, broadcasters whose reception ranges have been extended by means of "distant" signal CATV rechanneling will merely have a different and larger viewer market. From the point of view of the broadcasters, such market-extension may mark a reallocation of the potential number of viewers each station may reach, a fact of no direct concern under the Copyright Act. From the point of view of the copyright holders, such market changes will mean that the compensation a broadcaster will be

8 *Id.*, at p. 407.
9 *Fortnightly Corporation* v. *United Artists Television, Inc.*, 392 U.S. 390 (1968).
10 415 U.S. 394 (1974).
11 *Id.*, at pp. 412–414.

> willing to pay for the use of copyrighted material will be calculated on the basis of the size of the direct broadcast market augmented by the size of the CATV market.

However, just like the *Fortnightly's*[12] dissenting opinion, the dissenting opinion of this case also highlighted copyright holders' right and expressed his dissent that CATV does perform and thus has to take license from the holders of copyright.[13]

The Copyright Act, 1976, amended the definition of public performance to expand the scope against the interpretations offered in *Fortnightly*[14] and

12 *Fortnightly Corporation* v. *United Artists Television, Inc.*, 392 U.S. 390 (1968).

13 *Ibid.* The dissenting judge Mr. Justice Blackmun held: "The CATV system involved in the present cases performs somewhat like a network-affiliated broadcast station which imports network programs originated in distant telecast centers by microwave, off-the-air cable, precisely as petitioners do here. Petitioners in picking up these distant signals are not managing a simple antenna reception service. They go hundreds of miles from the community they desire to serve, erect a receiving station and then select the programs from TV and radio stations in that distant area which they desire to distribute in their own distant market. If "function" is the key test as Fortnightly says, then functionally speaking petitioners are broadcasters; and their acts of piracy are flagrant violations of the Copyright Act. The original broadcaster is the licensor of his copyright and it is by virtue of that license that, say, a Los Angeles station is enabled lawfully to make its broadcasts. Petitioners receive today a license-free importation of programs from the Los Angeles market into Farmington, New Mexico, a distant second market. Petitioners not only rebroadcast the pirated copyrighted programs, they themselves unlike those in Fortnightly originate programs and finance their original programs and their pirated programs by sales of time to advertisers. That is the way the owner of these copyrighted programs receives value for his copyrights. CATV does the same thing; but it makes its fortune through advertising rates based in part upon pirated copyrighted programs. The Court says this is "a fact of no direct concern under the Copyright Act"; but the statement is itself the refutation of its truth. Rechanneling by CATV of the pirated programs robs the copyright owner of his chance for monetary rewards through advertising rates on rebroadcasts in the distant area and gives those monetary rewards to the group that has pirated the program. We are advised by an amicus brief of the Motion Picture Association that films from TV telecasts are being imported by CATV into their own markets in competition with the same pictures licensed to TV stations in the area into which the CATV a nonpaying pirate of the films imports them. It would be difficult to imagine a more flagrant violation of the Copyright Act. Since the Copyright Act is our only guide to law and justice in this case, it is difficult to see why CATV systems are free of copyright license fees, when they import programs from distant stations and transmit them to their paying customers in a distant market. That result reads the Copyright Act out of existence for CATV. That may or may not be desirable public policy. But it is a legislative decision that not even a rampant judicial activism should entertain".

14 *Ibid.*

Teleprompter Corp.[15] As a result, the opinion of the US Supreme Court was rejected by the Congress. According to Section 106 of the US Copyright Act, 1976, the authors are given different exclusive rights over their works. Among those rights, the right to perform publicly is the one which covers all types of transmissions including digital audio transmission. By virtue of this right, the authors' right of communication over all platforms would be covered by this provision. The definition of to perform or display a work 'publicly'[16] which is otherwise known as public performances reads as follows:

> To perform or display a work "publicly" means–
> (1) to perform or display it at a place open to the public or at any place where a substantial number of persons outside of a normal circle of a family and its social acquaintances is gathered; or
> (2) to transmit or otherwise communicate a performance or display of the work to a place specified by clause (1) or to the public, by means of any device or process, whether the members of the public capable of receiving the performance or display receive it in the same place or in separate places and at the same time or at different times.

In this definition, introduction of transmission clause makes clearer that all types of communication by using any device or process would amount to performance in public even the content of such transmission is received beyond the intended area of the initial communication. By this, the CATV system has been well covered within the scope of public performance as intended by the Congress.[17] Now the question is whether the authors' right over live streaming has been covered by the same public performance definition or not?

The second part of the definition clearly states that any transmission or communication by using any devices or process should be considered as performance. Though the definition was made in 1976, the same can very well cover the future technologies as well. Such interpretation would be the most appropriate one because, the Act has not been amended so far since 1976 to

15 *Teleprompter Corp.* v. *Columbia Broad. Sys., Inc.*, 415 U.S. 394 (1974).

16 US Copyright Act, 1976, Sec. 101.

17 See *American Broadcasting Cos., Inc.,et. al.* v. *Aereo, Inc.,FkaBamboom Labs, Inc.* 573 US 2014.H. R. Rep., at para 63 ("[A] cable television system is performing when it retransmits [a network] broadcast to its subscribers"); ("[T]he concep[t] of public performance ... cover[s] not only the initial rendition or showing, but also any further act by which that rendition or showing is transmitted or communicated to the public"). The Clause thus makes clear that an entity that acts like a CATV system itself performs, even if when doing so, it simply enhances viewers' ability to receive broadcast television signals.

accommodate any technological developments rather the technological advancements have been accommodated by using the same provision. The Congress was of the opinion that it would not only cover the existing modes of transmission which were so prevalent during the time of 1976 or before but also to cover the future technological developments too. This is more evident from the very language of the definition of public performance which says transmission by using 'any devices' or 'any process' that would inevitably cover live streaming as well. This interpretation has been adopted recently by the US Supreme Court in *American Broadcasting Cos., Inc., et. al.* v. *Aereo, Inc., Fka-Bamboom Labs, Inc.*[18]

Even much prior to this Supreme Court decision, Pennsylvania District Court had held that unauthorized streaming by using internet would be an infringement of public performance right.[19] In this case, the plaintiff(s) alleged that the defendant(s) captured the broadcasted content on which the plaintiff(s) owned copyright[20] then converted into transmittable streams over internet in the specific website i.e., iCraveTV.com. Therefore, the plaintiff(s) contented that the defendant(s) had infringed their exclusive right of public performance along with other statutory provisions. The defendant(s) had agreed to the fact that they had captured the broadcasted content and streamed on the website. However, it was contented that the same was made available only to the Canadian people and not for the US viewers. The same was refuted by the plaintiff(s) that the same content was made available even for the US viewers.[21] Therefore, the plaintiff(s) sought injunction. From the facts of the case, it could be presumed that the nature of transmission involved in this case is streaming of broadcasted content over internet. After hearing both parties, the Court held:

---

18 *Ibid.*

19 *Twentieth Century Fox Film Corp.* v. *iCraveTV*, 53 U.S.P.Q. 2d 1831 [2000 WL 255989 (W.D. Pa.)].

20 *Id., at* para 3.

21 *Ibid.*, where in stated: "… any Internet user may access iCraveTV.com by simply entering three digits of any Canadian area code, one of which is provided to the user on the site itself, and by clicking two other buttons. Further, Internet users from the United States and elsewhere easily may revisit the site because iCraveTV causes a small file, or cookie, to be deposited in a user's computer during his or her initial visit so that the user can automatically bypass defendants' screening process. Although defendants have ceased streaming of plaintiffs' copyrighted programming since entry of the temporary restraining order on January 28, 2000, there is no dispute that defendants streamed plaintiffs' programming continuously from November 29, 1999 through January 28, 2000, despite several requests from plaintiffs that defendants cease doing so".

> The evidence set forth above and other evidence in the record shows that plaintiffs are likely to succeed in showing that defendants are unlawfully publicly performing plaintiffs' copyrighted works in the United States. Defendants do so by transmitting (through use of "streaming" technology) performances of the works to the public by means of the telephone lines and computers that make up the Internet. This activity violates plaintiffs' rights to perform their works publicly and to authorize others to do so. These infringements occur in the United States and violate the U.S. Copyright Act. Defendants have also engaged in contributory infringement by making plaintiffs' copyrighted programming available on the Internet with the knowledge that third parties (such as streambox.com) could and would further infringe plaintiffs' copyrights by further transmitting (and publicly performing) the programming. Defendants' streaming of plaintiffs' programming through the Internet, even with supposed security controls, materially contributes to these further infringements.

Though the case was for preliminary injunction, it was decided based on correct interpretation of the law and held that unauthorized streaming of broadcasted content would be an infringement of copyright holders' exclusive right of public performance. Therefore, it is very clear that the authors' right of streaming has been recognized through public performance right. It is worth to be noted here that according to US Copyright Act, the broadcasting organizations have not been provided with any protection and thus the broadcasters do not enjoy any special protection under the copyright (neighbouring right under copyright law) unlike other jurisdictions, because, it is understood in US that the authors' public performance right would cover the program carrying signal aspects as well. This position is very much clear from the US Copyright Act infringement provision that 'the beneficial owner of the exclusive right' i.e., broadcasters have only been given with the right of taking infringement action against the unauthorized use of signal.[22]

---

22 See 17 U.S. Code § 501. The provision reads; "The legal or beneficial owner of an exclusive right under a copyright is entitled, subject to the requirements of Section 411, to institute an action for any infringement of that particular right committed while he or she is the owner of it. The court may require such owner to serve written notice of the action with a copy of the complaint upon any person shown, by the records of the Copyright Office or otherwise, to have or claim an interest in the copyright, and shall require that such notice be served upon any person whose interest is likely to be affected by a decision in the case. The court may require the joinder, and shall permit the intervention, of any person having or claiming an interest in the copyright". See for the same, Shyam Balganesh, "The Social

Therefore, it is clear from the above provision that even the infringement action can only be initiated by the exclusive right holder. As a market practice in the US, the broadcasters are assigned with the exclusive right of the authors' work. As a result, it could be stated that since the program carrying signal aspect is covered under the authors' public performances right, the legal gap which existed for which the Rome Convention was brought in, has been addressed in the US by the authors' right itself. Perhaps this approach could be justified based on the understanding that as the ultimate loss arising out of any unauthorized uses of signal is the program/content; the copyright owner is in a better position to take action rather than any other person.[23] Even though the broadcasters signal has been given a protection under the Telecommunication Code, the protection is only to deal with their signal out of which further use of signal could be prohibited. Thus the remedy given to the broadcasters' is outside the Copyright law for their signal[24] which is not relevant for our present discussion. However, when a broadcaster deals with copyright content, if the broadcaster wishes to take any legal actions against any of unauthorized rebroadcasting/simultaneous broadcasting, there are two options in front of him. One is to request the copyright holder to take action against such unauthorized uses and the other option is take action with the authorization of copyright holder. This interpretation is also further corroborated and more clarified by the US Supreme Court in the *Aereo* case.[25]

In this case, Aereo commercially retransmitted the TV broadcasting over the internet for which monthly payment was collected. In order to enjoy the Aereo service, the subscribers had to log on into the website of Aereo to watch live TV over internet rather than traditional model of digital terrestrial TV or satellite TV. In order to facilitate the access to the live TV content over internet, Aereo built its own novel system of retransmission over internet by using servers, transcoders and small antennas. Based on the number of subscribers, the deployment of antennas would be increased because for every subscriber, an individual antenna had been designated and then, when the subscriber places his request on the Aereo website, the dedicated antenna of the same subscriber would begin the receiving of live TV broadcasting signal which would be

Costs of Property Rights in Broadcast (and Cable) Signals," 22 *Berkeley Technology Law Journal*, (2007), pp. 1303–1387, p. 1345.

23 This inference is derived based on fact that the copyright owners' consent i.e., exclusive license is required for even to initiate infringement proceedings.

24 See Shyam Balganesh, "The Social Costs of Property Rights in Broadcast (and Cable) Signals," 22 *Berkeley Technology Law Journal*, (2007), pp. 1303–1387, at p. 1347.

25 *American Broadcasting Cos., Inc., et. al.* v. *Aereo, Inc., FkaBamboom Labs, Inc.* 573 US 2014.

converted into transmittable data over internet with the help of transcoders. Once the signal is converted into data, instead of directly transmitting to the respective subscriber, the data would be stored in the server of the Aereo as a personal copy of the concerned subscriber for few seconds and then the same stored data would be made available to the subscriber by using streaming. Thus the subscriber who requested for the content, would be able to enjoy the same either by using PC, laptop, tablet, smart phone or TV connected with internet, etc., the entire process of Aereo system of streaming would be delayed by less than few seconds of the live TV broadcast.

According to Aereo, it had designated separate antennas for every subscriber and then the same would be stored in the server as the respective subscriber's personal copy in a dedicated folder. Such stored content in a specific folder would not be transmitted to anyone else. Even if there is more than one request for a same live TV broadcasting, then the Aereo would dedicate individual antennas for each subscriber. It means, for illustration, if there are five persons and they place requests for the same live TV broadcasting, then Aereo would activate five dedicated antennas of those subscribers rather than receiving from one antenna and then communicate to all five subscribers by making five temporary copies of the programme content.

According to the plaintiffs, as Aereo was offering streaming service of live TV broadcasting in its website without any permission from the copyright holders of those broadcast content unlike the cable and satellite broadcasters, Aereo could offer the service at a lower subscription fee. Without paying any due royalty to the copyright holders, as Aereo was streaming the live broadcasting content, Aereo was making profit out of the free to air broadcasting signals. Therefore, it was strongly contented that Aereo's streaming would amount to infringement of public performance rights under the Copyright Act, 1976. However, Aereo refuted the question of copyright infringement by contending that it was merely retransmitting the live TV broadcasting signals over internet and the deployment of individual antennas for every subscriber would amount to receiving the signals by the respective subscribers. Even the content that is streamed is also out of the signal received out of the individual antennas exclusively dedicated for a customer. Therefore, Aereo strongly contended that all such streaming would only amount to individual performances as a dedicated antenna is involved for every subscriber and the subscriber is enjoying his right to receive the content from the signal in the form of streaming. As this would only mean the private performance of the over the air live broadcasted copyright content, it was argued that there is no question of public performances out of this streaming and hence no copyright infringement.

While deciding the preliminary injunction, the United States District Court for the Southern District of New York decided that though the plaintiffs established the likelihood of irreparable damage to the plaintiffs in the absence of an injunction, the plaintiffs failed to establish a '*likelihood of success on the merits*'. Thus, the District Court denied injunction to the plaintiffs. In order to decide '*the likelihood of success on the merits*',[26] the judge relied on the decision of *Cablevision Case*[27] wherein the Second Circuit decided that in order to consider a transmission as public performance, the transmission has to be made available to the public. If the same transmission is made available to a single viewer, it would not constitute public performance.[28] Based on the *Cablevision ratio,* the District Court came to the conclusion that Aereo did not perform as it used individual antenna for signal reception. The Court observed:

> Indeed, in light of this Court's factual determination that each antenna functions independently, in at least one respect the Aereo system is a stronger case than Cablevision for attaching significance to such copies because, unlike Cablevision in which multiple copies were all created from a single stream of data, each copy made by Aereo's system is created from a separate stream of data.[29]

Against this order, the plaintiffs appealed before the Second Circuit.[30] The Second Circuit also confirmed the decision of the District Court and held that Aereo did not perform. While deciding the case, the Second Circuit also relied on the *Cablevision*[31] and held:

---

26 *Am. Broad. Cos.* v. *Aereo, Inc.* 874 F.Supp.2d 373, 405 (S.D.N.Y. 2012), it held: "Because the Court concludes that it cannot accept Plaintiffs' novel attempt to distinguish Cablevision, Plaintiffs have not shown a likelihood of success on the merits. And although they have demonstrated that they face irreparable harm, they have not demonstrated that the balance of hardships decidedly tips in their favor. As such, the Court DENIES Plaintiffs motion for a preliminary injunction." Available at: https://casetext.com/case/am-broad-cos-v-aereo-inc, (Last visited on 29/06/2019).

27 *Cartoon Network LP* v. *CSC Holdings, Inc.*, 536 F.3d 121 (2d Cir.2008).

28 *Ibid.* It held: "the transmit clause directs us to identify the potential audience of a given transmission, i.e., the persons "capable of receiving" it, to determine whether that transmission is made "to the public." Because each RS-DVR playback transmission is made to a single subscriber using a single unique copy produced by that subscriber, we conclude that such transmissions are not performances "to the public," and therefore do not infringe any exclusive right of public performance".

29 *Am. Broad. Cos.* v. *Aereo, Inc.* 874 F.Supp.2d 373, 405 (S.D.N.Y. 2012).

30 *WNET, Thirteen* v. *Aereo, Inc.*, 712 F.3d 676, 680 (2d Cir. 2013).

31 *Cartoon Network LP* v. *CSC Holdings, Inc.*, 536 F.3d 121 (2d Cir.2008).

> We conclude that Aereo's transmissions of unique copies of broadcast television programs created at its users' requests and transmitted while the programs are still airing on broadcast television are not "public performances" of the Plaintiffs' copyrighted works under Cablevision. As such, Plaintiffs have not demonstrated that they are likely to prevail on the merits on this claim in their copyright infringement action. Nor have they demonstrated serious questions as to the merits and a balance of hardships that tips decidedly in their favor. We therefore affirm the order of the district court denying the Plaintiffs' motion.[32]

However the dissenting opinion focused on the public performance from a different perspective as decided in *IVI*[33] than in *Cablevision*.[34] The dissenting opinion highlighted how and why *Cablevision*[35] cannot be applied in the present case. The dissenting Judge *Chin* observed thus:

> The RS-DVR was not designed to be a substitute for viewing live television broadcasts. Aereo's system, however, was designed to be precisely that. It does not exist only, or even primarily, to make copies; it exists to stream live television through the Internet. Its users can choose to "Watch" live television instead of "Record" a program, but the system begins to produce a full-length copy anyway because, even under its own theory, Aereo cannot legally retransmit a television signal to them without such a copy. Aereo's system is much different than a VCR or DVR – indeed, as Aereo explains, it is an antenna, a DVR, and a Slingbox rolled into one – and for that reason Cablevision does not control our decision here.
>
> I note also that in Cablevision this Court "emphasize[d]" that its holding does not generally permit content delivery networks to avoid all copyright liability by making copies of each item of content and associating one unique copy with each subscriber to the network, or by giving their subscribers the capacity to make their own individual copies.

By making clear distinction between Cablevision and the Aereo, the dissenting opinion voiced out that Aereo's act is nothing but public performance as it streams the content rather than merely storing in DVR. However, this could not change any legal position as it was merely the dissenting opinion. It is worth to

32 *WNET, Thirteen* v. *Aereo, Inc.*, 712 F.3d 676, 680 (2d Cir. 2013).
33 *WPIX, Inc.,* v. *IVI, Inc.*, 691 F.3d 275.
34 *Cartoon Network LP* v. *CSC Holdings, Inc.*, 536 F.3d 121 (2d Cir.2008).
35 *Cartoon Network LP* v. *CSC Holdings, Inc.*, 536 F.3d 121 (2d Cir.2008).

point here that the majority of the Second Circuit had failed to look back at its own decision in *IVI*.[36]

Against the opinion of the Second Circuit, the Writ of Certiorari was filed before the US Supreme Court. The Supreme Court decided the case in favor of the Petitioners. The Court held that Aereo's streaming would amount to public performance which is similar to the CATV model and therefore, the interests of the copyright holders should be protected.[37] Even assuming

---

36 *WPIX, Inc.,* v. *IVI, Inc.,* 691 F.3d 275. In this case, the defendant was involved in unauthorized streaming of the plaintiffs' copyrighted contents. In addition to that, the plaintiffs' broadcasted contents were also retransmitted live via internet i.e., live streaming by the IVI. The Court held that the IVI's live streaming would be an infringement of the public performance right and thus injunction was granted. It held: "Plaintiffs are copyright owners of some of the world's most recognized and valuable television programming. Plaintiffs' television programming provides a valuable service to the public, including, inter alia, educational, historic, and cultural programming, entertainment, an important source of local news critical for an informed electorate, and exposure to the arts. Plaintiffs' desire to create original television programming surely would be dampened if their creative works could be copied and streamed over the Internet in derogation of their exclusive property rights./Further, there is a delicate distinction between enabling broad public access and enabling ease of access to copyrighted works. The service provided by IVI is targeted more toward convenience than access, and the public will still be able to access plaintiffs' programs through means other than IVI's Internet service, including cable television. Preliminarily enjoining defendants' streaming of plaintiffs' television programming over the Internet, live, for profit, and without plaintiffs' consent does not inhibit the public's ability to access the programs. A preliminary injunction, moreover, does not affect services that have obtained plaintiffs' consent to retransmit their copyrighted television programming over the Internet."

37 *American Broadcasting Cos., Inc., et.* al. v. *Aereo, Inc., FkaBamboom Labs, Inc.* 573 US 2014. It held: "When an Aereo subscriber selects a program to watch, Aereo streams the program over the Internet to that subscriber. Aereo thereby "communicate[s]" to the subscriber, by means of a "device or process," the work's images and sounds. §101. And those images and sounds are contemporaneously visible and audible on the subscriber's computer (or other Internet-connected device). So under our assumed definition, Aereo transmits a performance whenever its subscribers watch a program./But what about the Clause's further requirement that Aereo transmit a performance "to the public"? As we have said, an Aereo subscriber receives broadcast television signals with an antenna dedicated to him alone. Aereo's system makes from those signals a personal copy of the selected program. It streams the content of the copy to the same subscriber and to no one else. One and only one subscriber has the ability to see and hear each Aereo transmission. The fact that each transmission is to only one subscriber, in Aereo's view, means that it does not transmit a performance "to the public."/In terms of the Act's purposes, these differences do not distinguish Aereo's system from cable systems, which do perform "publicly." Viewed in terms of Congress' regulatory objectives, why should any of these technological differences matter? They concern the behind-the-scenes way in which Aereo delivers television programming to its viewers' screens. They do not render Aereo's commercial objective any different from that of cable companies./Nor do they significantly alter the

that Aereo's streaming would constitute performance, the remaining issue would be whether the same is transmitted/communicated to public? It is precisely because, Aereo system communicates to one person only using individual antenna. In this regard, the Supreme Court held that Aereo's streaming would further amount to communicating to the public and observed thus:[38]

> Moreover, the subscribers to whom Aereo transmits television programs constitute "the public." Aereo communicates the same contemporaneously perceptible images and sounds to a large number of people who are unrelated and unknown to each other. This matters because, although the Act does not define "the public," it specifies that an entity performs publicly when it performs at any place where a substantial number of persons outside of a normal circle of a family and its social acquaintances is gathered.

Based on the above reasons, the Court equated the CATV with Aereo and held that Aereo's act would be very much covered by the Copyright Act and declared that Aereo performs publicly though it streams to individuals. Though there are criticisms against the decision,[39] it seems that the Court was right in deciding the case because, the authors' interest should be protected from unauthorized exploitations.[40] As result of this decision, the unauthorized streaming would be stopped.

---

viewing experience of Aereo's subscribers. Why would a subscriber who wishes to watch a television show care much whether images and sounds are delivered to his screen via a large multisubscriber antenna or one small dedicated antenna, whether they arrive instantaneously or after a few seconds' delay, or whether they are transmitted directly or after a personal copy is made? And why, if Aereo is right, could not modern CATV systems simplycontinue the same commercial and consumer-oriented activities, free of copyright restrictions, provided they substitute such new technologies for old? Congress would as much have intended to protect a copyright holder from the unlicensed activities of Aereo as from those of cable companies."

38 *American Broadcasting Cos., Inc., et. al.* v. *Aereo, Inc., FkaBamboom Labs, Inc.* 573 US 2014.

39 Sarah E. Claypool, "Aereo, Unlicensed Retransmissions, and Emerging Technologies: The Case for Congressional Action," 100 (4) Iowa Law Review, (May 2015), pp. 1789–1812, Aereo K Consiglio and FilmOn, "Technology's Latest Copyright War and Why Aereo Should Survive", 71(4) Wash & Lee L. Rev., (2014), 2557. EFF, "Copyright Law Shouldn't Control How and Where Viewers Watch TV", available at https://www.eff.org/press/releases/eff-files-supreme-court-brief-defending-internet-streaming-service (last accessed on 29/06/2019).

40 See for the same view, *WPIX, Inc.*, v. *IVI, Inc.*, 691 F.3d 275.

From Aereo's decision, it has been made clear that streaming would be part of the public performance right of the author of the work. By this way, the US Supreme Court has also recognized the authors' right over the new technology i.e., streaming. Even when we closely analyse Aereo's system, over the air live broadcasting signal is being captured by a dedicated antenna, with the help of transcoder, the signal is being converted into transmittable data via streaming. Thus, the content is only transmitted and not the signal as the signal does not exist after its reception. Therefore, the sole right of the copyright holder is being violated and there is no question of broadcasters' protection.

As pointed above, since USA does not provide any protection for broadcasting organizations, the broadcasters have to depend on the copyright holders. Moreover, the dependency can be very well determined between both. However, it is worth remembering that it is only the authors' right not the broadcasters' right which was addressed due to unauthorized live streaming in USA. Even though the broadcasting organization brought the case they argued it based on the rights of the author rather than their independent right to safeguard their economic interest. From the USA experience, it may be safe to conclude that the copyright holders' streaming right itself is sufficient to address the unauthorized transmissions. Even the retransmission of broadcasting over internet, would require authors' permission since it constitute a new communication over new medium. This permission should be in addition to the permission given for broadcasting the work since traditional broadcasting would not cover streaming. Therefore, it may be well concluded that the authors' right over internet i.e., live streaming has been recognized by the US Copyright Act, 1976 and the broadcasting organizations are protected from the unauthorized simultaneous retransmission over internet of the content from TV broadcasting provided they take separate authorization for the same from the author.

As we discussed in the previous chapters, the technological features are different, there is no technological gap which would facilitate streams being pirated. Hence, there is no economic loss involved. If so, authors' public performance right itself is adequate to address the concerns of live streaming, if any.

As far as, simulcasting (simultaneous retransmission of TV broadcast over internet) issue is concerned, the broadcasters have been demanding right of simultaneous transmission of broadcast over internet. As we discussed and concluded in the previous chapters, once the broadcast signal is decrypted, the received signal is exhausted and the content is further modified for the IP based transmissions and not the signal. If the traditional broadcasters' rights are based on signal, as there is no signal once the signal is decrypted, further transmissions such as simultaneous or deferred are based on content. Thus, the broadcaster has to get necessary permission to exploit the content over the IP network from the copyright owner as IP based transmission is considered a separate platform. Hence, there is no merit in considering the broadcasters' right beyond the signal. It was also observed in the previous chapter that there is no economic loss to the broadcasting organization on their traditional platform due to simultaneous streaming since internet is a new medium and a new market for the author.

Even if somebody captures the broadcasted signal and streams the content received out of the signal over IP network without authorization, obviously, there would be a revenue loss due to the unauthorized use of content over IP network. This is the problem of the copyright owner because his streaming right is infringed by illegal streaming and thus his revenue loss could be well addressed with the help of authors' right over live streaming i.e., through public performance right. As the US model does not provide any special protection to the broadcasters under copyright, there is no scope of extending the broadcasters' right to internet based transmissions. This is the position of live streaming in the US, let us discuss the legal position in the UK context.

5.3 EU Copyright and Live Streaming

One of the most important Directives of the EU on copyright is Copyright Directive, 2001/29/EC which is otherwise known as Information Society Directive.[41] Although the Directive has been brought so as to comply with its international obligations under the WCT and WPPT by the EU,[42] it has been further aimed to harmonise the copyright law in EU. The Directive intended to consolidate the exclusive rights of the copyright holders in the digital era by which a higher degree of protection could be offered to the authors.[43] Thus, the core objective of the Directive is to ensure that the exclusive rights of right

41 Directive 2001/29/EC of the European Parliament and of the Council on the harmonisation of certain aspects of copyright and related rights in the information society, 22 May 2001 available at http://eur-lex.europa.eu/LexUriServ/LexUriServ.do?uri=OJ:L:2001:167:0010:0019:EN:PDF, (last accessed on 29/06/2019).

42 See Directive 2001/29/EC, Recital 15.

43 See Directive 2001/29/EC, Recital 9. It reads: "Any harmonisation of copyright and related rights must take as a basis a high level of protection, since such rights are crucial to intellectual creation. Their protection helps to ensure the maintenance and development of creativity in the interests of authors, performers, producers, consumers, culture, industry and the public at large. Intellectual property has therefore been recognized as an integral part of property".

holders cover new platforms or new means by which they can exploit the works in the digital environment.[44] Further it advocates for the technological protective measures by which unauthorized access in the digital environment could be tackled.[45] In order to ensure uniformity among the Member State copyright laws on the neighbouring right protection, the Directive mandates a set of protection to be offered to them.[46] Therefore, the Directive plays an important role in clarifying the complex emerging new issues in digital context in copyright among the Member States. Let us discuss the communication to the public right in detail so as to find out whether live streaming has been covered under this right or not.

According to Recital 9 of the Directive,[47] the communication to the public right should be understood in a broad sense and should also cover all types of transmission including broadcasting. As it highlights both wire and wireless mode of transmissions, it may be termed as an attempt to cover all types of transmission and should cover the future means of communication too. Article 3 of the Directive covers the entire aspect of the communication to the public right.[48] According to the Article 3 (1) of the Information Directive,

---

44 See Directive 2001/29/EC, Recital 5.

45 See Directive 2001/29/EC, Recital 35 and 39.

46 See Directive 2001/29/EC, Art. 1.

47 See Directive 2001/29/EC, Recital 23. It reads: "This Directive should harmonise further the author's right of communication to the public. This right should be understood in a broad sense covering all communication to the public not present at the place where the communication originates. This right should cover any such transmission or retransmission of a work to the public by wire or wireless means, including broadcasting. This right should not cover any other acts".

48 Article 3, Right of communication to the public of works and right of making available to the public other subject-matter:

1. Member States shall provide authors with the exclusive right to authorise or prohibit any communication to the public of their works, by wire or wireless means, including the making available to the public of their works in such a way that members of the public may access them from a place and at a time individually chosen by them.
2. Member States shall provide for the exclusive right to authorise or prohibit the making available to the public, by wire or wireless means, in such a way that members of the public may access them from a place and at a time individually chosen by them:
   (a) for performers, of fixations of their performances;
   (b) for phonogram producers, of their phonograms;
   (c) for the producers of the first fixations of films, of the original and copies of their films;
   (d) for broadcasting organisations, of fixations of their broadcasts, whether these broadcasts are transmitted by wire or over the air, including by cable or satellite.
3. The rights referred to in paragraphs 1 and 2 shall not be exhausted by any act of communication to the public or making available to the public as set out in this Article.

authors have been provided with the exclusive right to authorize/prohibit 'communication to the public' of their works. Further it states that all the communication by means of wire and wireless would be covered. It also covers the on-demand communication as well. As the Directive is aimed to cover all the possible means through which the communication could be done including the future technologies, it is possible to infer that it covers live streaming over internet. Therefore, it could be inferred that the authors' right over the internet especially in the context of live streaming has been recognized. The same view has been recognized by the ECJ in *ITV Broadcasting Ltd.,* v. *TV Catchup Ltd.*[49]

One of the very novel provisions of the Directive is Article 3(3) which emphasizes on the nature of the authors' right of communication to the public. It says that communication to the public right is generally not exhausted by any act of communication to the public. The same is explained in the form of following illustrations.

1. If an author has authorized Mr. X to communicate the work to the public by a particular means/medium, then the remaining means of transmission would be with the authors. If Mr. X wishes to use another medium, then author's approval is required for any further communication.
2. In the same way, if an author has authorized Mr. X to include his works in the broadcasting, then the authorization has been given only for broadcasting. If the broadcaster wishes to retransmit the same over internet by using live streaming, then there should be a specific authorization from the author for live streaming. As the technical means are different and the market is different, for each mode of exploitation, specific authorization has to be taken from the author.

This particular view has also been reemphasized by the ECJ in its judgment on ITV.[50] Let us discuss the case in detail.

49 *ITV Broadcasting Ltd.,* v. *TV Catchup Ltd.,* (Case C-607/11) 2013.

50 *Ibid.* In this case, the claimants are commercial broadcasting organizations based in UK, owned copyright over their TV broadcasts and films. Their revenue generation was based on advertisements. The TV Catchup (hereinafter referred as TVC) which is the respondent, was offering streaming services of the free to air channels of the claimants to the people in UK only. Further, TVC ensured that those who possessed a valid license of claimants, they could only access its streaming service. Though the TVC was merely transmitting the contents of the broadcasting as such. However, prior to the commencement of the live streaming, the users were shown with an AV advertisement through which the revenue generation was done. Against this the act of TVC, claimants initiated the legal proceedings.

5.3.1 *ITV Broadcasting Ltd., v. TV Catchup Ltd.*

In this case, TV Catchup ('TVC') was a website based live streaming service provider which merely retransmitted the TV programs over internet by using streaming and hence the TV programs could be enjoyed over internet via live streaming.[51] In order to access TVC's streaming, users had to have a login account in which they had to disclose their possession of valid permission/authorization to enjoy the same broadcasted content by using TV. In a way, it merely enabled the persons who were the valid subscribers to TV channels to enjoy the same TV broadcast content over internet on TVC's website without any alteration in the original broadcast including the advertisements.[52] However, at the beginning of the streaming, different advertisements were displayed through which TVC mobilized its revenue.[53] As the login mechanism was technology neutral and device neutral, the users could use their PC, laptop, tablet, smart phone, etc., and the same broadcasted TV content would be accessed by providing the login details and the same enabled only for valid subscribers of the TV broadcast.[54]

In order to provide access to the broadcasted content over internet by using live streaming, the digital terrestrial signal and the digital satellite signals were captured with the help of a single TV aerial and a single satellite dish located in the particular location.[55] Due to digital broadcasting, the digital signal which was captured would be converted into content with the help of TV tuner cards which were generally in the MPEG-2 compression format.[56] When it was streamed over website, then the MPEG-2 was further compressed with MPEG - 4 format and then streamed with the help of software. As and when the server got a request, each subscriber would be provided with an individual stream with the help of the same streaming software rather than one stream for all.[57]

When a request was placed by one of the subscribers of TVC, they at first verify the login credentials and then possession of a valid TV subscription. After the details were confirmed the user was provided with the streaming with the help of its server.[58] While providing access to the streaming, the server would initially store content for few seconds and then transmit it to the viewers.[59]

51 See *ITV Broadcasting Ltd., v. TV Catchup Ltd.*, [2011] E.W.H.C. 1874 (Pat), para 1.
52 *Id.*, at para 2.
53 *Id.*, at para 3.
54 *Id.*, at para 9.
55 *Id.*, at para 5.
56 *Id.*, *at* para 6.
57 *Id.*, at para 7.
58 *Id.*, at para 12.
59 *Id.*, at para 13.

However, in all the cases, only few seconds of delay would be there. Even the delay is essential to complete the entire process involved in streaming.[60] Finally the subscriber is provided with the requested content over on its website in real time.[61]

According to the claimants, they owned the copyright i.e., over films, content of the broadcast and the broadcast itself under the CDPA, 1988 of UK and the same was accepted by the High Court as well. As TVC streams the broadcast over internet, it is alleged that it has infringed the work of broadcast[62] and work of films[63] by communication to the public and the unauthorized copying of the broadcast content as per the provisions of UK Copyright law. The claimants contented that intervention of the broadcast and retransmission of the same over internet by using streaming technology to the public who are not otherwise entitled to enjoy the content over the internet would amount to infringement of the communication to the public right[64] of the copyright owner of the content.[65] By denying the contentions of the claimants, the TVC argued that its act would only amount to technical assistance with which the broadcasted content would be enjoyed over internet in the same catchment area.[66] As the technical assistance is given to catchment area in which the broadcast is already made available, the technical assistance is merely given to the same old public not any new public. The argument is worth quoting:[67]

> TVC submit that the point made here shows that not every physical act of distribution of a broadcast signal is an act of communication to the public. Merely providing technical means which assist people more easily or

60 *Id.,* at para 13.
61 *Id.,* at para 14.
62 According to the UK Copyright law, broadcast is treated as work of authors and the same is discussed in the next part of this chapter. See for the same, UK CDPA, 1988, Sec. 6.
63 UK CDPA, 1988, Sec. 5B.
64 UK CDPA, 1988, Sec. 20. It reads: Infringement by communication to the public: (1) The communication to the public of the work is an act restricted by the copyright in— (a) a literary, dramatic, musical or artistic work, (b) a sound recording or film, or (c) a broadcast. (2) References in this Part to communication to the public are to communication to the public by electronic transmission, and in relation to a work include— (a) the broadcasting of the work; (b) the making available to the public of the work by electronic transmission in such a way that members of the public may access it from a place and at a time individually chosen by them.
65 *ITV Broadcasting Ltd., v. TV Catchup Ltd.,* [2011] E.W.H.C. 1874 (Pat), at para 84.
66 *Id.,* at para 85.
67 *Id.,* at para 86.

> readily to receive what they could in principle receive by other means does not amount to a communication to the public.

Further it advocated that according to the Inter-Governmental Committee of the Rome Convention, distribution of broadcast by cable would not constitute infringement and thus the distribution over internet would be covered by this cable provision. However, the Court did not accept the contentions of TVC. It held that TVC's intervention is in direct competition with the original broadcaster as the audience is deviated from the direct reception of broadcasted signal. The Court opined:[68]

> In my judgment, these limitations are all concerned with excusing from liability acts whose purpose is purely supportive of the original broadcaster's intention to have its signal received in its catchment area. Where, by contrast, the acts concerned are aimed in competition with the original broadcaster, and intended to attract the audience of the original broadcaster away from direct reception of its signals, they are within the notion of communication to the public.

By citing the above point, the Court differentiated TVC's intervention from mere technical assistance. It was held that TVC's streaming would amount to communication to the public of the content and thus it is an alternative service to the original broadcast. Therefore, it provisionally held:[69]

> TVC do not in my judgment merely provide technical means to ensure or improve reception in the catchment area of the broadcast. The service which TVC provide is an alternative service to that of the original broadcaster, including its own advertising content, and which is in competition with the service provided by the original broadcaster. It is operated for profit. It is intended to attract its own public audience. Its activities are therefore, in my view an independent exploitation, of the works and other subject matter. They are not merely supportive of the original exploitation of the work.

As the streaming access is given to the individual users and that is based on one to one streaming, TVC contented that it would not amount to communication

68 *Id.*, at para 91.
69 *Id.*, at para 98.

to public as the nature of communication is one to one and relied on *RecordTV* case[70] of Singapore Court of Appeal. However, the High Court did not agree with the same proposition and ruled that as the Directive provides technology neutral approach to the communication to the public, it would cover all types of communications of the present and future. Therefore, it held:[71]

> It would be an unfortunate result if a point-to-multipoint communication were to be actionable but a number of point to point transmissions were not.

To the argument that the communication is not to the 'new' public, the Court ruled:[72]

> I do not think that the fact that subscribers would be entitled to receive the broadcasts direct on their domestic televisions or computer screens means that the recipients of the TVC service are not a "new public". The Directive and the Act require only that the communication be to "the public", subject to the narrow limitations which I have discussed. If there is a communication to a new class of the public, then that is a clear indication that one is outside the exception.

Based on the above reasons, the Court finally reached to a preliminary conclusion that TVC's live streaming over internet to the mobile devices would

70 *RecordTV Pte Ltd.* v. *MediaCorp TV Singapore Pte Ltd.* [2010] SGCA 43. It held: "26 In any case, in view of the modus operandi of RecordTV'siDVR service, we find that any communications made by RecordTV to Registered Users who had requested the recording of a particular MediaCorp show were made privately and individually. We see no reason why the aggregate of the private and individual communications made to each of the aforesaid Registered Users should transform the nature of such communications into "public" communications. Although any member of the public could register with RecordTV to become a Registered User, he had no immediate access to all (or any) of the MediaCorp shows already recorded by RecordTV. This was because RecordTV's iDVR service was not a video-on-demand service whereby RecordTV shared a library of recorded works with Registered Users. Rather, a Registered User was only allowed to access and view time-shifted recordings of the specific MediaCorp shows which he had requested to be recorded. Thus, each Registered User had to make a request for a particular MediaCorp show to be recorded for him, and only he could access the show recorded at his request."

71 See *ITV Broadcasting Ltd.,* v. *TV Catchup Ltd.,* [2011] E.W.H.C. 1874 (Pat), at para 102.

72 *Id.,* at para 99.

amount to 'communication to the public'.[73] With respect to retransmission, the Court equated the internet transmissions i.e., the OFC broadband services with cable which cannot otherwise be equated with cable due to the technology, and held that the defence in Section 73 is available for such a transmission.[74] The High Court further stayed the proceedings with respect to the retransmission issues[75] and then referred the same to Court of Justice of the EU.

---

73 *Id.*, at para 95. It held: "*In my provisional view, the acts of TVC in intercepting the claimants' broadcasts (and works comprised therein) and making them available via the internet amount to acts of communication to the public.*"

74 The Court held: "I see no reason why the cabling system inherent in the internet should not be regarded as "cable" for the purposes of the sec. 73 defence. So I reject the bald "internet is not cable" argument. However, to take advantage of the section it seems to me that the whole of the transmission must be by cable. If that were not so, the defence would be available if the initial re-transmission was by cable to an antenna intended for widespread broadcast. It is clear to me that the signal must reach its destination by cable for the defence to bite. Accordingly I would hold that TVC cannot take advantage of the defence where their re-transmissions are for reception by mobile phone."

75 *ITV Broadcasting Ltd.*, v. *TV Catchup Ltd.*, [2011] E.W.H.C. 2977 (Pat), at para 24. The Reference reads:

1. Does the right to authorise or prohibit a 'communication to the public of their works by wire or wireless means' in Article 3(1) of [Directive 2001/29] extend to a case where:
   (a) Authors authorise the inclusion of their works in a terrestrial free-to-air television broadcast which is intended for reception either throughout the territory of a Member State or within a geographical area within a Member State;
   (b) A third party ([that is to say,] an organisation other than the original broadcaster) provides a service whereby individual subscribers within the intended area of reception of the broadcast who could lawfully receive the broadcast on a television receiver in their own homes may log on to the third party's server and receive the content of the broadcast by means of an internet stream?
2. Does it make any difference to the answer to the above question if:
   (a) The third party's server allows only a 'one-to-one' connection for each subscriber whereby each individual subscriber establishes his or her own internet connection to the server and every data packet sent by the server onto the internet is addressed to only one individual subscriber?
   (b) The third party's service is funded by advertising which is presented 'pre-roll' ([that is to say,] during the period of time after a subscriber logs on but before he or she begins to receive the broadcast content) or 'in-skin' ([that is to say,] within the frame of the viewing software which displays the received programme on the subscriber's viewing device but outside the programme picture) but the original advertisements contained within the broadcast are presented to the subscriber at the point where they are inserted in the programme by the broadcaster?
   (c) The intervening organisation is:
      (i) providing an alternative service to that of the original broadcaster, thereby acting in direct competition with the original broadcaster for viewers; or
      (ii) acting in direct competition with the original broadcaster for advertising revenues?

5.3.2 *ITV Broadcasting Ltd., v. TV Catchup Ltd.: Before the CJEU*

As we discussed above on the EU position of live streaming, the CJEU, after examining the Directive 2001/29, emphasized that the Directive is aimed to have much stronger protection to the authors by which they could reap the benefit of the exploitation of their works at the possible extent including communication to the public.[76] Further it pointed out that the definition of communication to the public under the Directive is not an exhaustive one.[77] It should be construed very broadly so as to cover the possible ways of communication. If this is the objective of the concept of the communication to the public, then it is very much possible to point out that the concept of communication to the public would be a technology neutral one and thus would include future modes of exploitation as well.

In this context, the Court held that mere authorization of the work to be included in a mode of communication or over a particular medium of communication, it cannot preclude the authors to use the same work in other modes of communication and the same is the intention of the EU Directive 2001/29.[78] Therefore, it is highly essential to get authorization for each mode/medium of communication separately from the authors.[79] Even the simultaneous transmission of the initial broadcast over satellite and cable for the same catchment area where it was already broadcasted, technology specific authorization is essential according to the EU law.[80] Thus CJEU held:[81]

> Given that the making of works available through the retransmission of a terrestrial television broadcast over the internet uses a specific technical means different from that of the original communication, that retransmission must be considered to be a 'communication' within the meaning of Article 3(1) of Directive 2001/29. Consequently, such a retransmission cannot be exempt from authorisation by the authors of the retransmitted works when these are communicated to the public.

Based on the above reasoning, the CJEU rejected the TVC's contention of mere technical assistance and held that mere technical assistance should be very

76 See *ITV Broadcasting Ltd., v. TV Catchup Ltd.*, [2013] F.S.R. 36, at para 20.
77 *Id.,* at para 22.
78 *Id.,* at para 23.
79 *Id.,* at para 24.
80 *Id.,* at para 25.
81 *Id.,* at para 26.

much restricted only to improve the quality of the reception of pre-existing transmission and not beyond that. The Court further observed:[82]

> Thus, the intervention of such a technical means must be limited to maintaining or improving the quality of the reception of a pre-existing transmission and cannot be used for any other transmission.
>
> In the present case, however, the intervention by TVC consists in a transmission of the protected works at issue which is different from that of the broadcasting organization concerned. TVC's intervention is in no way intended to maintain or improve the quality of the transmission by that other broadcasting organization. In those circumstances, that intervention cannot be considered to be a mere technical means within the meaning specified in [28] above.

With respect to 'one to one communication', the Court clarified the position by saying that it would be highly irrelevant to look into the nature of the communication.[83] Based on the above reasoning, the CJEU held that TVC's act would squarely fit into the concept of communication to the public of content.[84] As TVC does not possess an authorization to transmit the content of the broadcast, its live streaming would amount to the communication to the public of content.[85] Even the broadcasters have to take multiple technology/medium

82 *Id.,* at para 29 and 30.

83 *Id.,* at para 35. The only relevant aspect would be whether the technology facilitates considerable number public to access the same work at the same time. Therefore it held: "Thus, the retransmission in question is aimed at an indeterminate number of potential recipients and implies a large number of persons. Consequently, it must be held that, by the retransmission in question, the protected works are indeed communicated to a "public" within the meaning of Art. 3(1) of Directive 2001/29."

84 *Id.,* at para 39. It reads: By contrast, the main proceedings in the present case concern the transmission of works included in a terrestrial broadcast and the making available of those works over the internet. As is apparent from [24]–[26] above, each of those two transmissions must be authorized individually and separately by the authors concerned given that each is made under specific technical conditions, using a different means of transmission for the protected works, and each is intended for a public. In those circumstances, it is no longer necessary to examine below the requirement that there must be a new public, which is relevant only in the situations on which the Court of Justice had to rule in the cases giving rise to the judgments in SGAE [2006] E.C.R. I-11519, FA Premier League [2012] F.S.R. 1 and Airfield [2012] E.C.D.R. 3.

85 *Id.,* at para 48. After having the detailed discussion, based on the above analogy, the CJEU answered to the referred questions as follows:
"1. The concept of "communication to the public", within the meaning of Art.3(1) of Directive 2001/29/EC of the European Parliament and of the Council of 22 May 2001 on the harmonisation of certain aspects of copyright and related rights in the information

specific licenses from the authors to exploit the same in each medium. The concept of retransmission is subjected to the authors' authorization. Based on the facts, TVC's act would amount to simulcasting. As far as simulcasting is concerned, as deliberated under the EU's position, exploitation of works over each and every platform should be authorized separately by the authors. If so, simulcasting of the broadcast is possible only with the permission of authors as each and every simulcasting could be nothing but new transmission of the broadcasted content. Thus, the content owners' authorization is required even when you communicate to the same public through another mode of transmission. Further, it was observed that the profit element would be irrelevant and not an essential condition for the existence of communication to the public.[86]

As per the decision of the CJEU's in the TV Catchup -1, it has been made clear that that each transmission over different medium should be authorized by the copyright owner separately. It has been further clarified in the TV Catch-up -2 that retransmission over internet could be possible only with the authorization of copyright owners.

5.3.3 *Broadcasters' Protection in EU*

Unlike the US, EU has given protection to the broadcasting organizations under its copyright regime. The broadcasting organizations have been deriving

---

society, must be interpreted as meaning that it covers a retransmission of the works included in a terrestrial television broadcast

- where the retransmission is made by an organisation other than the original broadcaster;
- by means of an internet stream made available to the subscribers of that other organisation who may receive that retransmission by logging on to its server; and
- even though those subscribers are within the area of reception of that terrestrial television broadcast and may lawfully receive the broadcast on a television receiver.

2. The answer to Question 1 is not influenced by the fact that a retransmission, such as that at issue in the main proceedings, is funded by advertising and is therefore of a profit-making nature.
3. The answer to Question 1 is not influenced by the fact that a retransmission, such as that at issue in the main proceedings, is made by an organisation which is acting in direct competition with the original broadcaster."

86 *Id.*, at para 42 and 43. They read: "In that connection, the Court has indeed held that it is not irrelevant that a "communication" within the meaning of Art.3(1) of Directive 2001/29 is of a profit-making nature (FA Premier League [2012] F.S.R. 1 at [204]). However, it has acknowledged that a profit-making nature is not necessarily an essential condition for the existence of a communication to the public (see, to that effect, SGAE [2006] E.C.R. I-11519 at [44]). 43 Consequently, a profit-making nature does not determine conclusively whether a retransmission, such as that at issue in the main proceedings, is to be categorised as a "communication" within the meaning of Art.3(1) of Directive 2001/29."

their rights from the InfoSoc Directive, 2001/29.[87] Article 2[88] and Article 3[89] enable the broadcasters to enjoy certain rights. The relevant provisions are extracted here for further discussion.

> Article 2: 'Member States shall provide for the exclusive right to authorise or prohibit direct or indirect, temporary or permanent reproduction by any means and in any form, in whole or in part:
>
> ... (e) for broadcasting organisations, of fixations of their broadcasts, whether those broadcasts are transmitted by wire or over the air, including by cable or satellite.'
>
> Article 3: (2) Member States shall provide for the exclusive right to authorise or prohibit the making available to the public, by wire or wireless means, in such a way that members of the public may access them from a place and at a time individually chosen by them:
>
> ... (d) for broadcasting organisations, of fixations of their broadcasts, whether those broadcasts are transmitted by wire or over the air, including by cable or satellite.

From the above provisions, it could be inferred that the broadcasting organizations can use the wireless, wire and satellite mediums for broadcasting purposes. It is evident from these provisions that the rights conferred are post fixation rights i.e., reproduction of the fixation of broadcast and making available of the fixed broadcast content. It is not clear whether these rights also include retransmission of the broadcast by wire or over the air? Though the Directive uses the term broadcast but there is no definition for the same. In order to have clarity on the right of retransmission of broadcast by wire or over the air, it is worth examining the 2002 recommendations of the Committee of Ministers' for the broadcasters' neighbouring right protection.[90]

According to the 2002 recommendations, it is reiterated that the broadcasting organizations would have rights specified in Articles 2 and 3 throughout the Member States. According to this document, both broadcast and pre-broadcast

87 Directive 2001/29/EC of the European Parliament and of the Council on the harmonisation of certain aspects of copyright and related rights in the information society, 2001. Hereinafter, referred as InfoSoc Directive, 2001/29.

88 *Id.*, at Art. 2.

89 *Id.*, at Art. 3.

90 Recommendation Rec(2002)7 of the Committee of Ministers to member states on measures to enhance the protection of the neighbouring rights of broadcasting organisations, 2002, available at https://www.ebu.ch/CMSimages/en/leg_ref_coe_r2002_7_nr_110902_tcm6-4398.pdf (last accessed on 29/06/2019).

programme carrying signal should be protected. Of the different rights, recognized for the broadcasters for both pre and post broadcast signal, retransmission right is more significant.[91] It reads:[92]

> a) the exclusive right to authorise or prohibit the retransmission of their broadcasts by wire or wireless means, whether simultaneous or based on fixations;

From the above clause, it is clear that retransmission through different means of technology is recognized for broadcasting organization for their both pre and post broadcast signal. Use of the phrase *"retransmission of their broadcasts by wire or wireless means, whether simultaneous or based on fixations"* covers simultaneous retransmission of the content received from their signal over computer network (simulcasting). Thus, it appears the broadcasters' right on simulcasting coexists with the authors' right of communication to public on live streaming as recognized Directives and interpreted by the ECJ.[93] Though the Directive could not accommodate simulcasting initially,[94] it was through the 2002 regulation; the simulcasting has been extended to the broadcasters.

---

91 The relevant part reads: a) the exclusive right to authorise or prohibit the retransmission of their broadcasts by wire or wireless means, whether simultaneous or based on fixations;

b) the exclusive right to authorise or prohibit the fixation of their broadcasts;

c) the exclusive right to authorise or prohibit the direct or indirect reproduction of fixations of their broadcasts in any manner or form;

d) the exclusive right to authorise or prohibit the making available to the public of fixations of their broadcasts, by wire or wireless means, in such a way that members of the public may access them from a place and at a time individually chosen by them;

e) the exclusive right to authorise or prohibit the making available to the public through sale or other transfer of ownership of fixations and copies of fixations of their broadcasts;

f) the exclusive right to authorise or prohibit the communication to the public of their broadcasts if such communication is made in places accessible to the public against payment of an entrance fee.

Pre broadcast programme signal: Member states should consider taking measures to ensure that broadcasting organisations enjoy adequate protection against any of the acts referred to in a) to f) above in relation to their pre-broadcast programme carrying signals.

92 *Ibid.*

93 *ITV Broadcasting Ltd.*, v. *TV Catchup Ltd.*, [2013] F.S.R. 36.

94 Irini Stamatoudi and Paul Torremans, *EU Copyright Law: A Commentary*, Edward Elgar, (2014), p. 413. It reads: " 'Making available to the public' covers all on-demand services such as video on demand, pay per view TV, the selection of works (or subject matter) from online databases of, for example, films or songs where one can retrieve a work with the aid of a such engine or special software and choose the time and place to use it. This right

Though there was an attempt in 2008 to strengthen further the broadcasters' protection by bringing a new legal document for the EU on the protection of broadcasting organizations at par with the WIPO's ongoing discussion on broadcasters' protection, the same was annulled by the CJEU.[95] Therefore, the position remains same even today. However, as an example, let us look at how the EU Directives and interpretation on the authors' right of live streaming and the simulcasting right of broadcasting organizations is implemented under the Copyright Designs and Patent Act, 1988 of the UK.

5.4 UK Copyright: Live Streaming and Simulcasting

Being a member state of the European Union, the UK has also complied with the EU Directive, 2001/29 by amending its Copyright Designs and Patent Act, 1988. Like Article 3 of the EU Directive, the CDPA also provides the communication to the public right to the authors of the works. Unlike the US Copyright Act of 1976, the CDPA provides an independent right called 'communication to the public'[96] which is entirely different from the 'public performance right'.[97]

According to Section 20 of the CDPA, the communication to the public right is available for the following works. They are:

(a) literary, dramatic, musical and artistic works,
(b) sound recordings and films
(c) broadcasts.

Therefore, the general communication to the public is available to all these works. In addition to the general communication right, a specific right i.e., all electronic transmissions including broadcasting and other transmissions has been extended to the authors. It reads:

---

even applies in cases where one can choose works incorporated in broadcasts, which are available online to the extent that it is not the broadcast as such that one selects from a variety of broadcasts but rather the works in it. Podcasts where the user chooses to access a work from pre-existing materials are also covered by the 'making available' right. If one cannot chose when and where to retrieve a work then it is not the right of 'making available to the public' that applies but rather the right of 'communication to the public'. Such examples are broadcasting, simulcasting, webcasting, streaming and near-video-on-demand (NVOD) services."

95 *European Commission. v. Council of the European Union*, Case C-114/12, (2014).

96 The Copyright Designs and Patent Act, 1988 of UK, Sec. 19.

97 *Id.*, at Sec. 20.

> (2) References in this Part to communication to the public are to communication to the public by electronic transmission, and in relation to a work include–
> (a) the broadcasting of the work;
> (b) the making available to the public of the work by electronic transmission in such a way that members of the public may access it from a place and at a time individually chosen by them.

As the right is much wider in nature, it would cover all types of internet based transmissions including live streaming. This inference is precisely based on the EU's position as clarified by the ECJ. If so, the authors' right of live streaming would also be covered by the same definition as it is also an electronic transmission by which copyright works could be communicated. In the light of the above discussion, it can be summarized here that the authors' right of live streaming has been recognized and the same has been covered under the ambit of 'the communication to the public' as mandated by the EU.

As far as the broadcasting organizations' simulcasting right is concerned,the nature of protection given under the UK CDPA seems to be the same as that of the EU. Hence, it is worth examining in detail the nature of protection being offered to broadcasting organization under the CDPA, 1988.

Under the CDPA, the broadcast is considered as an independent work of copyright. The definition reads as follows:

> 6. (1) In this Part a "broadcast" means an electronic transmission of visual images, sounds or other information which -
> (a) is transmitted for simultaneous reception by members of the public and is capable of being lawfully received by them, or
> (b) is transmitted at a time determined solely by the person making the transmission for presentation to members of the public,
> and which is not excepted by subsection (1A); and references to broadcasting shall be construed accordingly.
> (1A) Excepted from the definition of "broadcast" is any internet transmission unless it is -
> (a) a transmission taking place simultaneously on the internet and by other means,
> (b) a concurrent transmission of a live event, or
> (c) a transmission of recorded moving images or sounds forming part of a programme service offered by the person responsible for making the transmission, being a service in which programmes are transmitted at scheduled times determined by that person…

As amended in 2003, the definition of broadcast has been modified to cover all types of electronic transmissions which are intended for simultaneous reception. However, the threshold to determine which type of internet transmissions could be covered under this definition is 'simultaneous reception'. As per Section 6 (1A), there are only three types of internet transmissions that could be covered under the definition of 'broadcast'. These are; a) any transmissions done simultaneously over internet; b) concurrent transmission of live events over internet and c) transmission for simultaneous reception of recorded content. Thus, it is clear that live streaming is covered under the definition, provided the content is taken from broadcast. Thus, the definition of broadcast refers not only to the in broadcasting but also refers simulcasting i.e., the 'streams' for the simultaneous internet transmissions of the content taken from the broadcast. If so, then it is pertinent to inquire who would be the owner of the work of broadcast under the CDPA, 1988?

According to the CDPA, 1988, the person who makes the broadcast shall be the author/owner of the copyright over the broadcast.[98] In order to determine the ownership of the work of the broadcast, it is highly essential to examine Section 6(3) of the 1988 Act. It reads:

> (3) References in this Part to the person making a broadcast, or a transmission which is a broadcast are-
> (a) to the person transmitting the programme, if he has responsibility to any extent for its contents, and
> (b) to any person providing the programme who makes with the person transmitting it the arrangements necessary for its transmission;
> and references in this Part to a programme, in the context of broadcasting, are to any item included in a broadcast.

According to Section 6(3)(a), the person who transmits the program shall be considered as an owner of a broadcast provided he has at least a minimum responsibility over the content of the said broadcast. However Section 6(3)(b) says that the programme provider i.e., the content creator or the owner of the

98 *Id.*, at Sec. 9 reads: Authorship of work.
9.-(1) In this Part "author", in relation to a work, means the person who creates it.
(2) That person shall be taken to be-
(aa) in the case of a sound recording, the producer;
(ab) in the case of a film, the producer and the principal director;
(b) in the case of a broadcast, the person making the broadcast (see section 6(3)) or, in the case of a broadcast which relays another broadcast by reception and immediate re-transmission, the person making that other broadcast;................

copyright works shall also be the owner of the broadcast. Since 'and' is used at the end of Section 6(3)(a), it is clear that both the broadcasters and the content creators are the authors of the broadcast. Thus, the ownership over the 'program carrying signal' is given as a joint ownership of copyright owner of the content and the broadcasting organizations.

Though the EU Directive mandates to protect the broadcasters under the neighbouring rights category, the CDPA provides protection to the content carrying signal of the broadcasters as work of authors, since it is jointly owned by the authors and broadcaster. Thus the authors' right of broadcasting under the communication to the public right and the broadcast right i.e., right over the content carrying signal would coexist. In the light of the above discussion, let us analyze the judicial decision related to live streaming in *Europeennes de Football* (UEFA) v. *Briscomb*[99] case. Union of the European Football Association i.e., (UEFA) which is the governing body of football matches in Europe organized championship league matches and the same was communicated to the public by licensing the broadcasters. The UEFA authorized many broadcasters to broadcast the sports through contract. 'Multilateral Signal' was generated by the host broadcaster for its own broadcasting and then the same was made available to other broadcasters for their modification based on the local needs. In this case, the first claimant i.e., UEFA along with other claimants i.e., the licensed broadcasters sued the defendants who were involved in streaming of the UEFA sports content which was broadcasted and the streaming was made available in real time on its website. By this real time streaming/live streaming, they captured the broadcast signal and then converted into content. The same would be streamed over internet in real time by which the defendants' subscribers were allowed to enjoy the sport content on the website rather than subscribing to the original broadcaster.

According to the facts of the case, it is clear that based on the contractual arrangements copyright over the sports content was with the UEFA. Even the copyright over other claimants' broadcasts were also with the UEFA. This copyright aspect was also accepted by the court.[100] UEFA contented that the

99 [2006] E.W.H.C. 1268 (Ch) and 2006 WL 1635072.

100 *Europeennes de Football* (UEFA) v. *Briscomb*, 2006 WL 1635072, at p. 3. The Court observed: "Paragraph 9 of the particulars of claim asserts that UEFA is the owner of the copyright in every broadcast of a UEFA Champions League match made on Sky or ITV channels and Mr Speck has carefully taken me to the particular contracts with broadcasters which lead to that conclusion. Then the particulars of claim deal with how the various ancillary works which are included within the live broadcasts come to have been created and come to have had their copyrights owned by UEFA. There is then detail in the particulars of claim as to the creation of the star ball logo, the UCL music, the break bumpers and the programme content roll. Mr Speck has then taken me through the relevant contracts

defendants had infringed their rights under Sections 17 & 20 of Copyright Designs and Patent Act, 1988. Section 17[101] prohibits copying of a work by others who do not have permission from the owner of the work. In this case, the defendants captured the broadcast using digital equipment and then streamed it. In the course of streaming they made illegal copy of the broadcast and allowed their subscribers to store it on their computers. Thus, it was contended that the defendants' acts were in violation of Section 17 of CDPA, 1988. In addition to the copying, the defendants streamed the broadcasted content without any change, though the broadcasters also enjoy the copyright along with the UEFA by virtue of their work of broadcast as given by Section 6 CDPA, as the case was not only related to live streaming but also connected with ancillary works, it was argued specifically that UEFA's copyright was infringed.[102]

After hearing the contentions of the claimants, the Court came to the conclusion that the defendant had infringed the copyright of the UEFA and held:[103]

> … rightly in my view, that this is a case where it is plain beyond peradventure that UEFA's rights have been infringed, and have, indeed, been infringed for some considerable time. He argues, and I agree with him, that there is no reason for the matter to await trial.

From the above case discussion it is very clear that the court had recognized the copyright owners' right of communication to the public by using live streaming and held that the defendants act would amount to infringement of

and I am satisfied that the copyrights are owned as the particulars of claim claim them to be."

101 Copyright, design and Patents Act, 1988 (as amended in 2003), Sec. 17 reads: Infringement of copyright by copying. (1) The copying of the work is an act restricted by the copyright in every description of copyright work; and references in this Part to copying and copies shall be construed as follows. (2) Copying in relation to a literary, dramatic, musical or artistic work means reproducing the work in any material form. This includes storing the work in any medium by electronic means. (3) In relation to an artistic work copying includes the making of a copy in three dimensions of a two-dimensional work and the making of a copy in two dimensions of a three-dimensional work. (4) Copying in relation to a film or broadcast includes making a photograph of the whole or any substantial part of any image forming part of the film or broadcast. (5) Copying in relation to the typographical arrangement of a published edition means making a facsimile copy of the arrangement. (6) Copying in relation to any description of work includes the making of copies which are transient or are incidental to some other use of the work.

102 *Europeennes de Football* (UEFA) v. *Briscomb*, 2006 WL 1635072, p. 4.

103 *Id.*, at p. 5.

communication to the public right. The same view has been once again reiterated in *ITV Broadcasting Ltd., v. TV Catchup Ltd.,* (Case C-607/11) 2013.[104]

From the above detailed discussion on the UK CDPA provisions, it has been found that authors' right of live streaming has been recognized even prior to the *TV Catchup* case. In the same way, broadcasters' protection was also extended to the simultaneous live streaming of the content received from their broadcast. Being an EU Member State, UK has well complied with the EU mandate by creating a coexisting right on broadcast for the broadcasters and the authors' of the works which include simulcasting right.

5.5 Conclusion

From the above discussion, it is evident that the authors' right of live streaming is part of communication to the public in USA, EU and UK. When we analyze the public performance right provision of the US Copyright Act of 1976 by tracing its evolution, it is possible to understand that the public performance right would cover not only the existing modes of communication but also the future once. The same view has been reiterated once again by the US Supreme Court in *Aereo*.[105] Therefore, the authors' right of live streaming has been recognized and well protected. Interestingly the USA does not recognize the broadcasters' neighbouring rights under the Copyright Act of 1976. The right of the broadcasting organization to initiate action to protect the signal from unauthorized uses is based on the contractual relationship with the author of the work. It is also noticed that the broadcasting organizations' interest over retransmission of the content received from the broadcasting signal is also protected based on contractual relationship.

When we analyze the EU position along with the UK, it is very clear from the Directive of 2011/29 and Section 20 of the CDPA, 1988 that the concept of communication to the public has been construed very broadly to cover all possible types of communication methods. This view has been corroborated by the judiciary in the *UEFA case*[106] and in the *TV Catchup case.* Therefore, it is safe to conclude that live streaming is now expressly recognized as authors' right. Regarding the protection of broadcasting organization on simulcasting, the reading of EU Directive and the 2002 recommendation, it is now well settled that

104 See *ITV Broadcasting Ltd., v. TV Catchup Ltd.,* [2013] F.S.R. 36.

105 *American Broadcasting Cos., Inc., et. al. v. Aereo, Inc., FkaBamboom Labs, Inc.* 573 US 2014.

106 *Europeennes de Football* (UEFA) v. *Briscomb,* [2006] E.W.H.C. 1268 (Ch) and 2006 WL 1635072.

the broadcasters enjoy simulcasting right. This is also recognized under CDPA by considering broadcast as an independent work jointly owned by the owner of copyright and broadcasting organizations. Based on the legal position of the authors' right of live streaming and the simulcasting in USA, EU and UK, the Indian position is examined in the next chapter.

CHAPTER 6

Indian Copyright Act and Live Streaming: a Critical Analysis

6.1 Introduction

The evolution of broadcasting in India dates back to the year 1923[1] when programmes were broadcasted by the Radio Club of Bombay. Since then, the broadcasting industry anchored by the state run All India Radio (AIR) and *Doordarshan* has witnessed considerable development. Local broadcasting from *Calcutta* and *Madras* continued till 1930, when the Indian Broadcasting Company took over the service with a capital of Rs. 15 lakhs. In 1930, India had a total of 7775 radio sets and this number went up gradually, yet, the Company was under financial stress due to global financial recession which prompted it to shut down its services temporarily. However, the resentment against the closure prompted the British Government to immediately resume the services. From 1940 to 1947, under A.S.Bukhari, the broadcasting sector witnessed momentous events and the AIR expanded at an aggressive pace. The broadcasting under British Government concluded on June 3, 1947 with the historic broadcast of the Viceroy, Lord Mountbatten, Jawaharlal Nehru and Mohammad Ali Jinnah's announcement on the partition of India.[2] At the time of its Independence, India had six radio stations (at *Delhi, Bombay, Calcutta, Madras, Lucknow* and *Tiruchirappalli*) which broadcasted Nehru's 'Tryst with Destiny' speech. When India became independent, AIR's network had a total complement of only 18 transmitters, six of them on medium wave (MW) and the remaining on short wave (SW). At present, AIR possesses 146 MW, 47 SW and 400 FM transmitters.[3]

1 See for the same details, available at https://archive.india.gov.in/knowindia/radio.php (last accessed on 30/06/2019).

2 The Times reports on Lord Mountbatten's radio broadcast on partition, 4 June 1947, " available at http://www.nationalarchives.gov.uk/education/resources/the-road-to-partition/mountbatten-radio-broadcast/ (last accessed on 30/06/2019).

3 "Genesis and Growth of Indian Broadcasting", available at http://www.indiantelevision.com/indianbrodcast/legalreso/Chapter2.htm (last accessed on 20/10/2017) and see further details available at: http://allindiaradio.gov.in/wpresources/ -AIRstationslist.pdf (last accessed on 20/10/2017).

 | DOI:10.1163/9789004419155_007

This was also the period which witnessed the emergence of television as a broadcasting medium in India. In 1950, the Indian Express reported that a demonstration of a television had taken place at *Teynampet* in Madras.[4] However, it was only nine years later, on 15 September 1959 in Delhi, India started with a pilot telecast which flagged off the use of terrestrial television in India; it was broadcasted from a makeshift studio with a small transmitter. The regular daily transmission started in 1965 as a part of All India Radio and was extended to Bombay and Amritsar in 1972. During that period, only seven Indian cities had a television service.[5]

Successive five year plans poured in funds to the development of the sector including the conceptualization of Satellite Instructional Television Experiment (SITE)[6] to promote television in India. During the initial days, when *Doordarshan* was still a part of AIR, it telecasted twice a day, once in the morning and once in the evening. In October 1959, an agreement was signed with UNESCO for providing a grant of US $ 20,000 to be utilized towards programme production, training, organization of tele-clubs for community viewers, supply of TV receivers for the tele-clubs and evaluation of project for expanding TV services. During 1977, when the *Janata Party* came to power, it brought a proposal to make two separate autonomous institutions for *Doordarshan* and AIR.[7] It also introduced frequency modulation (FM) stations at Madras, Bombay and Calcutta.

The year 1982 was a watershed moment which saw the introduction of a regular satellite link between Delhi and different transmitters. Prabir Roy, had the distinction of introducing colour television coverage in India during the 1st Nehru Cup which was held at Eden Gardens, Kolkata.[8] *Doordarshan* switched over to colour transmission during the Asian Games held in Delhi in 1982. This was also the year when national telecast started. After 1982, there was rapid

---

4 See for the same, available at https://news.google.com/newspapers?id=B8c-AAAAIBAJ&sjid=lUwMAAAAIBAJ&pg=4191%2C543248 (last accessed on 30/06/2019).

5 "Brief history of the TV in India", available at http://shodhganga.inflibnet.ac.in/ – bitstream/10603/94199/7/07_chapter%202.pdf (last accessed on 30/06/2019).

6 "TV in India", available at http://download.nos.org/srsec335new/ch13.pdf (last accessed on 30/06/2019).

7 While doing so, The Working Group on Autonomy for Akashvani and Doordarshan, known as the Verghese Committee, was constituted in the wake of the stranglehold of the Government on the media during the Emergency. Public opinion asserted itself in favour of creation of an independent professional body, protected from the day-to-day incursions of politics and free from the rigid regimen of rules and regulations of the Government. However this proposal fell through.

8 See "Cable TV", available at https://psmali.wordpress.com/2014/12/05/cable-tv/ (last accessed on 30/06/2019).

expansion owing to the setting up of Low Power Transmitters (LPT) throughout the country. The number of transmitters grew from 46 to 553 in just one decade. During the early 1980s, there was only one television channel namely *Doordarshan* and popular programmes televised were series on Mahabharata and Ramayana. *Doordarshan* added a second channel during the latter half of the decade called DD 2 came to be known as DD Metro which included both national and regional programs owing to high viewership.[9]

Post liberalization of the Indian economy in 1991, the broadcasting sector faced the arrival of foreign private television channels which challenged the erstwhile monopoly enjoyed by *Doordarshan*. The coverage of the Gulf War by the American news channel, Cable News Network (CNN) brought satellite television to India. CNN used satellite dishes to catch signals and then cable operators commenced exploitation of satellite broadcasting immediately. In 1995, the Supreme Court ruled in *Union of India* v. *Cricket Association of Bengal*[10] that air waves were not to be monopolized by the government and this judgement ushered in private players into the market and saw the emergence of Zee TV, STAR Network and Sun TV.[11]

In 1997, *Prasar Bharati* was established through the Prasar Bharti (Broadcasting Corporation of India) Act, 1990 and it also saw the emergence of an alternate method of broadcasting content through cable networks as against the conventional method of terrestrial transmission in which an antenna connected to the television was used to receive the signals telecasted by the broadcaster's transmitter. An alternative to over-the-air transmission used by *Doordarshan* was free-to-air transmissions used by private channels. These two forms of transmission were prevalent until the arrival of cable networks.[12] The launch of Star TV and Zee TV was a watershed movement for the industry; this coupled with post liberalized economy and the ascendance of Indian middle class fuelled the expansion of cable TV in India. In the first half of 1992, almost 4,500 households were being cabled up daily. That figure increased to 9,450 homes daily in the second half of the year.[13] The popularity of private entertainment channels provided impetus for the exponential growth not only

---

9 See for the same "DD Metro to stay terrestrial channel", http://www.thehindubusinessline.com/2002/06/11/stories/2002061102600300.htm (last accessed on 30/06/2019).

10 A.I.R. 1995 S.C. 1236.

11 "Media in Globalising India", available at http://shodhganga.inflibnet.ac.in/bitstream/10603/ – 27658/13/13_chapter%205.pdf (last accessed on 30/06/2019).

12 *Ibid.*

13 According to a study conducted by market research firm – Frank Small for Star TV., available at http://indiancabletv.net/cabletvhistory.htm (last accessed on 30/06/2019).

in cable TV but also in number of TV households. As of now, according to the BARC[14] India Universe Update-2018,[15] India has over 197 million households with television sets, with a 66% TV penetration.

In 2001, CAS or conditional access system, a digital mode of transmitting TV channels through a set-top box (STB) was first mooted by the government. Though, this initiative faced stiff resistance from cable network operators, government ploughed through resistance and implemented the digitalization. Dish TV was the first to enter this wagon. In December 2012, India had 7 major DTH service providers namely Dish TV (a ZEE TV subsidiary), Tata Sky, Videocon D2H, Sun Direct DTH, Reliance Digital TV (now Independent TV), Airtel Digital TV and the public sector DD Direct Plus (now DD Free Dish) with a total of over 54 million subscriber households. As of 2019, there are five DTH operators in India namely, Dish TV, Tata Sky, Sun Direct DTH, Independent TV (previously known as Reliance/ Big TV) and Airtel Digital TV with a cumulative subscriber base of 70.49 million.[16] The rapid growth of DTH in India propelled an exodus of cabled homes and India achieved 100% digitization of cable TV network in 2018.[17]

Earlier, the services were provided by indigenous satellites from ISRO such as INSAT 4CR, INSAT 4A, INSAT-2E, INSAT-3C and INSAT-3E as well as private satellites such as Dutch-based SES, Global-owned NSS 6, Thaicom-2 and Telstar 10.[18] Today, the DTH platform uses either the cable network or the satellite route to deliver content to the public. All DTH services in India currently use the MPEG-4 standard of signal compression. As of 2019, the country has a collection of over 880[19] channels of which 330 are pay channels with a total viewership of 197 million households.

14 Since 2016, BARC India is the sole TV viewership data provider in India, the committee consists of representatives from TRAI and industry experts.

15 See for the same details, available at https://www.barcindia.co.in/resources/pdf/BARC%20India%20Universe%20Update%20-%202018.pdf (last accessed on 30/06/2019).

16 See for the same details, *The Indian Telecom Services Performance Indicators*, available at https://main.trai.gov.in/sites/default/files/PIR_04042019_0.pdf p. 74 (last accessed on 30/06/2019).

17 *Ibid* p. 76.

18 See for the same details, available at http://www.indiantelevision.com/ – satreckon/satelliteindia/satellitesoverindia.htm (last accessed on 30/06/2019).

19 List of Permitted Private Satellite TV Channels as on 31-01-2016, available at http://mib.nic.in/writereaddata/documents/Master_List_of_Permitted_Private_Satellite_TV_Channels_as_on_31.01.2016.pdf (last accessed on 30/06/2019) and also see *The Indian Telecom Services Performance Indicators*, available at https://main.trai.gov.in/sites/default/files/PIR_04042019_0.pdf p. 74 (last accessed on 30/06/2019).

Digitization remains the key growth driver for the broadcasting industry. DTH services witnessed a steady growth of 4.3% percent in net subscriber base, adding 3 million subscribers to its existing customer base in 2018.[20] The constant regulatory push by the government and its emphasis on digitization, the advent of 3G and 4G spectrums, and the increase in penetration of mobiles and broadband connections have broadened the subscriber base of digital distribution. The new breed of smart TVs and high speed broadband cables have presented an excellent opportunity for the prevalence of IPTV.[21]

Live streaming in India is limited to sites like hotstar.com which also offers videos on demand. However, all major news channels in India offer live streaming services for free.[22] While Bloomberg,[23] being one of the latest additions to this ever-growing list, charges a certain amount for its premium content. There were many sites like newtvworld, myindian.tv etc., which offered the content provided by conventional television channels online for free however, they were blocked in 2018 on request.

With these details on the technological penetration and the market structure of the Indian broadcasting industry, we need to examine the provisions of the Indian Copyright law[24] in order to find out whether communication of works using new technologies including live streaming have been recognized as authors' right of communication to the public. It is also important to discuss the scope of broadcast reproduction right of broadcasting organizations and examine the need to expand the same to simulcasting. Let us do the same by analyzing the response of the copyright law from its very inception to accommodate the technological developments in the area of communication in India.

---

20 See for the same, available at http://www.business-standard.com/article/technology/23-77-mn-dth-subscribers-by-june-2010-trai-110100500228_1.html (last accessed on 30/06/2019).

21 See generally for the features of the new generation TVs and its capability of accommodating streaming, Lan Morris, "Smart TV Explained: Apps, Streaming, Upgrades and More", available at http://www.expertreviews.co.uk/tvs-entertainment/8080/smart-tv-explained-apps-streaming-upgrades-and-more (last accessed on 30/06/2019).

22 See for an example of the same, available at https://www.ndtv.com/video/live/channel/ndtv24x7 (last accessed on 30/06/2019).

23 Taruka Srivastav, "Bloomberg Quint aims to capture Indian business audience with its new digital live streaming service", available at http://www.thedrum.com/news/2017/09/25/bloomberg-quint-aims-capture-indian-business-audience-with-its-new-digital-live (last accessed on 30/06/2019).

24 The Copyright Act, 1957.

6.2 Technological Advancements in Communication and Copyright Law: a Rational Approach

The historical evolution of copyright law in India could be traced from the beginning of the 20th century. The copyright law in England has been extended to India from 1837 onwards.[25] Even the Indian Copyright Act, 1914 which existed in India at the time of independence was merely, an extracted portion of the UK Copyright Act, 1911.[26] The first schedule of the British –India Copyright Act, 1914 provided for the portion of the Imperial Copyright Act, 1911 that is applicable to British –India.[27]

The portion applicable to British-India described the rights provided to the authors' of works. In relation to the literary, dramatic and musical work, the following rights related to communication were provided under the same. It reads:[28]

> ... in case of a literary, dramatic or musical work, to make any record, perforated roll, cinematograph film, or other contrivance by means of which the work may be mechanically performed or delivered.

From a plain reading of the above provision of the 1911 Act which was made applicable to British India through the 1914 Act, it is understood that mechanical performance or mechanical delivery refers specifically to the then existing communication technologies. The legislature intended to cover only the musical sheets and loud speakers that were performed in public. The reason for such construction was that only those technologies penetrated into the British society and its colonies at that time. Radio diffusion was at its infancy at the time of the enactment of the UK Copyright Act, 1911 and the commercial aspects of the radio broadcasting was not known till 1920s in the UK.[29] Therefore, it is safe to conclude that this was not intended to be covered

---

25 T. G. Agitha and N.S. Gopalakrishnan, "The Imperial Copyright Act 1911 and the Indian Copyright Law" in Uma Suthersanen and Ysolde Gendreau, *A Shifting Empire 100 Years of the Copyright Act 1911*, Edward Elgar Publishing, (2012), at pp. 116–140 and Ilse Sternberg, " The British Museum Library and Colonial Copyright Deposit", available at https://www.bl.uk/eblj/1991articles/pdf/article4.pdf (last accessed on 20/10/2017).

26 T. G. Agitha and N.S. Gopalakrishnan, "The Imperial Copyright Act 1911 and the Indian Copyright Law" in Uma Suthersanen and Ysolde Gendreau, *A Shifting Empire 100 Years of the Copyright Act 1911*, Edward Elgar Publishing, (2012), at pp. 116–140.

27 The British-India Copyright Act, 1914, Sec. 3.

28 The Copyright Act, 1911.

29 Even BBC commenced its broadcasting in 1922. See generally for the evolution, Makeen Fouad Makeen, *Copyright in a Global Information Society: The Scope of Copyright Protection*

in the definition of mechanical performance or delivery. However, there were a few attempts made to cover the radio diffusion/broadcast under the public performance as the works were made available to the public to be heard. Thus, the post radio diffusion context was equated to public performance and the same was accepted[30] by the Australian Court.[31] Thus, the issue emerged out of new medium was somehow addressed in the Commonwealth. However, the associations which were entrusted to collect the revenue arising out of the performance of their work in public did not share the income in an appropriate manner.[32] Though the issues that arose out of the technology were addressed by expanding the scope of public performances, the authors did not have appropriate remedies to address all these issues. This position continued till the enactment of UK Copyright Act, 1956. Being a colonial country, the legal

---

under International, US, UK and French Law, Kluwer Law International, London, (2000), at p. 35.

30 See Staniforth Ricketson, *The Law of Intellectual Property: Copyright, Designs & Confidential Information*, LBC Information Services, (2nd edn., 1999), at p. 114.

31 See *Chappell & Co Ltd* v. *Associated Radio Co of Australia Ltd* [1925] V.L.R. 350 (9th June, 1925). In this case, the plaintiff, a publishing company of musical works, alleged that the defendants, without its license or permission, published and performed through their broadcasting stations thereby its performance right was infringed by the defendant. Therefore, the plaintiff sought restraining the defendant from doing so. However, the defendant contended that the performances were done in a studio which is in a close room and therefore it was not a public performance. By refering to the US case of *Remick and Co.* v. *The American Automobile Accessories Company*, the Court held: "the radio was not developed at the time the Copyright Act was enacted in 1909 may raise some question as to whether it properly comes within the purview of the Statute, it is not by that fact excluded from the statute. In other words, the Statute may be applied to a situation not anticipated by Congress; if fairly construed, such situation comes clearly within the intent and meaning of the Statute. A Performance, in our judgment, is no less 'public because the listeners are unable to communicate with one another or are not assembled within an enclosure or gathered together in some open stadium or park or other public place. Nor can a performance, in our judgment, be deemed private because each listener may be alone in the privacy of his home. Radio-broadcasting is intended and in fact does reach a very much larger number of the public at the moment of the rendition than any other medium of performance. The artist is constantly addressing a great and widely scattered audience, and is therefore participating in a public performance." The Court also deals with the question whether the performance was "for profit," and holds that certain advertising benefits were equivalent to direct profit; but as this question is, under our Act, not directly of importance, we need not further refer to this part of the judgment. The case was remitted to the lower Court for further proceedings. For the reasons we have stated we think that the plaintiff is entitled to succeed."

32 See Benedict Atkinson, *The True History of Copyright 1905–2005: The Australian Experience*, Sydney University Press, (2007), Chapter 4.

position of UK was applicable to India as well under the 1914 Act which was in force till the enactment of the Indian Copyright Act, 1957.

In UK, the Imperial Copyright Act was replaced with the Copyright Act, 1956 based on the Gregory Committee Report.[33] But, the provisions dealing with the rights of the authors of communication to public[34] and broadcasting organizations on broadcast reproduction right[35] in the 1956 Act seems to have had very limited influence on the Indian Copyright Act, 1957, since, the bill to enact

33 The Committee was meant to study and suggest the reforms in Copyright law of UK in 1951.

34 The 1957 Act adopted with suitable modifications many key provisions of the UK Copyright Act of 1956. Before discussing the authors' right of broadcasting under the 1957 Act, it would be ideal to examine the position of authors' right of broadcasting under the 1956 Act in brief so as to understand the position under the 1957 Act. According to the 1956 Act, the authors of literary, dramatic and musical were given with the following rights which are generally communication rights. They were: performing the work; broadcasting the work and transmission through radio diffusion. Further, the authors of the sound record is concerned, they were given with the public performance right and the broadcasting right. In addition to the public performance right and the broadcasting right, the authors' of the cinematograph film were given with the right of radio diffusion. The use of radio diffusion was to cover the wireless mode and the broadcast was to cover cable or wire.

35 As far as authors' right of broadcasting right is concerned, as discussed above, among the communication related rights, broadcasting and the radio diffusion are the focal point of our present discussion. From the very language itself, it is clear that the authors were given with the communication rights among those communicating their works by broadcasting and radio diffusion were given to the authors. When the scope of these authors' rights are analyzed, the broadcasting right and the radio diffusion right, it is worth to refer the definition of 'broadcasting' as defined. The definition refers "broadcasting by wireless telegraphy (within the meaning of the Wireless Telegraphy Act, 1949), whether by way of sound broadcasting or of television." The definition of broadcasting again refers broadcasting. While this is the definition, in general, from the authors' point of view, broadcasting refers to 'the act of transmission'. It means the transmission right is with the authors', hence the broadcasters require a license to communicate by broadcasting or radio diffusion. Though, it may be possible to argue that the scope and ambit of the broadcasting right and the radio diffusion right is to refer the act of communication/transmission, then we need to examine the scope of broadcasters' right. In the UK, the broadcast has been given with the status of 'work' and the same position remains, even today. Though, the 1956 Act did not have a definition for broadcast, as the broadcast is for the purpose of fulfilling the authors' right of communication i.e., by broadcasting and radio diffusion, after getting proper authorization of the authors' consent to transmit the work by generating a signal. It means, broadcast refers to the signal which is generated for broadcasting the work. As we analysed and discussed in the international scenario of the authors' right of broadcasting, because of the inadequacy of the authors' right of broadcasting to address the signal piracy due to which the legal gap was found and envisaged to be addressed internationally by Rome. That the same signal issue was addressed well before the Rome Convention under the 1956 Act.

independent India's first Copyright Act was introduced in the Parliament in 1955 and passed in 1957. This is evident from the difference in language used in the Indian Act, the details of which are discussed below.

With regard to the right of communication to the public of the works, two specific rights were recognized under the 1957 Act – the public performance right and the right of radio-diffusion[36] so as to cover the then available

---

36 The Copyright Act, 1957 (without amendment), Sec. 14 which recognized the radio diffusion as authors' right of communication. It read: Meaning of copyright:- (1) For the purposes of this Act, "copyright" means the exclusive right, by virtue of and subject to the provisions of, this Act, – (a) in the case of a literary, dramatic or musical work, to do and authorize the doing of any of the following acts, namely:
   (i) to reproduce the work in any material form;
   (ii) to publish the work;
   (iii) to perform the work in public;
   (iv) to produce, reproduce, perform or publish any translation of the work;
   (vi) to communicate the work by radio-diffusion or to communicate to the public by a loud-speaker or any other similar instrument the radio-diffusion of the work;
   (vii) to make any adaptation of the work;
   (viii) to do in relation to a translation or an adaptation of the work any of the acts specified in relation to the work in clauses (i) to (vi);
   (b) in the case of an artistic work, to do or authorise the doing of any of the following acts, namely:
   (i) to reproduce the work in any material form;
   (ii) to publish the work;
   (iii) to include the work in any cinematograph film;
   (iv) to make any adaptation of the work;
   (v) to do in relation to an adaptation of the work any of the acts specified in relation to the work in clauses (i) to (iii).
   (c) in the case of a cinematograph film, to do or authorise the doing of any of the following acts, namely:
   (i) to make a copy of the film;
   (ii) to cause the film, in so far as it consists of visual images, to be seen in public and, in so far as it consists of sounds, to be heard in public;
   (iii) to make any record embodying the recording in any part of the sound track associated with the film by utilising such sound track;
   (iv) to communicate the film by radio-diffusion;
   (d) in the case of a record, to do or authorise the doing of any of the following acts by utilising the record, namely:
   (i) to make any other record embodying the same recording;
   (ii) to cause the recording embodied in the record to be heard in public;
   (iii) to communicate the recording embodied in the record by radio-diffusion.
   (2) Any reference in sub-section (1) to the doing of any act in relation to a work or a translation or an adaptation thereof shall include a reference to the doing of that act in relation to a substantial part thereof.

technologies. These include performances by radio-diffusion, loud-speaker or any other similar instrument of the radio-diffusion of the work. By this express inclusion, the authors were given with the right of exploiting their work over the technologies which reached the Indian society. It is interesting to note that even the definition of the performance also referred radio diffusion and it appears that this was aimed to cover the exhibition of the cinematograph film and radio diffusion.[37] In order to understand the scope and meaning of radio diffusion, we need to trace the definition of the same. It reads:[38]

> Radio-diffusion includes communication to the public by any means of wireless diffusion whether in the form of sounds or visual images or both.

While reading the authors' right of radio diffusion and the definition of performance in the light of the definition of radio diffusion, it is clear that radio diffusion under the 1957 Act refers to the act of diffusion of the work. The use of term 'communication to the public' in the beginning of the definition also makes it clear that the authors were given with the right of transmission only based on the then existing technology of diffusion. The terminology, 'radio diffusion' gives an impression that the right is covered only for radio. But, the definition covers "sound or visual images or both" giving an indication that the legislative intent was to cover both radio and televisions. In this context, it may be interesting to note that the language used in the UK Act 1956 is 'broadcasting' covering the act of diffusion through both radio and television.[39] Reading of the definition of broadcasting used in the UK Act and radio-diffusion used in the India Act gives the impression that nature of the right given to the authors is same even though the language is different i.e., the right to give permission to diffuse the work through radio or television. Thus, the authors' right of radio diffusion i.e., act of transmission was aimed to cover both radio diffusion and TV broadcasting which started slowly penetrating to India. From the analysis of the technology for radio diffusion in the earlier chapter, it is very clear that it was the signal technology that was intended to be captured in this

37 See Copyright Act, 1957(without amendment), Sec. 2 (q). It read: "performance" includes any mode of visual or acoustic presentation, including any such presentation by the exhibition of a cinematograph film, or by means of radio-diffusion, or by the use of a record, or by any other means and, in relation to a lecture, includes the delivery of such lecture.

38 See Copyright Act, 1957(without amendment), Sec. 2 (v). The same has been deleted by the 1984 Amendment Act.

39 See UK Copyright Act, 1956, Sec. 48.

definition. When we look at the nature of the definition, as the word 'includes' was used, it could very well be considered as an inclusive definition and extensive in nature and thus it might accommodate other similar wireless diffusion techniques. Thus, use of the term '*any means*' of wireless diffusion would cover even future signal technologies such as satellite, which emerged as one of the important modes of communication in the 1970s. Hence, it is possible for one to argue that, since, satellite is also wireless communication through the diffusion of signal, and the same could be covered under the definition of radio diffusion. Therefore, the authors' right of communication could be extended to the satellite as well without amending the 1957 Act. However, the language of the legislature was not flexible enough to cover the future technologies in the same definition, since, it is confined to wireless. Since the right of the author covers only the right to diffuse the content carrying signal and not the signal, there was a need to protect the signal (broadcast) generated by broadcasting organizations for diffusion. A separate right called 'broadcast reproduction right' was recognized to them in Section 37 of the Act and the details will be discussed separately.

When the satellite and cable based broadcasting started in India in the 1980s, there was a need for incorporating cable broadcasting also within the definition so that the authors could enjoy the economic benefit of enhanced broadcasting services. When the technology reached the market, the legislature incorporated the same technology by amending the Act in 1983.[40] For the purpose of incorporating the satellite communication, the Act was amended and new definitions 'broadcast' and 'communication to the public' were added. The definitions read thus:

> "Communication to the public" means communication to the public in whatever manner, including communication through satellite.'[41]
>
> "broadcast" means communication to the public–
>
> (i) by any means of wireless diffusion, whether in any one or more of the forms of
>
> signs, sounds or visual images; or
>
> (ii) by wire,
>
> and includes a re-broadcast;[42]

---

40 The same is available at http://www.egazette.nic.in/WriteReadData/1983/E-0919-1983-0026-40695.pdf (last accessed on 20/10/2017).

41 See Indian Copyright Act, 1957 (as amended in 1983), Sec. 2 (ff).

42 See Indian Copyright Act, 1957 (as amended in 1983), Sec. 2 (dd).

Though the radio diffusion definition was substituted with broadcast, in essence, the nature of the definition remains the same, but, it was extended to cover some more mediums such as cable in addition to wireless diffusion. The use of the word 'diffusion' in the definition also makes it clear that it is the signal based technology that is covered in this definition. Even though the word 'broadcast' was used rather than 'broadcasting', the definitions of broadcast and communication to public makes it clear that it is the right to diffuse the work to the public that is covered. Thus, it is evident that the term broadcast is used as a noun (broadcasting) to describe the act of diffusion of the work using signals (transmission) rather than to refer the signal.[43] It appears that the appropriate term should have been 'broadcasting' as used in the Bern Convention[44] and the UK Act[45] rather than 'broadcast' particularly in the context of the term broadcast appearing in Section 37 dealing with 'broadcast reproduction right' of the broadcasting organizations protecting the signals generated by them to diffuse the work to the public.[46] Thus, it could be safely concluded that it is the authors' right of broadcasting i.e., the act of diffusion of works, was given to the authors over the then existing signal based technologies and this also included the right of re-broadcasting of the broadcast.

The fast technological changes in the field of communication that took place in India during the 1980's forced the Parliament again to amend the Copyright Act in 1994.[47] This further expanded the scope of right of communication to pubic. The different technology specific rights given under Section 14 were consolidated to 'perform the work in public or communicate it to public'[48] by adding a new definition of 'communication to the public'.[49] However, regarding

43 The term "broadcast" is used as verb, noun and adjective. It is used as a noun to indicate the programme. See for details, *Cambridge Dictionary*, available at http://dictionary.cambridge.org/dictionary/english/broadcast. This term is used is also used interchangeably with broadcasting based on context (last accessed on 20/10/2017).

44 See Berne Convention, Art.11 *bis*.

45 See UK Copyright Act, 1956, Sec. 48.

46 The implication of the definition of broadcast to Section 37 and the overlap of it with the right of the author if any is discussed separately below.

47 The object and reasons of the Bill read: " to further clarify the law in respect of cable, satellite and other means of simultaneous communication of works to more than one household or private places of residence, including the residential rooms of a hotel or hostel."

48 See Sec. 14 (a) (iii).

49 Sec. 2 (ff) read: "communication to the public" means making any work available for being seen or heard or otherwise enjoyed by the public directly or by any means of display or diffusion other than by issuing copies of such work regardless of whether any member of the public actually sees, hears or otherwise enjoys the work so made available.

broadcasting, the technology based on signal diffusion was retained by reintroducing the term 'diffusion' in the expanded definition of communication to the public along with display.[50] This is further evident from the explanation added to the definition, extending the protection to communication of works through satellites and cable to households, residential area and hotels. Though the legislature wanted to have a technology neutral definition to cover the then existing technologies, it is indeed a technology specific definition, as it specifies technologies like display, diffusion, cable and satellite. Hence, it is safe to conclude that the definition of communication to the public included the right of broadcasting of the author though the word broadcast was deleted from Section 14. But, the only important implication is the failure to include the right of 're-*broadcasting*' of the author in the definition which was recognized under Berne Convention and was covered under the definition of broadcast. Further, the definition of the performance was substituted with a new definition[51] confining it to performers' rights provided to performers under this amendment Act.[52]

In this context, it is worth noting that the right of reproduction was extended from the traditional technology to new emerging digital technology by including the right of 'storing of it any medium by electronic means'.[53] This has the potential of protecting the reproduction right of the authors even in internet. It is also important to point out that the right of communication to public is extended to on demand services by use of the language 'regardless of whether any member of the public actually sees, hears or otherwise enjoys the works so made available'. It is to be noted that though the definition included 'any means', it is confined to display or diffusion. Thus, it is evident that the legislature had no intention to extend the right of communication to the public

Explanation – For the purposes of this clause, communication through satellite or cable or any other means of simultaneous communication to more than one household or place of residence including residential rooms of any hotel or hostel shall be deemed to be communication to the public.

50 It is to be noted that the definition of communication to public introduced in 1983 was technology neutral and the diffusion technology was included in the definition of broadcast.

51 Sec. 2 (q): "performance", in relation to performer's right, means any visual or accoustic presentation made live by one or more performers; and Sec. 2 (qq): "performer" includes an actor, singer, musician, dancer, acrobat juggler, conjurer, snake charmer, a person delivering a lecture or any other person who makes a performance.

52 See Sec. 38.

53 Sec. 14 (a) (i): to reproduce the work in any material form including the storing of it in any medium by electronic means;

to computer networks (internet) based transmissions. The reason seems to be the non availability of the technology and its penetration to the market at that time.

The coverage to then existing technology is further evident from the interpretation of the right of communication to public by different High Courts.[54] The Courts made it clear that this is a bundle of right for different means of communication that could be enjoyed separately and includes exhibition/distribution/exploitation using Traditional TV, Satellite TV, Cable TV, transmission over High Seas, Air, DVD or Video.[55]

Hence, if the term broadcast is retained in any provision dealing with right of author, it must be understood as the right of diffusion of work using signal based technology that forms part of the definition of communication to public.[56] It may be noted here that there are changes introduced in section 37 dealing with '*broadcast reproduction right*' in the 1994 Amendment and the implications of the definitions on this provision and overlap if any with the right of the authors is discussed in detail separately.

Therefore, historically, it has been the practice of the Indian legislature that as and when the technology penetrates into the market for exploitation of the authors' works, the same was included as authors' right by way of amendment. In this scenario, we need to examine whether the definition of '*communication to the public*' as amended in 2012, would include the live streaming technology or not? Let us examine the same in the next part.

6.3 Authors' Right of Live Streaming: an Unarticulated Area

The 2012 Amendment of the Copyright Act, 1957 added the words '*whether simultaneously*' and re-arranged the last part of the definition of communication to the public.[57] In order to understand whether live streaming is included

---

54 *Maganlal Savani* v. *Rupam Pictures (P) Ltd.*, 2000 P.T.C. 556 (Bom.), *Video Master* v. *Nishi Productions*, 1998 (18) P.T.C. 117, *Raj Video Vision* v. *K. Mohan Krishna*, A.I.R. 1998 Mad. 294 and *Entertainment Network (India) Ltd.*, v. *Super Cassette Industries Ltd.*, 2008 (37) P.T.C. 353 (S.C.).

55 *Maganlal Savani* v. *Rupam Pictures (P) Ltd.*, 2000 P.T.C. 556 (Bom.), at p. 560.

56 For example the term "broadcast" is retained in Section 31 dealing with compulsory licence. It is interesting to note that the new Section 31D introduced in 2012 also uses the term broadcast.

57 The Copyright Act, 1957, Sec. 14 deals with the rights of the authors with respect to various works.

within the scope of the communication to the public, the changes introduced in the definition should be examined in detail. It reads:[58]

> Communication to the public means making any work or performance available for being seen or heard or otherwise enjoyed by the public directly or by any means of display or diffusion other than by issuing physical copies of it, *whether simultaneously or at places and times chosen individually*, regardless of whether any member of the public actually sees, hears or otherwise enjoys the work or performance so made available.
>
> Explanation. – For the purposes of this clause, communication through satellite or cable or any other means of simultaneous communication to more than one household or place of residence including residential rooms of any hotel or hostel shall be deemed to be communication to the public.

It is to be noted that the words 'whether simultaneously' is used to qualify 'directly or by any means of display or diffusion'. As discussed earlier, the use of the term 'diffusion' refers to the right of broadcasting and hence the addition of 'simultaneously' is to expressly recognize the right of re-broadcasting left out in the previous definition. Since, the term 'display or diffusion' is retained without replacing it with the neutral term 'transmission' as done in other jurisdictions, it is difficult to argue that internet based live streaming using packet technology is covered in the definition only because the words 'any means' is retained in the definition and explanation. This is discussed in detail below.

The 2012 Amendment[59] was carried out to meet the expectations of the WCT and WPPT, even though India is not a signatory to both the treaties. In order to bring conformity with the international practices and trends, the authors' right has been strengthened further by introducing a new set of rights to meet the digital era.[60] If so, whether the internet based live streaming has been covered or not? While examining the position at the international level and in other jurisdictions, it was observed that the authors' right of live streaming was recognized only by judicial interpretations at a later stage as the use of the term 'transmission'[61] in the statutory language was capable enough to

58 The Copyright Act, 1957, Sec. 2 (ff).

59 The same is available at http://copyright.gov.in/Documents/CRACT_AMNDMNT_2012.pdf (last accessed on 20/10/2017).

60 See Zakir Thomas, "Overview of Changes to the Indian Copyright Law", 17(4) *J.I.P.R.*, (2012), pp. 324–334, at p. 324.

61 See for the detailed discussion on the same, Chapter 5 of this book.

accommodate new technologies. In the absence of any such technology neutral definition, the question is whether the 2012 amendment has been aimed to bring parity with the international trends?

While analyzing the historical legislative practices of India, it has been obvious to us that whenever a new technology reaches/penetrates the market, the same would be incorporated by an express inclusion and not by merely expanding the existing provision. Based on this analysis, it can be very well argued that since the 2012 Amendment Act does not expressly mention live streaming technology or use the term 'transmission', the same is not covered by the definition of the communication to the public. This view can very well be corroborated even with the help of the reach of the technology. When the amendment was proposed, the technology had not substantially penetrated into India. It was at an infant stage. It could not reach the society not because of technology but it was due to the absence of requirements for such transmission i.e., availability of internet access with reasonably good bandwidth. As discussed at the beginning of this chapter, the internet penetration was substantially low at the time of the amendment and even the speed of the internet was also substantially low. The live streaming service was not a reality at that time. The NTP, 2012 only proposed to upgrade the internet speed from the 256 kbps to 2 mbps. However, in many places, even in metro cities including Delhi, the basic internet speed was 256 kbps which has been slightly upgraded to 512 kbps now. The high speed connections are even now not affordable to common man. Thus, a good bandwidth internet penetration to major cities itself requires at least a few more years. Thus, the reach of the technology itself is at a minimal level even today.[62] Even though mobile internet has reached the market, availability of LTE at all places, lack of resources with service providers and affordability of the mobile internet are the factors for poor penetration of the technology. Of course, with the emergence of Jio LTE, the availability of the bandwidth has become affordable with an increase in speed. After the application of *Jio* TV was launched for mobile devices, rivals like Airtel, Vodafone followed pursuit and launched their mobile applications to enjoy the contents that are transmitted over TV

62 As we have pointed out in the technological chapter and the socio-economic analysis of the live streaming technology, it has been substantially used to retransmit the TV broadcast contents in many jurisdictions. Indian is not an exception to same. As of today most of the TV channels and their contents are made available simultaneously over the internet. In the Indian context, it is worth to note that with the availability of the limited bandwidth, in very low quality contents delivery, such transmissions are happening in a limited sense. It means the contents of such transmission would be critically low due to the bandwidth. However, there are exceptions.

channels.[63] However, it is not at the same pace in all the parts of the country due to lack of infrastructure and technical problems on the part of service providers. As pointed out above, it may take a few more years to get the same, at all places, from all service providers. Interestingly, BSNL, the public sector mobile service provider and some other service providers have announced their plan of launching 5G mobile communication service by 2020 due to which the speed of the data transmission would be much higher than 4G LTE service.[64] In addition to these developments in the mobile communication, many service providers have come out with high speed internet broadband services. Once these technological developments in the internet reach all, live streaming based IPTV and web TV would be affordable to many and also available at a higher quality. From the above stated points, it could be safely concluded that the penetration of the internet, even today, is at an average level. Back then in 2010, live streaming based transmission did not reach the market commercially and the legislature had deliberately left out the same from including it in the definition of communication to the public.

In addition to this argument, the technological terminology used in the definition of communication to the public i.e., 'diffusion' would play a crucial role in constructing the scope and ambit of the definition and would be in a position to clarify the technological perspectives behind the communication to the public. The word 'diffusion' has remained in the Act since its inception. It was used in the definition of 'radio-diffusion' at first to signify the signal based technology and then it got inserted into the definition of communication to the public. Even today, the definition has kept the term 'diffusion' and thus it covers the specified signal based technologies only. As we discussed in the technology part, it is clear that live streaming is an internet based transmission. In streaming, there is no signal instead it is based on stream i.e., packets and thus there is no scope of diffusing the same. Hence, the diffusion element is absent in live streaming and the same cannot be covered in the technological point of view as well.

Had it been the case of intending to cover all the electronic transmission including live streaming, the legislature should have used the phrase 'electronic means/transmission' rather than using the word 'diffusion'. It may be remembered that the Parliament updated the right of reproduction in 1994

63 As of November, 2017, it offers around 400 channels in its app. See for the same, available at https://www.jio.com/en-in/apps/jio-tv (last accessed on 15/11/2017).

64 "BSNL to roll out 5G services in India together with global launch", available at https://economictimes.indiatimes.com/tech/internet/bsnl-to-roll-out-5g-services-in-india-together-with-global-launch/articleshow/64648764.cms?from=mdr (last accessed on 26/06/2019).

itself by using the term 'electronic means'. Incidentally, this is the practice we have seen in other jurisdictions where the right of the author was extended to live streaming especially in the UK context. Either the legislature should have opted for such usage or they should have preferred a technology neutral definition. However, it is not the case. As the legislature has still carried out the amendment to the definition of communication to the public by retaining the terminology i.e., 'diffusion', it is obvious that the legislature had not intended to cover such live streaming transmission under the present copyright regime.

In the context of the fast penetration of live streaming technology in the market, there is a need for recognizing the authors' right over this new mode of internet transmission. This is inevitable to provide enhanced protection in the technologically advanced era. Since the existing definition is technology specific. It may be difficult for the Indian judiciary to expand it to live streaming as was done by their counterparts in other jurisdiction. If the judiciary does the expansion by undermining the techno specific definition to accommodate new technology, such expansion would lead to serious impact on other provisions of copyright law. Thus, the issue requires careful consideration by the legislature and an amendment is called for in this regard, so that it could bring clarity to the authors' right in live streaming.

While the authors' right of live streaming is yet to be recognized, the traditional broadcasters have been claiming that retransmission of the broadcast contents over internet by using live streaming for simultaneous reception by the public would be part of their broadcast reproduction right. Thus, it is highly imperative to analyse the provisions related to broadcasters' reproduction right in the 1957 Act. Let us discuss the same in detail.

6.4 Subject matter of Broadcasters' Protection: Broadcast or Broadcasting?

Generally broadcasting organizations are identified as institutions that are involved in the activity of broadcasting.[65] From the literal meaning, the word broadcast can be comprehended in two ways. When it is used as a 'verb', it refers to 'transmit' i.e., the act of emitting the signal generated for broadcasting

---

65 See WIPO 14th SCCR "Draft basic proposal for the protection broadcasters along with a non mandatory proposal for the protection of webcasters", Art. 2 (c), available at www.wipo.int/edocs/mdocs/copyright/en/sccr_14/sccr_14_2.doc (last accessed on 20/10/2017).

and if it is used as a 'noun', it refers to 'transmission' i.e., the process of diffusing the signal – broadcasting.[66]

As we discussed above, internationally, the right of broadcasting has been recognized as authors' right of communication to the public and the same has been made available to them since the Berne Revision, 1928. While the content creators are enjoying the authors' right of broadcasting, the signal was subjected to unauthorized interception which resulted in revenue losses to the broadcasting organizations with whose help; the authors' right of broadcasting was realized. The copyright protection was not available to the signal and it was only the content which was protected. As there was a gap while exercising the authors' right of broadcasting, in order to provide a very comprehensive protection to the entire act of broadcasting, protection to the signal generated by the broadcasting organization was provided. Thus, the Berne Convention protects the act of broadcasting as authors' right and the Rome Convention protects the right to transmit the signal of the broadcasters i.e., broadcast which is always subjected to the authors' right. However, as discussed in the previous chapter, the Rome Convention's definition lacks clarity as it covers the act of transmission rather than covering the right to transmit the signal. It is important to note here that since these words are used interchangeably both in the international conventions and domestic legislation, the meaning of the same has to be understood contextually.

If this is the scope and meaning of broadcast and broadcasting at the international level, it is interesting to find out how this is accommodated in the Indian Copyright Act from 1957 onwards.

6.5 Broadcasters' Reproduction Right and Live Streaming: a Critical Analysis

Protection to broadcasting organizations was envisaged from the very beginning of independent India's Copyright Act, 1957, even though broadcasting was not that prominent in India at that time. It appears that the Parliament was aware about this technology and its possible penetration in India in the context of Government taking steps to improve the availability of this technology. This is evident from the language used in Section 37[67] of the Act. The broadcast

66 See "Farlex's the free dictionary", available at http://www.thefreedictionary.com/broadcast (last accessed on 20/10/2017).

67 Sec. 37(1) as it existed originally read: "Where any programme is broadcast by radio-diffusion by the Government or any other broadcasting authority, a special right to be known as "broadcast reproduction right" shall subsist in such programme".

reproduction right was conferred to 'Government or any other broadcasting authority'. The right was given to the 'programme broadcast by radio-diffusion'. It is interesting to note that the word used is 'broadcast by radio-diffusion'. There is no definition for broadcast provided in the original Act in 1957. As discussed earlier, the right given to the author at that time was the right of radio-diffusion and it was defined to include communication to public of the work using radio and television. The permission of the author is required to communicate the work through radio and television diffusion. In this context, the word 'broadcast' must be understood as a right to transmit the signal generated by the broadcasters and must be confined to the signal and not to the content carried by it. This is further clarified in Section 39[68] of the Act making it clear that the broadcast reproduction right shall not affect the independent right of the authors in their work. It appears that though the word 'broadcast' is interchangeably used as a verb and noun, the Parliament has clearly separated the right of author from that of the broadcasting organizations. Thus, the broadcast reproduction right was given as a neighbouring right which would be always subjected to the copyright of authors.

While reading the provision on broadcasters' protection, in the rights context, the Parliament used the phrase 'broadcast reproduction right'[69] as the nomenclature for the provision. As per the provision, the nature of rights granted to the broadcasters includes rebroadcast or make the broadcast to be heard by the public or making record out of the broadcast. These rights were granted for a period of 25 years.

---

68 Sec. 39 read: Other rights not affected:- For the removal of doubts, it is hereby declared that the broadcast reproduction right conferred upon a broadcasting authority under this Chapter shall not affect copyright:
(a) in any literary, dramatic or musical work which is broadcast by that authority; or
(b) in any record recording any such work.

69 Sec. 37 read: Broadcast reproduction right:- (1) Where any programme is broadcast by radio-diffusion by the Government or any other broadcasting authority, a special right to be known as "broadcast reproduction right" shall subsist in such programme. (2) The Government or other broadcasting authority, as the case may be, shall be the owner of the broadcast reproduction right and such right shall subsist until twenty-five years from the beginning of the calendar year next following year in which the programme is first broadcast. (3) During the continuance of a broadcast reproduction right in relation to any programme, any person who, – (a) without the licence of the owner of the right – (i) rebroadcasts the programme in question or any substantial part thereof; or (ii) causes the programme in question or any substantial part thereof to be heard in public; or (b) without the licence of the owner of the right to utilise the broadcast for the purpose of making a record recording the programme in question or any substantial part thereof, makes any such record, shall be deemed to infringe that broadcast reproduction right.

While examining the scope and ambit of the broadcast reproduction right, it is understood that it is confined to signal used for radio diffusion. From the authors' right of radio diffusion, it is understood that the authors were given right over radio and TV broadcasting. But, the broadcasters' broadcast reproduction right was intended to cover only the radio broadcast, since the language used is 'causes the programme in question or any substantial part thereof to be heard in public;'. Had the legislature intended to cover both the radio and television, it could have used 'to be heard or seen' rather than confining to 'to be heard'. Thus, the scope of broadcasters' protection under the 1957 Act was confined to radio only.

The only right granted beyond the signal was fixation and post fixation uses. However, the same was subjected to authors' right as clarified in Section 38.[70] Thus, the broadcast reproduction right includes both rights based on use of signal which is exclusively enjoyed by the broadcasting organizations and on the content fixed from the signal to be enjoyed jointly with the author. When the broadcasters' protection under the 1957 Act is compared with the 1956 Act of UK,[71] it is evident that the broadcasters under the Indian law were given with very limited level of protection as compared to their counterparts in UK. The probable reason might be the level of the then existing technology and its penetration into the Indian market. It may also be remembered that the Government was the only agency that was involved in broadcasting at that time and private players entered the market only after 1990s.

When the Act was amended in 1983, though there were substantial changes introduced with respect to authors' right of broadcasting by incorporating the then existing technologies under a new definition of broadcast, the broadcast reproduction right was retained as such with the only change of deleting 'by radio-diffusion' in Section 37(1). As we discussed, the definition of broadcast which replaced radio diffusion was introduced to address the authors' right of broadcasting with respect to specified technologies. Since the word broadcast

---

70 Sec. 38 read: other Provisions of this Act to supply to broadcast reproduction rights:- Sections 18, 19, 30, 53, 55, 58, 64, 65 and 66 shall, with any necessary adaptations and modifications, apply in relation to the broadcast reproduction right in any programme as they apply in relation of the copyright in a work; "Provided that a license to utilize a broadcast for the purpose of making a record recording a programme in which broadcast reproduction right subsists or any substantial part of such programme, shall not take effect unless the person to whom such license is granted has also obtained a license to make records recording the work embodied in such programme from the owner of the copyright in such work."

71 UK Copyright Act, 1956. It had a provision to protect the broadcast as work of authors' i.e., Sec. 14.

was retained in Section 37, it is interesting to find out the application of the new definition of broadcast to protect the right of authors in new technology.

If the 'broadcast' as we discussed above is a noun and refers to '*transmission*', the definition introduced through the 1983 amendment was not to cover signal rather it was meant for covering the act of broadcasting by using specified mediums. It was meant for qualifying the previous radio diffusion definition only. But, deletion of words "by radio diffusion" in Section 37 leads one to ask the question whether the definition of broadcast has the same meaning in section 37 referring to the act of transmission. Since the word '*work*' is not used in the definition of broadcast, it is possible for one to interpret that in the context of 'broadcast reproduction right', it refers to transmission of content carrying signal, whereas, in the context of right of authors, it refers to transmission of works. Such an interpretation will retain the distinction between the rights of authors and broadcasting organizations originally intended by the Parliament in 1957. This is made clear since there was no other changes introduced in Section 37 and the right is confined to radio broadcasting as discussed earlier. But, since the definition of broadcast also includes re-broadcast, it creates an ambiguity, if it is extended to Section 37 which expressly recognizes rebroadcast as part of broadcast reproduction right. The definition of broadcast also covers 'by wire', but the right in Section 37(3)(a)(ii) is still confined to 'to be heard in public'. This also creates confusion and conflict with the rights of authors. Hence, it could be safely concluded that the definition of broadcast was introduced with the right of broadcasting of author in mind and not to be extended to the 'broadcast reproduction right'. It appears that the Parliament was ignorant about the technical implications of the term. Had it been aware about the problems, it would have used the term broadcasting for the right of the author referring it to the works and introduced a different definition for broadcast confining it to signal. These problems seem to have been solved to some extent by the 1994 amendment, when the term broadcast was removed from Section 14 and replaced with a new definition of communication to public, but it resulted in a new set of problems with reference to broadcast reproduction right.

The 1990s witnessed the entry of private players in the Indian market. After the private players were allowed in the area of broadcasting, through the 1994 Amendment Act,[72] the provision was modified substantially.[73] There was considerable

72 The same is available at http://www.egazette.nic.in/WriteReadData/1994/E-0392-1994-0054-15072.pdf (last accessed on 20/10/2017).

73 Sec. 37 read:.Broadcast reproduction right.-(1) Every broadcasting organisation shall have a special right to be known as "broadcast reproduction right" in respect of its broadcasts. (2) The broadcast reproduction right shall subsist until twenty-five years from the

change in the language of Section 37. The term broadcasting organization is used and the right is now on the 'broadcast' and not on the programme broadcasted by them. This brings clarity that the right is on the signal and not on the content carried by the signal. Since the word broadcast was removed from section 14, it is now clear that the definition of broadcast is confined to the transmission of the signal. The scope of protection was also extended to television and new post fixation rights were also added to strengthen the right of broadcasting organization. But, the retention of term 'communication to public' in the definition of broadcast and the inclusion of new definition to communication to public added more problems.

The definition of communication to public as introduced in 1983 did not create any problem since it was a neutral one.[74] The new definition of communication to public introduced in 1994[75] refers to 'work' and different forms of activities of communication of the work to public. If one reads the definition of broadcast along with communication to public, then it gives an impression that broadcast is confined to works and all the different activities of communication of work to public meant for authors. This means that the communication to public definition is also extended to broadcast reproduction right of broadcasting organizations. This seems an absurdity, to say the least, created by Parliament in its failure to understand the difference between the broadcasting right of the author and the broadcast right of the broadcasting organization. In

beginning of the calendar year next following the year in which the broadcast is made. (3) During the continuance of a broadcast reproduction right in relation to any broadcast, any person who, without the licence of the owner of the right does any of the following acts of the broadcast or any substantial part thereof,- (a) re-broadcasts the broadcast; or (b) causes the broadcast to be heard or seen by the public on payment of any charges; or (c) makes any sound recording or visual recording of the broadcast; or (d) makes any reproduction of such sound recording or visual recording where such initial recording was done without licence or, where it was licensed, for any purpose not envisaged by such licence; or (e) sells or hires to the public or offers for such sale or hire, any such sound recording or visual recording referred to in clause (c) or clause (d) shall, subject to the provisions of section 39, be deemed to have infringed the broadcast reproduction right.

74 Sec. 2 (ff) read: 'Communication to the public' means communication to the public in whatever manner, including communication through satellite.

75 Sec. 2(ff) read: "communication to the public" means making any work available for being seen or heard or otherwise enjoyed by the public directly or by any means of display or diffusion other than by issuing copies of such work regardless of whether any member of the public actually sees, hears or otherwise enjoys the work so made available.

Explanation – For the purposes of this clause, communication through satellite or cable or any other means of simultaneous communication to more than one household or place of residence including residential rooms of any hotel or hostel shall be deemed to be communication to the public.

this context, it is worth noting that broadcasting organizations not only diffuse the works protected by the copyright but also other signs, words and visual images. This seems to be the reason for using the word programme in Section 37, as it was originally enacted. But, since the definition of broadcast originally intended for the author is left without any change, the confusion regarding its relation with the definition of communication to public and re-broadcasting still continues. This leads to the question whether the rebroadcast right is confined to works, all activities of communication of the works to public, simultaneous diffusion of the signals or it extends even to repeat broadcast where the signal has to be created again for diffusion. It also raises the question whether the right over repeat broadcast co-exists with that of the right of re-broadcasting recognized by Berne Convention for authors. This is all the more important since the original Section 39 dealing with protection of the right of author was removed in a 1994 amendment and replaced by a new section dealing with infringement.[76] The new Section 39A which was introduced to extend the application of other provisions of the Act, failed to include section 13 dealing with coexistence of the right and the proviso to Section 39A was confined only to post fixation rights. It appears again that the Parliament is confused with the nature of right to be given to the broadcasting organizations and its overlap with the right of the authors. The expansion of the post fixation right is a clear indication in this regard. It is strongly felt that the clarity of the provisions originally introduced was distorted to give more powers to broadcasting organizations at the cost of authors.

The confusion created by the 1994 amendment to some extent was addressed by the Parliament in the 2012 amendment without changing the position of the broadcasters' protection as it existed in 1994. The major contribution was the clarification on the right of authors in the context of new rights given to the broadcasting organizations in 1994. The original provision of Section 39 was reintroduced in Section 39A by way of additional proviso[77] making it clear that the authors' rights are not affected by the introduction of new rights to broadcasting organization. Similarly, addition of words 'whether simultaneously' in the definition of communication to the public in the 2012

---

76 Sec. 39 read: Other rights not affected:- For the removal of doubts, it is hereby declared that the broadcast reproduction right conferred upon a broadcasting authority under this Chapter shall not affect copyright:
(a) in any literary, dramatic or musical work which is broadcast by that authority; or
(b) in any record recording any such work.

77 Sec. 39A proviso read: "Provided further that the broadcast reproduction right or performer's right shall not subsist in any broadcast or performance if that broadcast or performance is an infringement of the copyright in any work".

Amendment, also makes it clear that the author has a re-broadcasting right and this could not be enjoyed by the broadcasting organization without the permission of the authors. Through this, the position of authors and their control over the content during broadcasting and post fixation right of broadcasters' have been reemphasized. But, the failure of the Parliament to create a new definition for broadcast to confine it to signals and deleting its link with the definition of communication to public makes one wonder how the courts are going to interpret this provision keeping the balance between the rights of authors and broadcasting organizations. The solution is to redefine the term 'broadcast' confining it to the right to transmit the signal through diffusion technology. This is precisely what India is advocating in the WIPO negotiations for the protection of broadcasting organizations based on the GA mandate of signal based approach.[78] It is unfortunate to note that the Government of India which is trying to bring clarity to the broadcasting organizations right internationally has failed to bring it to the notice of Parliament in 2012, the much needed clarity in India and suggested changes in the law. The missed opportunity must be addressed at the earliest in the light of technological changes and litigations emerging in this area. In this context the new definitions for signal and broadcast suggested by India in WIPO could be considered for inclusion in the Copyright Act.

As far as live streaming is concerned, as we discussed above, since the definition of the communication to the public does not recognize the right of communication to the public by using live streaming to the authors, the same is not at all possible to be claimed by the broadcasters. In addition to this justification, according to the definitions of the broadcasting under the WPPT, the Beijing Treaty[79] and the WIPO Draft Treaty on Protection of Broadcasting Organization, it is very clear that the definitions have not been aimed to have a techno-neutral approach. Rather they had specified the technologies such as wireless, wire, cable and satellite. Further, interestingly, the WIPO draft Treaty specifies that transmission over the computer network shall not be considered as broadcasting. Even the definition of broadcast proposed under the draft WIPO Treaty also specifies that transmission over the computer network shall not be considered as broadcast. As specified in the definitions, the transmission over computer network should not be considered as broadcasting.

78 India's Specific Amendments and Comments to the Articles in the Non-paper on the WIPO Treaty on the Protection of Broadcasting Organizations, 20th April, 2007, aviable at http://www.wipo.int/edocs/mdocs/copyright/en/sccr_s2/sccr_s2_paper1.pdf (last accessed on 10/11/2017). The same is in file.

79 The Beijing Treaty on Audiovisual Performance, 2012.

Even such transmission cannot constitute broadcast. If this is the position advanced by India in WIPO, the same should also be followed in understanding the scope of broadcast reproduction right in India. Moreover, from the above discussions, it is very clear that in light of Rome Convention, the present form of protection for the broadcasters under the Copyright Act has been aimed to address the issue of unauthorized use of signals and the entire model has been justified based on 'signal based approach' and not to cover the internet based transmissions.. Hence, the retransmission of such broadcast contents over the internet shall not be available as a right for the broadcasters. When we examined the authors' position with respect to live streaming, it has been clearly understood that their position is an unarticulated premise which require more clarity and express covering of the same technology under the communication to the public. While authors' position itself is not clear, then there is no question of thinking beyond what has been given to the authors. Such an extension would lead to great injustice to the authors. Even from the conclusions of the technological and the socio-economic part, it is much obvious that the chances of streams being stolen is almost nil due to the encryption and decryption techniques which cause no economic burden to the live streaming provider. As there are no economic issues arising out of such live streaming based transmissions, in the absence of such problem unlike traditional analogue broadcasting, there is no need for conferring any special right to the person who does the internet live streaming as the technology itself would safeguard such transmissions. Even, if there is any issue, the same could be addressed by the authors' right of communication to the public in an effective manner.

In the light of above discussions on the authors' right of broadcasting and the broadcasters' broadcast reproduction right under the Indian Copyright Act, it is pertinent and inevitable to discuss the judicial pronouncements on the same. Let us examine few judicial pronouncements in this area in detail.

6.6 Broadcast Reproduction Right: a Dilemma for the Judiciary too?

Most of the cases decided in India are based on sports content. The broadcasters usually buy the medium rights from the organizer of the events through auctions. The issue of copyrightability of such content is much debatable one.[80]

80 M. Sakthivel, "Copyrightability of Sports Contents: Indian Scenario", *Entertainment Law Review*, (2012), pp. 91–95.

However, as the definition of performers[81] is wide enough to address sports as well, the same could be covered under the rights of performers.[82] Interestingly, even the Delhi High Court went to the extent of saying that broadcast of such live sports event would constitute a work of 'cinematograph work'.[83] Though the Supreme Court had an opportunity[84] to examine whether such live sports would constitute 'cinematograph work', the issue has been left unanswered.[85] As the focus of our discussion is on the scope of broadcasters' protection, the cases related to same alone are examined in detail.

ESPN Star Sports is engaged in generating live feed and broadcasting most of sports events by deploying its own team in the premises where the sports events take place. For doing so, it obtains the sole exclusive rights from the organizers of such events. In the present case,[86] it had the exclusive licenses of all the cricket matches to be broadcasted. For the live feed distribution, it had authorized ESPN Software India Pvt. Ltd. to coordinate with the local cable

81 Copyright Act, 1957, Sec. 2 (qq). It reads: "performer" includes an actor, singer, musician, dancer, acrobat, juggler, conjurer, snake charmer, a person delivering a lecture or any other person who makes a performance.

82 See for the same argument, M. Sakthivel, "Copyrightability of Sports Contents: Indian Scenario", *Entertainment Law Review*, (2012), pp. 91–95.

83 *Star India Pvt. Ltd.* v. *Piyush Agarwal & Ors.*, 2014 (58) P.T.C. 169 (Del.). It held: Section 37 of the Act, in a way could be said to be duplication, if not otiose, inasmuch as, once really a combination of audio and visual recording creates a video recording/cinematographic film which is broadcasted, there would come into existence a 'cinematograph film' as per the provision of section 2(f) of the Act, and a cinematograph film is itself a subject matter of the copyright as per section 13(1)(b) of the Act. Once a cinematograph film is a subject matter of the copyright then surely no one can broadcast or rebroadcast or communicate to the public or in any manner utilize the cinematograph film except with the consent of and the permission of the owner/author of the cinematograph film, otherwise there would result infringement by the broadcast or rebroadcast in terms of section 51 and the related sections of the Act.

84 *Union of India and Ors.* v. *Board of Control for Cricket in India and Ors.*, MANU/SC/1041/2017.

85 *Ibid.* It held: Though such rights may seemingly come under Section 37 (Chapter VII) of the Copyright Act, 1957, it is argued that the telecast of the cricket matches is like production of a cinematograph film within the meaning of Section 2(f) of the Copyright Act. BCCI as the organizer is the author of the Copyright who has assigned the same to Star India Pvt. Ltd. There is a statutory 29 curtailment of the said right under Section 3 of the Sports Act, 2007, the extent of which must be understood to be confined to the explicit contours of the said provision which cannot be readily and easily extended. Any unwarranted extension would amount to an invasion of the copyright/broadcasting right of the respondents Nos. 3 and 4. The legislation is expropriatory in character.

86 *ESPN Stars Sports* v. *Global Broadcast News Ltd and Ors*, 2008 (38) P.T.C. 477 (Del.).

operators. ESPN contented that the Global Broadcast News Limited and other news channels were showing the cricket matches beyond the reasonable duration for reporting the current events without ESPN's authorization. Therefore, it prayed to the Court to restrain the Respondents/Defendants from doing so. While deciding the matter, the Single Judge,[87] dismissed the same due to non-compliance of Section 61 of the Copyright Act.[88] Aggrieved by this, ESPN appealed to the Division Bench (Two Judges) of the Delhi High Court.

After hearing the both side arguments, the Court came to the conclusion that Section 61 is not required to deal with Section 37 of the Act and held:[89]

> … we have found that the broadcast reproduction right in respect of telecast of live event like a Cricket match are separate and distinct right as from the copyright and as such Section 61 is not applicable to broadcast reproduction right. Even assuming that a copyright includes broadcast reproduction right and Section 61 applied, we are of the view that the eventual telecast by the appellant being different and distinct from the telecast of the host broadcaster, the independent copyright owner of the eventual product is the appellant itself. In light of the above observations, it is not incumbent upon us to rely on the above said Agreement or go into the effect of suppression of its portions.

---

87 ESPN *Stars Sports* v. *Global Broadcast News Ltd and Ors,* 2008 (36) P.T.C. 492 (Del.).

88 *Ibid.* It held: No doubt, Chapter VIII deals with a species of rights known as broadcast reproduction rights. The content and extent of that right has been defined in Section 37. Section 39A of the Act refers to certain provisions of the Act; it has inspired an argument that the absence of a reference to Section 61 means that the requirement of impleading the owner of copyright in a sporting event does not apply to broadcast rights and that such rights are 'special'. Facially, the argument seems logical; yet a careful examination would reveal several flaws in it. Firstly, there is no legislative intention to elevate 'broadcasting rights' to a special status, whereby the Chapter dealing with it operates in a special zone within the statute, immune from the operation of the other parts of the Act. If such intention were there, Parliament would have used legislative devices such as non-obstante clauses, exclusions, etc. Secondly, the argument flies against well established canone of legislative interpretation that a statute must be read as a whole and the legislature should be deemed to have intended application of each part for the situations intended. If the plaintiff's contentions were accepted, Section 61 would operate only in some situations and not all, even though no express provision manifests such intention nor can it be drawn by necessary implication. The requirements of Section 61, procedural in nature, apply with equal vigor to all nature of rights that are subject matter of the Act.

89 ESPN *Stars Sports* v. *Global Broadcast News Ltd and Ors,* 2008 (38) P.T.C. 477 (Del.), at pp. 505 & 506.

Based on the above reasoning, the Court held:[90]

> We hold that the broadcast reproduction right as contended by the appellant are to be treated as separate, distinct and independent rights.

In this context, we need to examine whether the broadcast reproduction right is a separate, distinct and independent right? As we discussed and concluded in the previous chapters and the discussion on the broadcast reproduction right of the broadcasters' under this chapter, it has been clearly established that the broadcasters have been given with a separate protection under the copyright, due to the inability of the authors' right of broadcasting which is covered under the communication to the public to address the signal piracy issue. In a way, the protection given to the broadcasters is only for their signal and not beyond that. If this is the underlining objective behind the broadcasters' protection under the copyright, while analyzing the nature of broadcast reproduction right of the broadcasters, it is clear that it is a bundle of rights given to them. Among those rights, the rebroadcast of the broadcast for simultaneous reception, if the authorization has been taken for medium through which rebroadcast is intended, it is considered as an independent right. Likewise, 'causes the broadcast to be heard or seen by the public against the payment' is also an independent right. The rationale for such conclusion is that both the rights do not deal with the content. As long as the broadcasters deal with the signal, they enjoy the independent right over the content carrying signal. In this context, it may be possible for one to argue that the broadcasting organizations can take action without impleading the owner of copyright of the content carried by the signal. However, these rights could be enjoyed only if they have taken permission from the owner of copyright to broadcast the work. If this is the position, it is important also to bring the owner of content into the litigation to ensure that the broadcasting organization is not violating the rights of the author of the work for which Section 61 has been incorporated. Hence, it appears that the court is wrong in concluding that the owner of copyright is not required to be impleaded. This shows the failure on the part of the court to understand the relationship between the authors' right of broadcasting and the broadcast reproduction right of the broadcasting organization and the need to ensure that broadcasting organizations are not going to violate the right of the author. In the context of the new proviso added to Section 39A(1)

90 *ESPN Stars Sports* v. *Global Broadcast News Ltd and Ors*, 2008 (38) P.T.C. 477 (Del.), at p. 506.

and sub-clause (2) to 39A, it is now clear that even for enjoying the independent right of broadcasting organization, the author need to be impleaded.

Remaining are the post fixation rights which are subjected to first proviso to Section 39A (1) and sub clause (2) of 39A, as they deal with contents of the broadcast. It is even worth to state that the post fixation rights are coexistence rights. However, though this is the original intended position of the broadcasters' protection under the Indian Copyright Act, due to poor articulation, this has led to serious confusion which has paved the way for judicial confusion as well. This is the case with respect to rebroadcast[91] and simulcast as well.[92]

6.7 Conclusion

While examining the evolution of the concept of broadcasting by tracing the amendments to the Copyright Act, 1957 at various point of time, It would be

91 ESPN *Stars Sports* v. *Global Broadcast News Ltd and Ors.* 2008 (38) P.T.C. 477 (Del.). Further, the Court held that eventual broadcast is different from original broadcast. It ruled: "… we are of the view that the eventual telecast by the appellant being different and distinct from the telecast of the host broadcaster, the independent copyright owner of the eventual product is the appellant itself." In this case, the feed is generated and provided by the parent company to its Indian subsidiary. Then the Indian subsidiary makes necessary modifications by adding some local advertisement and then the same is distributed to the public for simultaneous reception. While this is the actual happening of the case, then the natural question could be that how can it constitute an independent work? The same issue may arise even in a situation where initial and the subsequent broadcasters are not related to each other. As we discussed above, the initial broadcast is the original one and the subsequent broadcast is the simultaneous broadcast of the same to a defined geographical location with suitable adaptations such as adding advertise contents and clippings, it would not create a new work because the substantial part of the content, in this case 99%, remains same. This modifications are done in fraction of a second and then immediately broadcasted with a delay of few seconds only. In any case, the subsequent broadcast cannot constitute an independent work. The content owner would remain same irrespective of the fact that it is initial or subsequent broadcast. While this is the position, creating a legal position thereby calling the subsequent broadcast as an independent new work thereby conferring ownership is unwarranted and unacceptable one.

92 In *Star India Pvt. Ltd.* v. *Haneeth Ujwal & Ors.* 2014 (60) P.T.C. 504 (Del.) the plaintiff was the exclusive right holder of the 2014 India-England T20 cricket matches over all mediums i.e., TV Rights including analogue, digital, DTH and IPTV, Internet Rights, Mobile Rights, On-demand Rights. These exclusive rights were obtained by making huge investment. As a most demanded content, it was apprehended by the plaintiff that the defendants would potentially infringe their right by transmitting over internet and sought for a prohibitory order against the defendants. While granting the same, the Court even directed the ISPs to cooperate with the plaintiffs and further directed the Domain Name registration office to share relevant information in this regard.

very well concluded that whenever there were technical advancements in the context of communication, for the maximum exploitation of the work, the authors' right over the new technology for communication has been expressly incorporated in the Copyright Act, 1957 through amendments. When radio diffusion reached the market, the same was incorporated by the 1957 Act. When TV penetrated into the commercial market, satellite and cable technology were used for the communication in India, the same were incorporated by amending the 1957 Act in 1983. Even the new dimensions of the communications such as to the hotel room and residential areas were also further covered by widening the scope of communication to the public through the 1994 amendment. Therefore, historically, it has been the practice of the Indian legislature that as and when the technology penetrates into the market for exploiting the authors' works, the same was included as authors' right through amendments.

When the Act was further amended in 1994 so as to accommodate then existing technologies, the authors' right of broadcasting was brought and kept under the authors' right of communication to public. While doing so, even after removal of the phrase 'radio diffusion' from Section 14, the scope of authors' right remained the same; this was further qualified by the newly introduced definition of broadcast which referred the act of transmitting the work through the then existed technology. In the light of above discussion, when we examined the scope of authors' right of broadcasting/radio diffusion by tracing the legislative changes, it has been made clear by the definition of radio diffusion and the broadcast that the authors' right refers to the act of communication. Even after the introduction of the communication to the public right by removing the then existing right of radio-diffusion, it has been established that the definition of broadcast is meant to refer exclusively to the authors' right of broadcasting which is bundled under the communication to the public right. As the 2012 amendment has not introduced any change in this regard, the authors' right of broadcasting has remained the same that of 1994 even today.

As the focus of our examination is to find out the position of the authors' right of live streaming under the definition of 'communication to the public' as amended in 2012, it was found that live streaming has not been expressly specified under the Act. In the absence of such an express inclusion, the possibility of widening the scope of 'communication to the public' by interpreting 'any other means of simultaneous communication' to include the live streaming as well was also examined. In this context, we conclude from the historical practices of this country that whenever a new technology reaches/penetrates the market, the same would be incorporated by an express inclusion and not by merely expanding the existing provision.

In addition to this reason, retaining the word 'diffusion' under the definition of 'communication to the public' even under the 2012 amendment, further corroborates and strengthens the argument. If the legislature had intended to cover live streaming, then it should have done by express inclusion under the definition of the communication to the public by making it a technological neutral definition. Then, they should have used the phrase 'electronic transmission' also while retaining the word 'diffusion'. Instead of doing so, the 2012 amendment has merely added re-broadcasting right and clarified the on-demand part of internet transmissions and retained the old provision substantially. Therefore, the definition of communication to the public is technology specific based on signals and not a technology neutral one to cover the future technology such as live streaming based on packets as far as Indian market is concerned due to the justifications highlighted. Therefore, it has been concluded that the live streaming mode of communication has not been addressed and covered by the 2012 Amendment Act.

If the authors' right of live streaming is not covered under the definition of 'communication to the public', it is impossible for the broadcasters to claim retransmission right over internet by using live streaming. In addition to the technological understanding and the conclusions reached, it is pertinent to note that mode of transmission in live streaming is entirely different from broadcasting. In addition, in the absence of unauthorized use of stream, there is no point in extending the broadcasters' right to this live streaming. As concluded in the previous chapters, the authors' right itself is sufficient. However, in the absence of such express inclusion of live streaming by adopting a technological neutral definition, it is impossible to extend the authors' right over this. Thus, in this context, a specific amendment is required.

In addition to that, the discussion on the broadcasters' broadcast reproduction right revealed that their subject matter of protection under the copyright is broadcast i.e., signal. Based on the international practices and experiences, while examining the authors' right of broadcasting, it has been well established that the definition of broadcast under the Indian Act has been meant to cover the authors' right of broadcasting. i.e., the act of transmitting the work and not the broadcasters' broadcast reproduction right given under Section 37. In this context, it can be well concluded that as definition of broadcast under the Indian Act is meant to cover broadcasting which is meant to qualify the authors' right of communication to the public, due to terminological usages, Section 2(dd) of Indian Act lacks clarity and provides room for unwarranted interpretations by using the definition of broadcast to understand the scope of broadcasters' right. Even the judiciary has added fuel to the flame by using the definition of broadcast to explain the broadcasters' broadcast reproduction right which is not acceptable. In the absence of such clarification, authors would be invariably adversely affected and thus, it is the right time to revisit the present provisions under the Copyright Act and suitable modifications are also required in this regard.

CHAPTER 7

Conclusion

Technological advancements in the field of communication have posed considerable challenges to the copyright law. An examination of the growth of technology from broadcasting to live streaming revealed that each new mode of exploitation of works is a new market and a source of additional revenue for the owner of a copyright. In the present context, one of the fastest evolving new medium of communication of authors' work over internet is live streaming technology. Within a short span of time, it has substantially penetrated into different parts of the globe, particularly in to the technologically advanced countries. The penetration level is relatively slow in countries where the internet connectivity is poor. However, the available data shows that many developing countries including India is taking special efforts to increase the bandwidth so as to facilitate live streaming of audio visual works including sporting events. The study of international history and evolution of the right of communication to the public of owners of copyright also indicates that as and when a new technology is widely used for the commercial exploitation of the copyright works, the same has been recognized expressly, thereby, conferring the authors with a right over the new platforms to exploit their works. In this context, the current challenge before the copyright system is to accommodate the commercial exploitation of copyright works through the emerging live streaming technology.

While tracing the evolution of the right of communication to the public, it has been found that it originated with the growth of broadcasting technology. With the emergence of radio broadcasting, copyright works, particularly songs, were exploited by the broadcasting organizations without the authorization of the owners of the copyright. This was due to the lack of clarity on the scope of right of public performance of work to accommodate the new technology. It was the judiciary that started recognizing the authors' right in the new medium.[1] This resulted in the emergence of international norms for protecting the broadcasting right of author. Authors' right of radio diffusion was expressly recognized by the Berne Convention through its Rome Revision, 1928 and the same was further expanded to accommodate TV broadcasting in 1948. This was again revised in 1972 to accommodate cable and satellite communications. The

1 For the detailed discussion, see Chapter 4.

 | DOI:10.1163/9789004419155_008

language of Berne Convention as it stands even today is technology specific covering only signal based broadcasting technology through different platforms such as terrestrial, cable and satellite which cannot be used for accommodating the newly emerging internet based technologies.

Due to the technological advancements in communication of works to the public using internet, the authors' right to exploit their works over internet was initially recognized by individual jurisdictions and then taken up internationally. The authors' right over the newly emerged medium has been expressly recognized by the WCT, 1996. Interestingly, it is WCT that for the first time used the term 'right of communication to public' so as to cover different technologies used for transmission of the work to public. An analysis of the scope of Article 8 of WCT dealing with the right of communication to public also revealed that it is also technology specific like the Berne Convention. The language used in Article 8 is to cover all the technology accommodated in the Berne Convention and to further expand it to 'any communication to public – by wire or wireless means' including communication based on on-demand services. It is observed that this language may be inadequate to cover the live streaming technology based on 4G P2P that is currently growing fast. This has been corroborated by the records of the Diplomatic Conference of the WCT which is confined to on-demand transmission of works using digital technology and silent on future technologies. This is preciously because of the fact that at the time of negotiation of WCT, the live streaming technology was at an infant stage of development even in developed countries. Further, it is noticed that it is the WIPO Guide to the WCT in 2003, which, for the first time discussed the possibility of accommodating future technologies especially the live streaming technology under Article 8. Due to these reasons, it is felt that WCT did not expressly intend to accommodate live streaming transmission under Article 8 and thus the authors' position over live streaming needs to be read into this provision for countries to recognize it as and when needed. Considering the fact that live streaming is a fast emerging medium of future communication industry of the globe, it is advisable to clarify that this is covered under the existing international copyright regime. In this context, on examination of the recent practices followed in developed countries, especially in US and EU where live streaming technology has been a commercial success, it is noticed that the judiciary, by interpretation of the technology neutral language in the domestic legislation, has recognized live streaming as part of authors' right of communication to public. Thus, the *Aereo case*[2] in USA and the *ITV case*[3] in

2 *American Broadcasting Cos., Inc., et al.* v. *Aereo, Inc., FkaBamboom Labs, Inc.* 573 US 2014.
3 *ITV Broadcasting Ltd.,* v. *TV Catchup Ltd.,* (Case C-607/11) 2013.

UK[4] and the EU recognized live streaming as a separate technology facilitating commercial exploitation of copyright works in a new market which is different from broadcasting. The judiciary is categorical in mandating specific permission from the owner of copyright before enjoyment of the works in this medium. But these decisions are not free from dissent and critical comments showing reservations on expanding the rights in the absence of specific provisions in the legislation. In this context, it is important to note that many countries which are parties to Berne Convention are yet to become members of the WCT. Due to this reason, assuming that Art. 8 of WCT covers live streaming as interpreted by EU, this is not going to be the international standard. Hence, it is strongly suggested to revisit the Berne Convention so as to accommodate the newly emerged communication medium for better protection of authors.

In the light of the above observations, a critical analysis of the Indian copyright law discloses that based on international copyright regime, India followed a technology specific approach to recognize the right of communication to the public of authors. The historical analysis of the provisions in the Copyright Act, 1957 divulge that it has been the practice of the Indian Parliament to make changes in the law to recognize authors' right over a specific technology as and when the same is commercially exploited in India in a large scale. The amendments introduced in 1983 and 1993 and the use of technology specific terms like radio-diffusion, broadcast, display, diffusion, communication through satellite and cable while defining authors' right of communication to public are illustrative of this approach. Even after the 2012 amendment to the definition of communication to public, the approach is technology specific since, the word 'display or diffusion' is retained. This creates serious doubt as to whether live streaming technology is covered in the definition. This is all the more important in the context of including 'electronic storage' in the right of reproduction to cover digital technology. Had it been the intention of the Parliament to cover this new mode of communication under the copyright regime, it would have used technology neutral language such as 'any electronic transmission' in addition to retaining the word diffusion in the definition of communication to the public. Instead of doing so, the 2012 amendment has merely added rebroadcasting right and clarified the on-demand part of internet transmissions and substantially retained the old definition. The absence of the penetration of technology and the associated problems in the Indian market seems to be the reason for this. However, due to the speed at which the live streaming technology is penetrating into the Indian market, it is strongly felt that there is an

4 *ITV Broadcasting Ltd., v. TV Catchup Ltd.,* [2011] EWHC 1874 (Pat).

urgent need for incorporating the same under the Copyright Act as an authors' right. This could be achieved through an amendment to the definition of communication to public in Section 2(ff) of the Copyright Act, 1957 which could read as follows:

> "communication to the public" means making any work or performance available for being seen or heard or otherwise enjoyed by the public directly or by any means of display, diffusion *or electronic transmission including computer network* other than by issuing physical copies of it, whether simultaneously or at places and times chosen individually, regardless of whether any member of the public actually sees, hears or otherwise enjoys the work or performance so made available.
>
> Explanation. – For the purposes of this clause, communication through satellite or cable *or computer network* or any other means of simultaneous communication to more than one household or place of residence including residential rooms of any hotel or hostel shall be deemed to be communication to the public

The analysis of the technology specific approach followed internationally by the copyright system when the broadcasting technology emerged shows that while enjoying the authors' right of broadcasting using the traditional analogue broadcasting, the broadcasters' signal which is generated for carrying the contents has been subjected to unauthorized access and use. Further, it was also found that the reason for this is the limitation of the technology itself i.e., the weak carrier waves that were generally used in the analogue broadcasting that was responsible for the unauthorized access and use of content carrying signal. Due to the technological limitations, even with the aid of the authors' right of broadcasting, the unauthorized use of signal could not be effectively addressed. Since, authors' right is confined to expressions of works and not to content carrying signals, there was a need to address the signal piracy issue to protect the economic interest of the broadcasting organizations which made huge investments in setting up the infrastructure for broadcasting the work. Considering the economic loss suffered by the broadcasting organizations and the authors, broadcasters' protection was internationally demanded and was recognized in the Rome Convention, 1961 as a neighbouring right. Unfortunately, due to lack of clarity on the broadcast reproduction right including the concept of broadcast and considerable flexibility provided in the Convention for member countries, only a few countries joined this Convention. Thus, the Rome Convention failed to be evolved as a minimum international standard for the protection of broadcasting organizations. This also resulted in adopting a very limited and flexible approach in the TRIPS Agreement for the protection of broadcasting organizations. Even though, the rights of performers and phonogram producers provided under the Rome Convention were revised through WPPT in 1996, it did not address the cause of broadcasting organizations. This resulted in a wide gap in the protection for broadcasting organizations not only in the new and emerging technologies but also in traditional broadcasting based on wire.

In order to address the concerns of broadcasting organizations in the context of new technological developments, WIPO in 1998 initiated discussions to update the protection of the broadcasting organizations. During the negotiations which was primarily confined to issues relating to traditional broadcasting, the broadcasters' have demanded the expansion of their traditional broadcasting right to computer network based live streaming technology, due to the commercial success of the 4G P2P live streaming. The main reason advocated by the broadcasting organizations is the unauthorized simultaneous retransmission of the programmes (simulcasting) received from their signal through computer networks. Unauthorized retransmission of the sports content was projected as the main cause for concern.

While examining the demand of the broadcasters to expand their traditional broadcasting rights to simultaneous live streaming of the content received from their signal, it has been found that from the end users' point of view, cable broadcasting, satellite broadcasting, radio diffusion and TV broadcasting could be treated as one and the same due to the non-interactive character of these technologies. In these traditional modes of broadcasting of copyright works, the users have no freedom of interacting with the service providers and could only remain as passive viewers. Similarly, on the examination of the internet based technology, it has been found that communications using live streaming technology such as IPTV, Web TV and mobile streaming also possess the same feature of not allowing the users' to determine the contents to be enjoyed. This particular feature from the end users' perspective has favored to form an opinion that all these technologies are one and the same and should be treated together as 'broadcasting' for determining the scope of protection for broadcasting organizations. However, a detailed examination of the possibility of equating all the technologies revealed that they are not one and the same and differs substantially deserving differential treatment both from economic and legal perspective.

From a detailed analysis of the technologies, it is found that the traditional radio and TV broadcasting, cable broadcasting, satellite broadcasting could be grouped into one, because of the signal based technology. The rationale behind such grouping is that all these technologies have the radio magnetic waves, i.e., signal, as a commonality. Even in the digital broadcasting context, it is noticed that it is the digital signal that favors it to be in the same grouping. Generally, in all these modes, the content is first converted into signal to communicate the content to the public through the content carrying waves i.e., radio magnetic signals at different frequencies. It is clearly established that it is the content carrying signal which is diffused in case of traditional TV & Radio broadcasting and satellite broadcasting and it remains as signal (encrypted/encoded for protection) till it is received by the receiving equipment for enjoyment. The same is the case with cable broadcasting (termed as cablecasting in WIPO negotiations) as well. In cable broadcasting, it is the signal that is captured and further diffused to the individual subscribers' home through cable. Since it is the signal that is diffused and it remains as signal till it is received by an equipment such as radio/TV, it would be justified in using the word 'broadcasting' for these technologies. However, in case of cable broadcasting, there could be some reservation in using the term broadcasting because of the fact that the diffused signal by the broadcasting organizations is not meant for direct public reception. In this mode of broadcasting, the signal is first received by a common antenna and then communicated to the public again in the form of signal using cable by the local service provider. As the signal is further diffused through wire to the public with the help of intermediary for the enhancement of viewing quality and that too simultaneously, this form of diffusion of signal was also covered under the category of broadcasting.

However, in the internet based 4G P2P live streaming model of communications such as IPTV, Web TV and mobile TV, the analysis of the technology shows that it is based on Internet Protocol (IP) using packets. While comparing these technologies with the traditional broadcasting models, it is established that the concept of signal is a misnomer in the live streaming context. However, there is a corresponding factor equivalent to that of signal which is known as 'streams'. In live streaming, the content is dissected into small packets i.e., streams by compressing and encoding methods with the help of a specific software and then transmitted to the streaming server which regulates the delivery of the streams in the prescribed order for the enjoyment of the content. Here, the content is transmitted as a stream throughout the process. In this context, it is observed that broadcasting and streaming are different because of the fundamental differences in technology, model of communication, medium of communication, infrastructure and investment requirements. Due to these reasons, it is concluded that IPTV, Web TV and Mobile TV cannot be considered as broadcasting and they can only be treated as internet transmissions.

In the light of above technological differences, while examining the socio-economic rationale for protecting broadcasting and live streaming, it is noticed that signal piracy has been persisting in the analogue signal based traditional broadcasting and the same has been addressed by introducing neighbouring right protection under the copyright regime. Since, a substantial part of the globe has already switched over to digital broadcasting as mandated by the ITU, it is possible that within five years, analogue broadcasting will be completely replaced with digital broadcasting at least in major parts of the world. The examination of the technological protection measures such as encryption with high end keys for decryption used in digital broadcasting revealed that the signal piracy as persisting in traditional analogue broadcasting is no more in existence, due to the complexities in breaking the keys, time and cost factors. However, the contents received from digital broadcasting could be retransmitted over internet, due to which the internet TV streaming organizations and owners of copyright could face revenue losses out of the unauthorized retransmission of contents. Hence, the unauthorized retransmission of works received from digital broadcasting over computer network is all about the content and not signal, since, signal has to be fixed before the content is converted into streams. The experience of developed countries shows that this issue could be effectively addressed through contractual arrangements with the owners of copyright rather than through right of broadcasting organizations. It is the established law that the copyright owner has a separate right over live streaming of his work. The Courts in USA and the EU clarified that it is a different technology and a new market for the copyright owners. Hence, permission of the author is required to transmit the work using streaming technology either by the broadcasting or streaming organizations.

Similarly, the study of technology used for streaming revealed that due to the use of advanced encryption techniques, there is no possibility of unauthorized use of stream/packets either prior to or post streaming of content in internet TV and IPTV. If the stream piracy is not feasible either in the pre or post streaming stage in both internet TV and IPTV, then there is no question of economic loss or gap in law to be filled so as to protect the investment of streaming organizations. This seems to be the reason why there was no demand similar to the demand of the broadcasting organizations from streaming organizations to protect their streams. Further, it is concluded that since the issue, if any, is based on content, and the same could be effectively addressed by the authors' right of communication to public, if it is extended to internet based transmission. In the absence of unauthorized use of digital signal or streams, the permission from the owner of copyright is adequate to prevent the content being retransmitted without authorization.

As to the question whether the broadcasting organization must also be provided with a right over streaming of the content received from their digital signal, the study divulges that there is no reported evidence of any economic loss suffered by the broadcasting organization due to simulcasting. Since, it is a different market for the author, it is the author who is going to suffer by simulcasting and not the broadcasting organization. As it is the right of the author and there is no economic loss to broadcasting organization, a streaming right co-existing with that of author is found to be unjustified. Thus, it is concluded that since there is no economic loss suffered as in the case of traditional broadcasting based on analogue signal, there is no need to address the issue of additional protection to broadcasting organization in digital broadcasting by the copyright system. Based on the above analysis of the changes in technology and the socio-economic conditions of broadcasting, it can be inferred that there is no justification for the extension of the rights of broadcasting organizations. Thus, in the absence of possible signal piracy in digital broadcasting, there is no justification for retaining the neighbouring rights for broadcasting organizations, once the analogue broadcasting is completely replaced with digital broadcasting.

Irrespective of the above factual situations, the WIPO, in its ongoing discussions for the protection of broadcasting organizations, has been striving to expand the broadcast reproduction right to the computer networks. The attempt of the WIPO's proposed treaty to expand the broadcasters' right to the cable broadcasting which has been left out in the TRIPS Agreement is also unwarranted today, as digitalization has taken care of the piracy issue in this mode of broadcasting. As already stated, due to the use of much sophisticated encryption techniques, digital signal piracy has become highly complicated. It can be categorically asserted that it is practically impossible due to technological advancement. This situation has actually rendered the current model of protection under TRIPS infructuous. Thus, in the absence of unauthorized use of digital signals, the WIPO's efforts to provide enhanced protection to the broadcasting organization for simulcasting should be taken as an attempt to expand the protection to content as well, undermining the legitimate exclusive right of the authors in live streaming. Since the issue of simulcasting could be effectively addressed through the contractual relationship with the authors as followed in US, it is strongly suggested to abandon the WIPO's current deliberations on Broadcasting Treaty.

However, it is interesting to note that the analysis of the legal protection of broadcasting organizations for simulcasting in US and EU shows a difference in approach. As far as US is concerned, since the copyright law does not provide any separate protection to the broadcasting organizations, based on contractual agreements, right of the author to enjoy live streaming is used to prevent unauthorized steaming of contents received from broadcasting.

However, in the EU context, the broadcasters have been provided with right of simulcasting. As mandated by EU Directives, the study of UK copyright law shows that in UK, broadcast is an independent work jointly owned by authors and broadcasting organizations. It has also recognized simulcasting right for broadcasting organization which is jointly enjoyed with the authors. In the context of the technological changes taking place in digital broadcasting, the EU approach of extending the protection of broadcasting organizations over the computer network using live streaming is highly questionable.

The analysis of the protection of broadcasting organization in India from the very inception makes it clear that the intention of the Parliament was to protect them from the unauthorized use of their programme carrying signal. Unfortunately, this clarity was blurred when amendments were carried out from 1993 onwards. The failure of the Parliament to amend the definition of 'broadcast' included originally in 1983 to protect the broadcasting right of authors work created considerable confusion as to the nature of protection of the broadcasting organization. The judiciary also failed to examine the concept of broadcast reproduction right properly in the light of the definition of broadcast and concluded that it is an independent right giving an impression that the authors' permission is not required to enjoy the right by the broadcasting organization. The broadcast reproduction right in addition to providing protection for signal also provided for post fixation rights to the broadcasting organizations and this was considerably strengthened by the 1993 amendment at the expense of authors. To mitigate the implications, the 2012 amendment introduced a new provision in Section 39A to clarify that all the rights of broadcasting organizations are subject to the copyright of authors and the post fixation right can be enjoyed only with the additional consent of the owner of works. But, the Parliament left the conceptual issue open since it made no effort to change the definition of broadcast irrespective of the fact that the Government of India is strongly arguing for a signal based approach for the protection of broadcasting organization in the ongoing WIPO negotiations. In the context of India completely shifting to digital broadcasting by 2020 and absorbing 4G P2P streaming technology at an unprecedented speed and the fact that digital signal piracy is going to be practically unfeasible due to the availability of technological protection measure, it is strongly felt that the present nature and content of protection afforded to broadcasting organizations require serious reconsideration of especially the definition of broadcast. The current definition of broadcast needs to be replaced with the focus on signal rather than on the content.

Annexures

Preliminary Draft International Convention Regarding the Protection of Performers, Manufacturers of Phonographic Records and Broadcasting Organisations, 1951 (The ILO Draft)

Article 1[1]

1. Without prejudice to the rights belonging to the authors of literary and artistic works the contracting countries undertake to protect performing artist who recite, present or perform works, manufacturers of phonographic records and similar instruments, and broadcasting organisations when the country of origin as defined in Article 2 below is bound by the present convention.
2. The obligation provided for in the previous paragraph shall exist only if the country of origin defined as above and the country wherein the protection is claimed are bound by a bilateral or multilateral agreement for the protection of authors of literary and artistic works.[2]

Article 2

The country of origin shall be considered to be –

a) In the case of recitations, presentations and performances: the country in which the recitation, presentation or performance takes place;
b) In the case of phonographic records and similar instruments, the country in which the first finished was produced in a non-contracting country, the country of origin shall be considered to be the first of the contracting countries in which a finished record was produced;
c) in the case of broadcasts: the country in which the head office of the broadcasting organisation is situated.

1 This preliminary draft did not form part of the report of the Sub-committee on Performers' Rights. It is included here for information.

2 This paragraph did not receive the unanimous support of the Committee of Experts.

 | DOI:10.1163/9789004419155_009

Article 3

In the contracting countries, the protection shall be regulated by the legislation of the country in which this protection is claimed, subject to the rights specially granted by this convention. It shall not be subject to any formality. Nevertheless, every manufacturer of phonographic records and similar instruments shall make known, in the manner determined by the legislation of the country where the protection may be claimed, the country and the year in which the phonographic record has first been produced by him, whenever this information is requested in writing.[3]

Article 4

1. Any performer who gives a recitation, presentation or performance of a work shall enjoy the right to authorise:
   a) The recording of his recitation, presentation or performance with a view to the manufacture of phonographic records or similar instruments, intended to be sold to the public, and of cinematographic films intended to be exhibited in public halls;
   b) The communication to the public of his recitation, presentation or performance by means of loudspeakers or any similar instruments transmitting signs, sounds or images;
   c) The broadcasting of his recitation, presentation or performance when it is given for the purposes of a person or undertaking other than the body which proposes broadcast;
   d) The recording, by any person whatsoever, for broadcasting of the performer's recitation, presentation or performance when given under the conditions specified in subparagraph (c) above.
2. The right of authorisation is not granted to the performer –
   a) as against those who transmit by radio diffusion or communicate to the public his recitation, presentation or performance by the means referred to in paragraph 1(a) and (d);
   b) as against those who communicate to the public, whether over wires or not, or by whatever means, the broadcast of his recitation, presentation or performance.

---

3 *Variant proposed by certain experts:* "Nevertheless, the country and year of production of the first finished record shall be indicated on the phonographic records and similar instruments unless the legislation of the country in which the said record was produced provides for other means of making it possible for the public to know the said year and country".

3. Reservations and conditions relating to the application of the rights mentioned in paragraph in paragraph 1 (c) and (d) may be determined by legislation in each contracting country in so far as it may be concerned, but all such reservations and conditions shall apply exclusively in the country which prescribed them and shall in no case be prejudicial to the performer's right to obtain equitable remuneration fixed, failing prior agreement, by the competent authority.
4. It shall be a matter for the legislation of the contracting countries to determine the conditions under which the broadcasting, recording and communication to the public of short extracts from recitations, presentations or performances may be made for the purpose of reporting current events. It shall also be a matter for the said legislation to determine the regulations for ephemeral recording fixing recitations, presentations or performances and made by a broadcasting organisation by means of its own facilities and for its own emissions. The preservation of these recordings in official archives may, on the ground of their exceptional documentary character, be authorised by the said legislation.

Article 5

1) It shall be a matter for the legislation of the contracting countries to designate the physical or legal person or persons whom each performer may appoint to exercise on his behalf the rights mentioned in Article 4.
2) When several performers participate in the same recitation, presentation or performance, and in the absence of a single assignee duly appointed by the said performers, it shall be a matter for national legislation to determine in what manner the rights given to these performers shall be exercised on their behalf either by one of their number or by a physical or legal person designated by the majority.

Article 5 bis

The performer may oppose the broadcasting, recording or reproducing of his recitation, presentation or performance in conditions likely to prejudice his honour or reputation.[4]

4 Some experts would wish this article to be inserted into the convention.

Article 6

1) The manufactures of phonographic records and similar instruments shall enjoy –
   a) The right to authorise the reproduction of their phonographic records and similar instruments by whatever means or process of recording;
   b) The right to obtain an equitable remuneration from whomsoever uses their phonographic records or similar instruments for broadcasting or for any other method or communication to the public.
2) The right to an equitable remuneration is not granted to manufacturers as against those who communicate to the public, whether over wires or not, or by whatever means, radio-emissions effected by means of their phonographic records or similar instruments.
3) Phonographic records or similar instruments manufactured in a non-contracting country which, on the one hand, copy phonographic records or other instruments protected by this convention and, on the other hand, are imported into a contracting country without permission from the manufacturer of the phonographic records or other instruments so reproduced, shall be liable to seizure.
4) It shall be a matter for the legislation of the contracting countries to determine the conditions under which the broadcasting, the recording and the communication to the public of short extracts from recitations, presentations or performances may be made for the purpose of reporting current events. It shall also be a matter for the same legislation to determine the regulations for ephemeral recordings fixing phonographic records or similar instruments and made by a broadcasting organisation by means of its own facilities and for its own emissions. The preservation of these recordings in official archives may, on the ground of their exceptional documentary character, be authorised by the said legislation.
5) It shall be a matter for the legislation of the contracting countries to designate the competent authority for fixing, in default of an amicable agreement, the amount of the equitable remuneration.
6) It shall be reserved for the legislation of contracting countries to waive the application of paragraph 1 (b) in the case of communication to the public without a view to profit.

Article 7

The term of protection granted by paragraph 1 of the preceding article shall be determined by the legislation of the country in which protection is claimed, but it shall not exceed the term fixed in the country or origin. Nevertheless, it shall never expire before the end of the tenth year following the year when the finished phonographic record or similar instrument was produced for the first time in a contracting country. This shall not affect protection for any longer term which may be afforded on any other ground in the contracting country.

Article 8

1) The broadcasting organisations shall enjoy the right to authorise –
   a) The re-emission, whether over wires or not, of all or a part of their emission;
   b) The recording or any other fixation of all or part of their emission or of the re-emission by whatever means;
   c) The communication to the public of all or a part of their emission by means of any instrument transmitting images.
2) It is reserved to the legislation of the contracting countries to protect the broadcasting organisations as against third parties who may communicate to the public all or part of their emission by means of loudspeakers or any other instrument transmitting sounds.
3) Recording of emissions or re-emissions protected by this convention manufactured in a non-contracting country and imported into a contracting country without permission from the broadcasting organisation from which they originate, shall be liable to seizure.
4) It shall be a matter for the legislation of the contracting countries to determine under which conditions the re-emission, the recording and the communication to the public of short extracts from emission may be made for the purpose of reporting current events. It shall also be a matter for the same legislation to determine the regulations for ephemeral recordings fixing emissions or re-emissions and made by a broadcasting organisation by means of its own facilities and for its own emissions. The preservation of these recordings in official archives may, on the ground of their exceptional documentary character, be authorised by the said legislation.
5) It shall be reserved for the legislation of contracting countries to waive the application or paragraph 1 (b) in the case of recordings and other fixations made for private use or without a view to profit.

Article 9

Subject to the provisions of this convention, the contracting countries may determine the procedure for the protection and, in particular, the means of redress for safeguarding the rights granted by this convention. They may prescribe transitory provisions for the application of this convention.

Article 10

The provisions of this convention shall not preclude the making of a claim to the benefit of any wider protection which may be afforded by legislation in countries in which this protection is claimed.

Article 11

The provisions of this convention cannot in any way affect the rigght of the government of each of the contracting countries to control or to prohibit, by legislation or regulations made in the public interest, any recitation, presentation or performance, the use of any phonographic records and any radio-emission. The do not prevent the said countries from repressing any abuse resulting from the exercise of the rights granted by this convention.

Article 12

1) This convention may be submitted to periodic revision. For this purpose, conferences may be held successively in the contracting countries by delegates of the said countries. The government of the country in which a conference is to meet shall undertake the preparatory work for the conference.
2) No alteration in this convention shall be binding except by the unanimous consent of the contracting countries.

Article 13

Any dispute between two or more of the contracting countries concerning the interpretation or application of this convention, not settled by negotiation, shall be brought before the International Court of Justice for decision, unless the countries concerned agree on some other method of settlement.

Article 14

1) This convention shall be ratified by the signatory countries. The ratifications shall be deposited with the Government of ………………………
2) Non-signatory countries may adhere to this convention. Their notification of adherence shall be addressed to the Government of …………………
3) The deposit of the instruments of ratification and of the adherences shall be notified in writing by the Government of …………… to the governments of the signatory countries, and to the governments of the countries which gave adhered to this convention in conformity with the provisions of paragraph 2.
4) This convention shall enter into force between any two signatory countries one month after the deposit of the second ratification and between them and any non-signatory countries which may have adhered to it before the deposit of the second ratification. Any subsequent ratifications shall enter into force one month after having been deposited with the Government of ……….. and any subsequent adherences one month after having been notified to the same government.

Article 15

1) Any contracting country may at any time notify, in writing, the Government of …….. that this convention shall apply to its overseas territories, colonies, protectorates, territories under trusteeship, or any other territory for the international relations of which it is responsible, and the convention shall thereupon apply to all the territories named in the notification one month after the receipt of this notification.
2) Any contracting country may at any time notify, in writing, the Government of ………. that this convention shall cease to apply to all or any of the territories which have been made the subject of a notification under the preceding paragraph, and the convention shall cease to apply to the territories named in this notification twelve months after the receipt of this notification by the Government of ………………..
3) The Government of ……………….. shall communicate the notifications given in conformity with the provisions of paragraphs 1 and 2 of this article to the governments of the signatory countries and to the governments which have adhered to this convention in conformity with the provisions of paragraph 2 of Article 14.

Article 16

1) This convention shall remain in force for an indefinite period. Nevertheless, each contracting country shall be entitled to denounce it at any time by means of a notification in writing addressed to the Government of ....
2) This denunciation, which shall be communicated by the latter to the governments of the signatory countries as well as to the governments of the countries which have adhered to this convention in conformity with the provisions of paragraph 2 of Article 14, shall take effect only in respect of the country making it and twelve months after the receipt of the notification of denunciation by the Government of ...., the convention remaining in full force and effect for the other contracting countries.
3) The right of the denunciation provided by this article shall not be exercised by any country before the expiry of five years from the day of ratification or adherence by such country.

Proposed International Convention Concerning the Protection of Performers, Manufacturers of Phonographic Records and Broadcasting Organisations, 1956 (The Geneva Draft)

Article 1

1. Each contracting country undertakes to protect performers who recite, present. or perform works,[1] manufacturers of phonographic records and similar instruments, and broadcasting organisations when that country is the country of origin as defined in Article 2 below, or when the country of origin as defined in the said Article is another country party to the present Convention
2. The protection granted under the present Convention shall leave completely intact and shall in no way affect the protection of the rights of authors of literary and artistic works. Consequently, no provision of the present Convention may be interpreted as prejudicing such rights.

Article 2

1. The country of origin shall be considered to be:
   (a) in the case of recitations, presentations and performances: the country in which the recitation, presentation or performance takes place; however, when the recitation, presentation or performance has not taken place in a contracting country, and when a phonographic record or similar instrument or a broadcast has been made thereof, its country of origin shall be considered to be the country defined in subparagraph (b) or (c) below;
   (b) in the case of phonographic records and similar instruments: the country in which the first finished record was produced; if the first finished record was produced in a non-contracting country, the country of origin shall be considered to be the first contracting country in which a finished record was produced;
   (c) in the case of broadcasts: the country in which the head office of the broadcasting organization is situated.

1 The question whether the word "works" should be retained or deleted was left open.

 | DOI:10.1163/9789004419155_010

2. The protection provided for by this Convention shall only be applicable to such copies of phonographic records and similar instruments as are manufactured in a contracting country.

Article 3

In the contracting countries, the protection shall be regulated by the legislation of the country in which this protection is claimed, subject to the rights specifically granted by this Convention. It shall not be subject to any formality. Nevertheless, every manufacturer of phonographic records and similar instruments shall indicate on the phonographic record and on the similar instrument the country of manufacture and the year in which was made the for recording from which the phonographic record or similar instrument was derived.

Article 4

1. Any performer who gives a recitation, presentation or performance of a work[2] shall enjoy the right to authorise:
   (a) the recording by any means for commercial purposes or for communication to the public;
   (b) the broadcasting and the recording by any means for broadcasting purposes;
   (c) any communication to the public;
   of his live recitation, presentation or performance.
2. He shall furthermore enjoy the right to authorise the recording by any means for commercial purposes or for communication to the public of the broadcast or recording of his recitation, presentation or performance.
3. If a recording of a recitation, presentation or performance of a work was originally made for a purpose other than those mentioned in paragraph 1(a), 1(b) or in paragraph 2 of this Article, the authorisation of the performer shall be obtained before such recording is used for any of the purposes so mentioned.
4. (a) An agreement by performers to give a recitation, presentation or performance for broadcasting shall imply authorisation to record for broadcasting.

2 The question whether the words "of a work" used in this Article should be retained or deleted was left open.

(b) The terms and conditions governing the use of recordings made for broadcasting shall be laid down either in a written individual contract or in a collective agreement concluded with the organisation of the performers concerned. In cases where the national laws do not permit the establishment of their terms and conditions by a collective agreement, such terms and conditions may be established by the competent authority after-consultation with the performers concerned or their organisation. Subject to national legislation, each contracting country shall encourage the conclusion of collective agreements as referred to above between broadcasting organisations and organisations representing performers.

(c) The rights laid down by paragraph 1 above or their exercise may be transferred by performers to an individual or a corporate body. However, notwithstanding such transference, it is in all cases reserved to performers to exercise the rights necessary for the carrying out of an engagement accepted by them for recording or broadcasting.

5. (a) Performers shall have the right to obtain from manufacturers of phonographic records and similar instruments intended for sale to the public an equitable remuneration in respect of the use of such records and instruments for broadcasting and for all forms of communication to the public. This remuneration shall be paid according to the provisions of the following subparagraph.

First Alternative Text[3]

(b) The said manufacturers shall make in each contracting country payments to performers collectively in such country. Each contracting country shall appoint one or more bodies acting in the interests of performers to receive these payments. In default of amicable agreement between this or these bodies and the manufacturers, each Contracting country shall decide the amountof such payments which shall be a reasonable proportion of the remuneration derived in such country by virtue of Article 6, paragraph 2, subparagraphs (a) and (b) hereafter.

Second Alternative Text[4]

(b) The said manufacturers shall make in each contracting country payments to performers collectively in such country. The manner in which these payments shall be made and the amount of such payments shall be a matter for amicable agreement between the manufacturers and the organisations

3 Proposed by the European Broadcasting Union.

4 Proposed by the three international organisations of performers.

representing performers. In default of such agreement each contracting country shall appoint one or more organisations representing performers to receive such payments. In all cases the said payments shall in each contracting country be a reasonable proportion of the remuneration derived in such country by virtue of Article 6, paragraph 2, sub-paragraphs (a) and (b) hereafter.

6. Reservations and conditions relating to the application of the rights mentioned in paragraph l (p) may be determined by legislation in each contracting Country in so far as it may be concerned, but all such reservations and conditions shall apply exclusively in the country which prescribed them and shall in no case be prejudicial to the performer's right to obtain equitable remuneration fixed, failing prior agreement, by the competent authority.[5]
7. It shall be a matter for the legislation of the contracting countries to determine the conditions under which the broadcasting, recording and communication to the public of short extracts from recitations, presentations or performances may be made for the purpose of reporting current events. It shall also be a natter for the said legislation to determine the regulations for the making of ephemeral recordings fixing recitations, presentations or performances and made by a broadcasting organisation by means of its own facilities and for its own emissions. The preservation of these recordings in official archives may, on the ground of their exceptional documentary character, be authorised by the said legislation.

Article 5

In the case of a collective recitation, presentation or performance, the rights of authorisation laid down by Article 4 shall be exercised by the performers in common, in conformity with the national laws.

Article 6

1. Manufacturers of phonographic records and similar instruments shall enjoy the right to authorise the reproduction of their records or similar instruments by whatever means or process of recording.

5 The Experts representing the interested parties agreed that the principle of compulsory licences contained in this paragraph should be settled at the proposed diplomatic conference.

2. Manufacturers of phonographic records and similar instruments intended for sale to the public shall enjoy:
   (a) the right to receive an equitable remuneration from the broadcasting organisations in respect of the direct use of their phonographic records and similar instruments; it shall be a matter for the legislation of the contracting countries to designate the competent authority for fixing in default of an amicable agreement, the amount of the equitable remuneration;
   (b) the right to receive an equitable remuneration in the event of the direct use of their phonographic records or similar instruments for any method of communication to the public; it shall be a matter for the legislation of the contracting countries to determine the legal procedure for this purpose.
3. Phonographic records or similar instruments manufactured in a non-contracting country which, on the one hand, copy phonographic records or other instruments protected by this Convention and, on the other hand, are imported into a contracting country without permission from the manufacturer of the phonographic records or other instruments so reproduced, shall be liable to seizure.
4. It shall be a matter for the legislation of the contracting countries to determine the conditions under which the broadcasting, the recording and the communication to the public of short extracts from recitations, presentations or performances may be made for the purpose of reporting current events. It shall also be a matter for the same legislation to determine the regulations for the making of ephemeral recordings fixing phonographic records or similar instruments and made by a broadcasting organisation by means of its own facilities and for its own emissions. The preservation of these recordings in official archives may, on the ground of their exceptional documentary character, be authorised by the said legislation.
5. It is reserved to the legislation of the contracting countries to limit the application of paragraph 2(b) of thin Article.[6]

Article 7

1. The broadcasting organisations shall enjoy the right to authorise:
   (a) the re-emission;
   (b) the recording or any other fixation for commercial purposes or for communication to the public;

6 The Experts representing the performers organisations suggested the deletion of this provision.

(c) the communication to the public by means of any instrument transmitting or projecting images;

of all or part of their emissions or of the re-emissions, whether direct or recorded.

2. It is reserved to the legislation of the contracting countries to protect the broadcasting organisations as against third parties who may communicate to the public all or part of their emissions by means of loudspeakers or any other instrument transmitting sounds.
3. Recordings of emissions or re-emissions protected by this Convention manufactured in a non-contracting country and imported, into a contracting country without permission from the broadcasting organisation from which they originate, shall be liable to seizure.
4. It shall be a matter for the legislation of the contracting countries to determine under which conditions the re-emission, the recording and the communication to the public of short extracts from emissions may be made for the purpose of reporting current events. It shall also be a matter for the same legislation to determine the regulations for the making of ephemeral recordings fixing emissions or re-emissions and made by a broadcasting organisation by means of its own facilities and for its own emissions. The preservation of these recordings in official archives may, on the ground of their exceptional documentary character, be authorised by the said legislation.
5. It is reserved to the legislation of the contracting countries to limit the application of paragraph 1 (c) of this Article.

Article 8

1. The period of protection granted by this convention to performers, to manufacturers of phonographic record and similar instruments and to broadcasting organisations, shall be determined by the law of the country where the protection is claimed, but shall not exceed the period provided for in the country of origin.
2. Nevertheless, this period of protection shall in no case expire before the twentieth year following:
   a) for recitations, presentations and performances, the year in which the recitation, presentation or performance took place; if the recitation, presentation or performance has taken place in a non-contracting country but has been made the subject of a phonographic record or similar instrument or of a broadcasting in a contracting country, the period of protection shall be calculated according to subparagraphs (b) or (c) below;

b) for phonographic records and similar instruments, the year in which was made the first recording from which the phonographic record or similar instrument was derived.
c) For broadcasts, the year in which the broadcast took place, or, if it took place in a non-contracting country, the year in which it was re-broadcast for the first time in a contracting country.

3. The provisions of this Article shall not affect protection for any longer period which may be granted in any contracting country on any other basis.

Article 9

Subject to the provisions of the convention, the contracting countries may determine the procedure for the protection and, in particular, the means of redress for safeguarding the rights granted by this convention.

Article 10

1) It is a matter for the laws of the contracting countries and for convention which may be concluded between them to determine to what extent this convention shall be applicable to recitations, presentations, performances, phonographic records and similar instruments and broadcasts realised in a contracting country prior to the date of the coming into force of this convention in such country.
2) This convention is without prejudice to rights acquired by virtue of conventions or agreements in force in any contracting country prior to the date of the coming into force of this convention in such country.

Article 11

The provisions of this convention shall not preclude the making of a claim to the benefit of any wider protection which may be afforded by legislation in countries in which this protection is claimed.

Article 12

The provisions of this convention cannot in any way affect the right of the Government of each of the contracting countries to control or to prohibit, by legislation or regulations made in the public interest, any recitation, presentation or performance, the use of any phonographic records and any radio-emission. They do not prevent the said countries from repressing any abuse resulting from the exercise of the rights granted by this convention.

Article 13

1) This convention may be submitted to periodical revision. For this purpose, conferences may be held successively in the contracting countries by delegates of the said countries. The Government of the country in which a conference is to meet shall undertake the preparatory work for the conference.
2) No alteration in this convention shall be binding except by the unanimous consent of the contracting countries.

Article 14

Any dispute between two or more of the contracting countries concerning the interpretation or application of this convention, not settled by negotiation, shall be brought before the International Court of Justice for decision, unless the countries concerned agree on some other method of settlement.

Article 15

1. This convention shall be ratified by the signatory countries. The ratifications shall be deposited with.......
2. Non-signatory countries may adhere to this convention. Their notification of adherence shall be addressed to ....
3. The deposit of the instruments of ratification and or the adherence shall be notified in writing by ...... to the governments of the signatory countries, and to the governments of the countries which have adhered to this convention in conformity with the provisions of paragraph 2.
4. This convention shall enter into force between any two signatory countries one month after the deposit of the second ratification and between them and any non-signatory countries which may have adhered to it before the deposit of the second ratification. Any subsequent ratifications shall enter into force one month after having been deposited with .... and any subsequent adherences one month after having been notified to..................

Article 16

1. Any contracting country may at any time notify, in writing, ... that this convention shall apply to its overseas territories, colonies, protectorates, territories under trusteeship, or any other territory for the international relations of which it is responsible, and the convention shall thereupon apply to all the territories named in the notification one month after the receipt of this notification.
2. Any contracting country may at any time notify, in writing,........ that this convention shall cease to apply to all or any of the territories which have been made the subject of a notification under the preceding paragraph, and the convention shall cease to apply to the territories named in this notification twelve months after the receipt of this notification by................
3. .... shall communicate the notifications given in conformity with the provisions of paragraphs 1 and 2 of this Article to the governments of the signatory countries and to the governments which have adhered to this convention in conformity with the provisions of paragraph 2 of Article 15.

Article 17

1. This convention shall remain in force for an indefinite period. Nevertheless, each contracting country shall be entitled to denounce it at any time by means of a notification in writing addressed to ....
2. This denunciation, which shall be communicated by .... to the governments of the signatory countries as well as to the governments of the countries which have adhered to this convention in conformity with the provisions of paragraph 2 of Article 15, shall take effect only in respect of the country making it and twelve months after the receipt of the notification of denunciation by ...., the convention remaining in full force and effect for the other contracting countries.
3. The right of denunciation provided by this Article shall not be exercised by any country before the expiry of five years from the day of ratification or adherence by such country.

Draft Agreement on the Protection of Certain Rights Called Neighbouring on Copyrights, 1957 (The Monaco Draft)

Article 1

1. This Agreement is open for signature and ratification, or adherence by any State invited to participate in the Conference held at from to 19.... or by any other State designated by...................................
2. This Agreement will be effective in respect to those Contracting States which are parties to the Universal Copyright Convention or the International Union for the Protection of Literary and Artistic Works.
3. The protection granted under the Agreement shall leave intact and shall in no way affect the protection of the rights of authors or other copyright proprietors in literary and artistic works. Consequently, no provision of this Agreement may be interpreted as prejudicing such rights.[1]

Article 2

1. Each Contracting State shall accord the same protection to performing artists in their performances taking place on the territory of another Contracting State as the former State accords to its own nationals in performances taking place on its own territory,
2. The protection provided for by the preceding paragraph shall include the prevention of fixation and broadcasting of a live performance when such fixation or broadcasting was not expressly or tacitly consented to by the performing artist. Live performances shall include broadcast live performances. However, if broadcasting was consented to by the performing artist, protection against rebroadcasting shall be left to domestic legislation.

1 Note: The following additional paragraph was proposed by the French and Italian experts: "4. In each Contracting State whenever literary or artistic works protected by copyright are used in connection with performances, phonograms or broadcasts, the protection provided by this Agreement may not be greater in content or extent than that accorded to the authors. Furthermore, this protection should be subject to the same legal restrictions as those affecting the said literary and artistic works in the country where protection is claimed."

 | DOI:10.1163/9789004419155_011

3. The protection provided for by paragraph 1 shall include the recognition of the right of the performing artist to authorize or prohibit the copying of a phonogram of his performance. Copying shall include off-the-air copying of the broadcast of a phonogram of a performance.
4. Protection provided for by this article shall not expire before the end of the tenth year following the year in which the performance took place.
5. No Contracting State shall be obliged to grant protection for a longer period than that fixed by the law of the Contracting State in which the performance took place.
6. Contracting State may provide exceptions to the protection of performing artists with respect to;
   (a) fixation or copying for private use;
   (b) fixation, broadcasting or copying, within reasonable limits, in connection with reporting of current events;
   (c) the making of ephemeral fixations by a broadcaster for his own broadcasts.
7. For the purpose of this Agreement, "performance" means the performance of literary or artistic works.
8. Any Contracting State may, by its domestic law, specify the conditions under which performing artists exercise their rights if several of them participate in the performance of the same work.

Article 3

1. Each Contracting State shall accord the same protection to recorders in their phonograms recorded on the territory of another Contracting State, as the former State accords to recorders in phonograms recorded on its own territory.
2. The protection provided in the preceding paragraph shall include recognition of the recorder's right to authorize or prohibit the copying of his phonogram. Copying shall include off-the-air copying of the broadcast of a phonogram.
3. Protection provided for by this article shall not expire before the end of the tenth year following the year in which the recording took place.
4. No Contracting State shall be obliged to grant protection for a longer period than that fixed bythe law of the Contracting State in which the phonogram was recorded.
5. If a Contracting State, under its domestic law, requires as a condition of protection of recorders, compliance with formalities, these requirements shall be regarded as satisfied if all the copies in commerce of the phonogram bear the symbol ℗ accompanied by the name of the State in which the recording took

place and the year date of the recording placed in such manner and location as to give reasonable notice of claim of protection.

6. A Contracting State may provide exceptions to the protection of recorders with respect to:
   (a) copying for private use;
   (b) copying, within reasonable limits, in connection with reporting of current events;
   (c) the making of ephemeral recordings by a broadcaster for his own broadcasts.
7. For the purpose of this Agreement:
   (a) "Phonogram" means the exclusively aural fixation of a performance or of other sounds.
   (b) "Recorder" means the person who first fixes a performance or other sounds in material form.
   (c) "Recording" means the act of first fixing a performance or other sounds in material form.

Article 4

If, in the case of phonograms recorded on its own territory, a Contracting State accords any rights to performing artists or recorders or both in connection with the broadcasting or other public communication of phonograms, such State may deny the same rights in respect to phonograms recorded on the territory of another Contracting State to the extent to which the latter does not accord similar rights in connection with phonograms recorded on the territory of the former.

Article 5

1. Each Contracting State shall accord the same protection to the rights of broadcasters in their broadcasts originating in the territory of another Contracting State, as the former State accords to broadcasts originating on its own territory.
2. Subject to the provisions of paragraph 3 of this article, the protection provided for by the preceding paragraph shall include the recognition of the broadcaster's right to authorize or prohibit:
   (a) the re-broadcasting of his broadcasts;
   (b) the off-the-air fixation of his broadcasts;
   (c) the public exhibition of his television broadcasts.
3. Any Contracting State may, by its domestic law:

(a) exclude from the application of this article broadcasts of phonograms;
(b) limit the application of paragraph 2(c) of this article to exhibitions to paying audiences.

4. A Contracting State may provide exceptions to the protection of broadcasters with respect to:
(a) off-the-air fixation for private use;
(b) re-broadcasting, off-the-air fixation or pubic television exhibition within reasonable limits in connection with the reporting of current events;
(c) the making of ephemeral off-the-air fixations by a broadcaster for his own broadcasts.

Article 6

No provision of this Agreement may be interpreted as applying to the copying or any use (exhibition, broadcasting or otherwise) of motion pictures or other visual and audio-visual fixations.

Article 7

Ratification or adherence by the Contracting States shall imply full acceptance of all the obligations and admission to all the advantages provided by this Agreement. However, a Contracting Mate may specify in its instrument of ratification or adherence that it is not bound by any or all of the provisions of Article 5, Between such a State and all other Contracting States the application of the reserved provisions shall not be mandatory.

Article 8

A dispute between two or more Contracting States concerning the interpretation or application of this Agreement, not settled by negotiation, shall, unless the States concerned agree on some other method of settlement, be brought before the International Court of Justice for determination by it.

The Draft International Convention Concerning the Protection of Performers, Makers of Phonograms and Broadcasters, 1960 (The Hague Draft)

(*As approved unanimously by the Committee of Experts*)

The Contracting States, moved by the desire to protect the rights of performers, makers of phonograms and broadcasters,

Have agreed as follows:

Article 1

This Convention shall be effective in respect to those Contracting States which are parties to the Universal Copyright Convention or members of the International Union for the Protection of Literary and Artistic Works.

Article 2

The protection granted under this Convention shall leave intact and shall in no way affect the protection of the rights of authors of literary and artistic works or of other copyright proprietors. Consequently, no provision of this Convention may be interpreted as prejudicing such rights.

Article 3

Each Contracting State shall grant to performers, makers of phonograms and broadcasters, in respect of their performances, phonograms and broadcasts, when the country of origin of such performances, phonograms or broadcasts is another Contracting State, the same protection which it grants to its own nationals in respect of performances taking place on its territory, phonograms recorded or published on its territory and broadcasts transmitted on its territory.

 | DOI:10.1163/9789004419155_012

Article 4

For the purpose of enjoyment of protection under this Convention, the country of origin shall be considered to be:

(a) in the case of performances, the country where the performance took place; however, when the performance has not taken place in a Contracting State, and when a phonogram or a broadcast has been made thereof, its country of origin shall be considered to be the country defined in subparagraph (b) or (c) below;

(b) in the case of phonograms: (i) if published, the country of first publication; in the case of phonograms published simultaneously in a non-Contracting State and in a Contracting State, the latter shall be considered exclusively as the country of origin; a phonogram shall be considered as having been published simultaneously in several countries which has been published in two or more countries within thirty days of its first publication; (ii) if unpublished, the country in which the first fixation of sounds was made, provided it was made by a national of a Contracting State;

(c) in the case of broadcasts, the country where the broadcaster has its headquarters or the country where the broadcast is transmitted; however, any Contracting State may, in a declaration made and deposited with the depository of this Convention, require, for protection under this Convention, that the headquarters of the broadcaster shall be located on the territory of a Contracting State and that such broadcasts shall be transmitted from such territory.

Article 5

1. The protection provided for performers by this Convention shall include the possibility of preventing:
   (a) the fixation, the broadcasting and the communication to the public of their live performances, without their consent;
   (b) the fixation without their consent of their live broadcast performances;
   (c) the reproduction without their consent of a fixation of their performances: (i) if the fixation itself is unlawful; (ii) if the reproduction is made for purposes different from those for which the performers had given their consent; (iii) if the fixation was made in accordance with the provisions of Article 14 and the reproduction is made for purposes different from those provided for by the said provisions.
2. If broadcasting was consented to by the performer, it shall be a matter for national laws and regulations to regulate the protection against rebroadcasting, fixation for broadcasting and the reproduction of such fixation for broadcasting purposes.

3. The terms and conditions governing the use by broadcasters of fixations made for broadcasting shall be determined in accordance with national laws and regulations.

Article 6

Any Contracting State may, by its national laws and regulations, specify the conditions under which performers exercise their rights, if several of them participate in the same performance.

Article 7

For the purpose of this Convention, "performance" means the recitation, presentation or performance of a literary or artistic work. It shall be a matter for national laws and regulations to extend the protection to artistes who do not perform literary or artistic works.

Article 8

Makers of phonograms shall enjoy the right to authorise or prohibit the reproduction of their phonograms either directly or when broadcast.

Article 9

If a Contracting State, under its national laws and regulations, requires as a condition of protection of phonograms compliance with formalities, these requirements shall be considered to be satisfied, as regards the makers of phonograms and the performers, if all the copies in commerce of the published phonogram bear the symbol (P) accompanied by the name of the Contracting State in which the first publication took place and the year date of this first publication placed in such a manner and location as to give reasonable notice of claim of protection.

Article 10

For the purpose of this Convention:

(a) "phonogram" means any exclusively aural fixation of a performance or other sounds;

(b) "maker of phonograms" means the person or corporate body who first fixes a performance or other sounds in material form;

(c) "publication" means the multiplication of copies of the phonogram and the offering of such copies to the public in reasonable quantity.

Article 11

If a phonogram published for commercial purposes, or a reproduction of such phonogram, is used directly by a broadcaster or for any method of communication to the public, a single equitable remuneration shall be paid by the user to the performers, to the makers of phonograms or to both. National laws and regulations may, in the absence of agreement between these parties, lay down the conditions as to the sharing of this remuneration.

Article 12

Broadcasters shall enjoy the right to authorise or prohibit:
(a) the rebroadcasting of their broadcasts;
(b) the fixation of their broadcasts;
(c) the reproduction of unlawful fixations or of fixations made in accordance with the provisions of Article 14, if the reproduction is made for purposes different from those provided for by the above-mentioned provisions;
(d) the communication to the public of their television broadcasts if such communication is made in places accessible to the public against payment of an entrance fee. It shall be left to national legislation to determine the conditions under which this right may be exercised.

Article 13

1. The period of the protection granted, under the terms of this Convention, to performers, makers of phonograms and broadcasters, shall be determined by the law of the country where the protection is claimed. However, no Contracting State shall be obliged to grant protection for a longer period than that fixed by the law of the country of origin.
2. Nevertheless, the period of protection under this Convention shall in no case expire before the twentieth year following:
   (a) for performances, the end of the year in which the performance took place;
   (b) for unpublished phonograms, the end of the year of the fixation; for published phonograms, the end of the year of first publication, if the latter took place within the period of protection provided for unpublished phonograms;
   (c) for broadcasts, the end of the year in which the broadcast took place,

Article 14

Any Contracting State may provide exceptions, under its laws and regulations, to the protection of performers, makers of phonograms and broadcasters, with respect to:
(a) private use;
(b) use of short excerpts in connection with reporting of current events;
(c) ephemeral fixation by a broadcaster by means of his own facilities and for his own broadcasts;
(d) use solely for teaching purposes.

Article 15

1. Ratification or accession by a Contracting State shall imply full acceptance of all the obligations and admission to all the advantages provided by this Convention. However, a Contracting State may specify, in its instrument of ratification or accession:
   (a) that it does not intend to grant the right provided for in Article 11 or that it intends to restrict it in relation to any of the uses mentioned in that Article;
   (b) that it does not intend to be bound by one or more of the provisions of Article 12.
2. If a Contracting State makes such a declaration, the other Contracting States shall not be obliged to apply the reserved provision or provisions in their relations with such a State.

Article 16

No provision of this Convention may be interpreted as applying to the reproduction or any use of motion pictures or other visual and audio-visual fixations, except the provisions contained in Articles 12 and 5, other than paragraph 1(c) (ii) of the latter.

Article 17

This Convention is without prejudice to rights acquired in any Contracting State prior to the date of the coming into force of this Convention in such State.

Index

www.ingramcontent.com/pod-product-compliance
Lightning Source LLC
LaVergne TN
LVHW020635300926
849161LV00004B/707